VOLUME ONE

# THE GOSPEL OF GOD

WATCHMAN NEE

*Living Stream Ministry*
Anaheim, California • www.lsm.org

First Edition, July 1990.

ISBN 978-1-57593-953-7

Published by

*Living Stream Ministry*
2431 W. La Palma Ave., Anaheim, CA 92801 U.S.A.
P. O. Box 2121, Anaheim, CA 92814 U.S.A.

*Printed in the United States of America*

12   13   14   15   16   /   10   9   8   7   6   5   4

# CONTENTS

## PREFACE TO THE ENGLISH EDITION

As has become manifest to Christian readers throughout the earth, Brother Watchman Nee was especially entrusted by the Lord with the burden to help the believers in the truth of God's full salvation. In the spring of 1937 Watchman Nee delivered a series of twenty-six messages on the basic truths of the gospel of God to the church in Shanghai, China. These messages compose the contents of this two-volume set. The matters covered are comprehensive, ranging from man's sinful condition before salvation to his destiny in the coming age. In the first volume, Watchman Nee presents the particulars of God's salvation, that is, man's sins; God's love, grace, and mercy; the nature of grace; the function of the law and God's righteousness; the work of Christ and of the Holy Spirit in God's salvation; and faith as the way of salvation. In the second volume, he covers in detail the issues of eternal security of salvation and God's way of dealing with the believer's sins both in this age and in the age to come. For both issues Watchman Nee presents persuasive reponses from the Scriptures to various understandings current among Christians.

The messages in this series were spoken by Watchman Nee in Chinese and were transcribed by hand as they were being given. The handwritten notes have been translated into English and edited as necessary. As much as possible, the spoken nature of the messages has been preserved. Many of the illustrations Brother Nee used were drawn from his life in China at the time.

These messages demonstrate the Lord's commission to our brother and His equipping of him with the revelation in His Word. May the Lord richly bless all who read and see these truths released by the Lord through our brother.

The Editor

# CHAPTER ONE

# SIN, SINS, AND THE SINNER

## THE NATURE OF THIS MEETING— THE TEACHING OF THE GOSPEL

Tonight we begin a series of Bible-study meetings. But before we begin, I would like to first say a few words concerning the nature of these meetings. I do not know if there are some here who are with us for the first time. Some who come for the first time find it very hard to locate our address. Many have complained that the street we are on is difficult to locate. Some have even said that though they were actually sitting here, they did not know how to leave from here after the meeting. They did not know which way to turn to get to that auto shop they saw as they came here, and they did not know how to walk from there to the tram stop or to the bus stop. Even though they were here, they were not sure of and could hardly remember the way they came. This is the case with many Christians in their Christian life. If you ask them if they have believed in the Lord, they will say yes. But if you ask them how they have believed, they will say that they are not sure. They are not clear at all about the way they were saved.

The meetings that we are having now are not revival or gospel meetings. And while the subject of these meetings is the gospel, they are not gospel meetings. We are not preaching the gospel this time; instead, we are teaching the gospel. Why do we need to teach the gospel? Many have been saved and have become Christians, but they still do not know how they have become Christians. What we are doing today is telling people how they have become Christians. In other words, we are telling them that they turned south from Aiwenyi Road and walked straight ahead to that auto shop they saw, that they turned from there to Wen-teh Lane where we are now, took a few steps from there to the window of our meeting hall, turned at the entrance of our hall and walked to a trash can by the door of the meeting hall, and then entered into the meeting hall. This time we are not persuading people to come in; rather, we are telling them how to come in.

If there are some sitting here who have not believed in the Lord, they may be disappointed. What we are doing this time is showing those who have believed how they have believed. Some brothers and sisters may be very clear about the gospel; they may already know what we are speaking about. But I hope that the Lord would bless us and grant us new light. You must be clear that these meetings are Bible-study meetings and are meant for those who have believed but do not know how they have believed. This time I am not trying to encourage you or revive you. I am merely pointing out the direction to you. In other words, in these meetings I am nothing more than a tour guide.

### SIN, SINS, AND THE SINNER

I will begin with a very basic foundation concerning the gospel. Yet I hope that in every meeting we will advance a little. In this first meeting, our subject is one which most people do not like to hear about, but one which is unavoidable. Our subject in this meeting is sin, sins, and sinners.

The Bible pays much attention to the matter of sin. Only when we are clear about sin can we understand salvation. If we want to know about the gospel of God and the salvation of God, we must first know what sin is. We must firstly see how sin has affected us and how we have become sinners. Only then will we be clear about what God's salvation is. We will first consider the ABCs. We need to see what sin is, what sins are, and who is a sinner.

### THE DIFFERENCE BETWEEN SIN AND SINS

We can easily tell the difference between sin and sins: *sin* is singular, and *sins* are plural. However, we need to distinguish between sin and sins. If you cannot differentiate between the two, it will be impossible for you to be clear about your salvation. If someone is not clear about the difference between sin and sins, even if he is saved, his salvation is probably an unclear one. What is sin according to the Bible? What are sins? Let me give a brief definition first. *Sin* refers to that power within us that motivates us to commit sinful acts. *Sins,* on the other hand, refer to the particular individual sinful acts that we commit outwardly.

What is sin? I do not like to use terms such as "original sin," "the root of sin," "the source of sin," or the like. These are terms created by theologians and are unnecessary for us now. We will remain simple and consider this matter from our experience. We know that there is something within us that motivates and forces us to have certain spontaneous inclinations; it compels us toward the way of lust and passion. According to the Bible this something is sin (Rom. 7:8, 16-17). But not only is there this sin within us that forces and compels us, there are also the individual sinful acts, the sins, which are committed outwardly. In the Bible sins are related to our conduct, while sin is related to our natural life. Sins are that which are committed by the hands, the feet, the heart, and even the whole body. Paul refers to this when he speaks of the practices of the body (Rom. 8:13). But what is sin? Sin is a law that controls our members (Rom. 7:23). There is something within us that compels us to sin, to commit evil, and this something is sin.

If we want to differentiate clearly between sin and sins, there is one portion of the Scriptures which we must consider. It is the first eight chapters of the book of Romans. These eight chapters show us the full significance of sin. In these eight chapters we find one outstanding feature: from chapter one through 5:11, only the word *sins* is mentioned; *sin* is never mentioned. But from 5:12 until the end of chapter eight, what we find is *sin,* not *sins.* From chapter one through 5:11, Romans shows us that man has committed sins before God. From 5:12 on, Romans shows us what kind of person man is before God: he is a sinner before God. *Sin* refers to the life that we have. Prior to Romans 5:12, there is no mention of the dead being made alive, for the problem there is not that one needs to be made alive, but that the individual sins that one has committed need to be forgiven. From 5:12 on, we have the second section. Here we see something strong and powerful within us as a law in our members, which is sin, that compels and drags us to commit sinful acts, that is, sins. For this, there is the need of being freed.

Sins have to do with our conduct. Hence, the Bible shows us that for our sins we need forgiveness (Matt. 26:28; Acts 2:38; 10:43). But sin is that which entices and compels us to commit sinful acts. Hence, the Bible shows us that we need to be freed from sin (Rom. 6:18, 22). Once I met a missionary who talked about "the forgiveness of sin." Right away I stood up and grasped his hand and asked, "Where in the Bible does it say 'the forgiveness of sin'?" He contended that there are many such cases. When I asked if he could find one for me, he said, "What do you mean? Can you not find even one place that says this?" I told him that nowhere in the entire Bible are the words *the forgiveness of sin* mentioned; instead, the Bible always speaks of "the forgiveness of sins." It is the sins that are forgiven, not sin. He did not believe my words, so he went to look this up in his Bible. Eventually he told me, "Mr. Nee, it is so strange. Every time this phrase is used, a little *s* is added in." I believe that you can see that it is the sins that are forgiven, not sin.

Sins are outside of us. That is why they need to be forgiven. But something else is inside of us, something strong and powerful that compels us to commit sins. For this we do not need forgiveness; for this our one need is to be freed. As soon as we are no longer under its power and have nothing to do with it, we will be at peace. The solution to sins comes from forgiveness. The solution to sin, however, comes when we are no longer under its power and have nothing to do with it. Sins are a matter of our actions and are committed one by one. That is why they need to be forgiven. But sin is within us, and we need to be freed from it.

Therefore, the Bible never says "forgiveness of sin" but "forgiveness of sins." Neither does the Bible speak about being "freed from sins." I can assure you that the Bible never says this. Instead the Bible says that we are "freed from sin," rather than from sins. The only thing that we need to escape and be freed from is that which entices us and compels us to commit sins. This distinction is clearly made in the Bible.

I can compare the two in this way:

Sin, according to the Scriptures, is said to be in the flesh; whereas sins are in our conduct.

Sin is a principle in us; it is a principle of the life we have. Sins are acts committed by us; they are acts in our living.

Sin is a law in the members. Sins are transgressions that we commit; they are activities and real acts.

Sin is related to our being; sins are related to our doing.

Sin is what we are; sins are what we do.

Sin is in the realm of our life; sins are in the realm of the conscience.

Sin is related to the power of the life we possess; sins are related to the power of the conscience. A person is governed by the sin in his natural life, but he is condemned in his conscience by the sins committed outwardly.

Sin is something considered as a whole; sins are something considered case by case.

Sin is inside man; sins are before God.

Sin requires our being made free; sins require our being forgiven.

Sin is related to sanctification; sins are related to justification.

Sin is a matter of overcoming; sins are a matter of having peace in one's heart.

Sin is in man's nature; sins are in man's ways.

Figuratively speaking, sin is like a tree, and sins are like the fruit of the tree.

We can make this matter clear with a simple illustration. In preaching the gospel, we often compare the sinner to a debtor. We all realize that to be a debtor is not a pleasant matter. But we must remember that it is one thing for a man to have debts; it is another thing for a man to have a disposition for incurring debts. A person who borrows again and again is not that concerned about using others' money. The Bible says that Christians should not be debtors (Rom. 13:8); they should not borrow from others. A person with a borrowing disposition may borrow two or three hundred dollars from someone today, then two or three thousand dollars from someone else tomorrow. Even if he is unable to pay back his debts, and his relatives or friends have to pay back the money for him, after a few days he will begin to consider borrowing again. This shows that to borrow is one thing, but to have a borrowing disposition is another. The sins that the Bible describes are like the outward debts, while sin is like the inward habit and disposition; it is like the mind that is inclined to borrow easily. A person with such a mind will not stop borrowing just because someone else has paid his debts. On the contrary, he may borrow even more because others are now paying his debts.

This is why God is dealing not just with the record of sins, but also with the inclination toward sin. We can see that it is important to deal with the sins, but it is equally important to deal with sin. Only when we see both of these aspects can our understanding of our salvation be complete.

### WHO IS A SINNER?

Now we need to ask the question: Who is a sinner? I know that some of the brothers and sisters here have been believers for over twenty years. Some have even worked for the Lord for over fifteen years. My question can be considered as one of the ABCs of the Bible. Who is a sinner? I believe that many would answer that a sinner is someone who sins. If you check Webster's dictionary, I am afraid that you would get the answer that a sinner is one who sins. But once you read the Bible, you will have to reject this definition, because it is not that the ones who sin are sinners, but that the sinners are the ones who commit sins. What does this mean? Many among us have read the book of Romans. I have heard many say that Paul, in proving that everyone in the world is a sinner, mentioned in chapter three that all have sinned and have come short of the glory of God (v. 23). God seeks the righteous and finds none; He seeks those who understand and who seek after Him and finds none; all have lied and have turned aside (vv. 10-13). Hence, it seems that Paul is saying that everyone in the world is a sinner. But be careful. Do not be too quick to say this. Does Romans 3 mention the sinner at all? If anyone can find the word *sinner* in Romans 3, I will thank him for it. Where is the sinner mentioned in this chapter? Please note that the sinner is never mentioned here. Some have said that because Romans 3 talks about man sinning, it proves that man is a sinner. But Romans 3 does not mention the sinner. It is Romans 5 that talks about the sinner. Therefore, we must make the distinction: Romans 3 is on the problem of sins, and Romans 5 is on the problem of the sinner. All that Romans 3 tells us is that all have sinned. It is only in Romans 5 that we are told who the sinners are.

Everyone who was born in Adam is a sinner. This is what Romans 5:19 tells us. If you open up J. N. Darby's New Translation, you will find that he used the words *have been constituted sinners*. We are all sinners by constitution. When you write a resume, there are two things that you must put in. One is your birthplace, and the other is your profession. According to God, we are sinners by birth, and we are those who sin by profession. Because we are sinners by birth, we are always sinners, whether we sin or not.

Once I was conducting a Bible study with the brothers in Canton. I told them that there are two kinds of sinners in the world—the sinning sinners and the moral sinners. But whether you are a sinning sinner or a moral sinner, you are still a sinner. God says that all who are born in Adam are sinners. It does not matter what kind of person you are; as long as you are born in Adam, you are a sinner. If you sin, you are a sinning sinner. And if you have not sinned, or to be more accurate, if you have sinned less, you are a moral sinner, or a sinner who sins little. If you are a noble person, you are a noble sinner. If you consider yourself holy, you are a holy sinner. In any case, you are still a sinner. Today the biggest mistake among men is to consider a man a sinner only because he has sinned; if he has not sinned, he is not considered a sinner. But there is no such thing. Whether you sin or not, as long as you are a man, you are a sinner. As long as you are born in Adam, you are a sinner. A man does not become a sinner because he sins; rather, he sins because he is a sinner.

Therefore, my friends, remember God's Word. We *are* sinners; we do not *become* sinners. We do not need to become sinners. Once I was talking to a brother. There was a thermal flask in front of him, and he said, "Here is a thermal flask. If it prays, 'I want to be a thermal flask,' what will happen?" I said, "It already is one. It does not have to be one." Likewise with us, once we are something, we do not have to become it.

Though our sins are forgiven, we remain sinners. We can call ourselves the forgiven sinners. But many believe that they are no longer sinners. They think that if we talk about being sinners, it means that we do not know the gospel that well. But this may not be all that true. Paul did not say that his sins were not forgiven. But he did say that he was a sinner (1 Tim. 1:15). Have you seen the difference here? If you were to ask Paul if his sins were forgiven, he could not be so humble as to say no. But Paul could humbly say that he is a sinner. He could not deny the work of God in him. But neither could he deny his position in Adam. Although we have received fresh grace in Christ, God has not fully removed the problem of sin; we are still sinners. The problem of sin will not be fully solved until the new heaven and new earth appear. However, this does not mean that we have not received a complete salvation. Please do not misunderstand me. In a few days we will come to this point.

The thing that we must see clearly and accurately is that everyone in the world is a sinner. Whether you have sinned or not, as long as you are a man, you are a sinner. When some listen to the gospel, they spend the whole time reasoning about how many or how few sins they have committed. But before God there is only one issue: Are you in Christ or in Adam? All who are in Adam are sinners, and as long as you are a sinner, nothing more needs to be said.

Why then did Paul have to tell us in Romans 1—3 about all the sins that man commits? These few chapters show us that sinners sin. The first three chapters of Romans prove that a sinner is known by the sins that he commits. But Romans 5 tells us what kind of person a sinner actually is. Once I went to Jian in Kiangsi and one evening met a brother who is a security guard. He did not believe that I was a preacher and a worker for the Lord. Here was a problem. I am a worker for the Lord and a servant of Christ, but he would not believe it. Therefore, I had to prove to him that I was one. I gave him many proofs. In the end he did believe. In the same way, we are sinners already. But this has not been proven to us. The first three chapters of Romans prove that we are sinners. They give us the evidence. By showing us that we have sinned in such ways, these chapters prove to us that we are sinners. Chapter five says that we are sinners, but the first three chapters prove that we are sinners.

Let me relate another story. In Fukien, there were some robbers and kidnappers who had previously been nominal Christians. Though they were robbers and kidnappers, their consciences were still somewhat exercised; therefore, if they realized that they had kidnapped a pastor or a preacher they would release him without ransom. By and by, when some were kidnapped, they said that they were pastors or preachers of such and such a denomination. What could the robbers do? After some time, they came up with a way. Every time someone said that he was a pastor, the robbers would ask him to recite the Ten Commandments, the Lord's Prayer, and the Beatitudes. Those who could recite them had to be pastors, and so they were let go. I heard this story recently and thought that it was very interesting. If you were a pastor, you had to prove it. The robbers required that these people prove to them that they were pastors. In the same way, God wants to prove to us that we are sinners. Without proving this to us, we may forget about our true self. This is why Romans 1—3 enumerate all those sins. It is to show us that we are sinners. After so many facts are presented there, we are proven to be sinners.

Therefore, one should never think that it is the many sins that makes us sinners. We have been sinners for a long time already. We do not become sinners after these sins are committed. We must lay this foundation clearly. Today you can walk out to the street and meet anyone, and take him by the hand and tell him that he is a sinner. If he says that he could not be a sinner because he has not murdered anyone or set fire to anyone's house, you can tell him that he is a sinner who has never murdered anyone or set fire to anyone's house. If someone tells you that he never robs or commits fornication, you can tell him that he is a sinner who never robs or commits fornication. But no matter whom you meet, you can say that he is a sinner.

In the whole New Testament, only Romans 5:19 tells us who a sinner is. All the other places in the New Testament tell us what the sinner does. Only this one place tells us who the sinner is. A sinner can do a million things, but these do not constitute him a sinner. As long as he is born in Adam, he is a sinner.

### THE GREATEST SIN

We have seen the matters of sin, sins, and the sinner. By birth, we are sinners, and our walk matches our birth. Because we are sinners, our conduct matches our title *sinner*. There are many "gentlemen" in this world who cover up their sins and will not admit that they are sinners. But this does not mean that they are not sinners. It only means that they have disguised themselves as ones without sins. We are sinners by birth, and our profession and walk is to commit sins. Let me repeat that it is not because we have sinned that we have become sinners; rather, it is because we are sinners that we have sinned. The fact that we are sinners causes us to sin. Those who can sin prove that they are sinners.

Tonight we have a few Western friends here with us. Perhaps they all speak the Shanghai dialect. The Shanghainese can of course speak the Shanghai dialect. But we cannot say that everyone who can speak the Shanghai dialect is Shanghainese. Many have put a lot of effort into learning the Shanghai dialect, but they are not Shanghainese. There also may be some Shanghainese who do not speak the Shanghai dialect. We cannot say that because they do not speak the Shanghai dialect, they are not Shanghainese. They are still Shanghainese, but they are Shanghainese who cannot speak the Shanghai dialect. However, there are very few Shanghainese who do not speak the Shanghai dialect. Generally speaking, all Shanghainese speak the Shanghai dialect. It is a natural thing for them to speak the Shanghai dialect. In the same way, it is all but unavoidable for those with a sinner's life to live a sinner's living.

Concerning the sins that sinners commit, I prefer not to list them in detail, as many have done. I would just like to briefly prove man's sin. Both in the New Testament, as well as in the Old, there are a few sins that are especially prominent. In the Old Testament, one sin which is particularly striking is the failure to love God. In the New Testament, there is also one sin that is particularly striking, the refusal to believe in the Lord. When the Bible says that man is condemned and has become a sinner in the eyes of God, it does not mean that he has committed a multitude of sins that incur God's wrath, such as murder, arson, fornication, pride, debauchery, prostitution, gambling, or other kinds of filthy and secret sins. This is not what the Bible emphasizes. What the Bible considers serious is the problem that has arisen between man and God. The end of the law is to love the Lord your God with all your heart, with all your soul, with all your mind, and with all your strength (Matt. 22:36-37; Mark 12:30). Hence, at issue is not whether one has stolen from others, or whether one has murdered or plotted arson. At issue are not personal lusts or thoughts or words. Rather, at issue is the problem of one's relationship with God.

Among all the sins, there is one which tops the list. This one sin brings in all sins. By this one sin, all other sins follow. The Bible says that sin entered into the world through one man (Rom. 5:12). I want to ask you, What sin did that one man commit? Was it fornication, theft, murder, arson? There were no such things in Eden. All the evil, filthy, and terrible things that happen in the world today come from one incident involving Adam. But what did Adam do? Adam did not murder; he did not commit fornication; he did not commit any of the evil and filthy sins in the world today. The sin that Adam committed was simple and pure. Adam thought that God was holding one thing back from him. He thought that if he were to eat of the fruit of that tree, he would be like God. The sin that Adam committed was actually a problem that developed between him and God. God expected Adam to be standing on his proper ground. But Adam did not believe that what God had given him was profitable for him. He began to doubt the love of God. A problem developed concerning the love of God.

Adam did not commit that many sins in this incident. He did not gamble; he did not set his eyes on evil things in the streets; he did not read evil books. Adam's sin was a problem that arose between him and God. Following that, many sins came. Once Adam sinned in this way, all kinds of sins followed. Sins are after their kind, and they all come one after another. However, the first sin was not the sin that we would have thought. The first sin was the unique sin in the Old Testament, the sin of not loving God. After a problem developed between man and God, problems among men began to develop. In the garden of Eden, a problem developed in man; then, outside the garden of Eden, the older brother murdered the younger, and all kinds of sins followed. Hence, we see that sins did not begin in a serious and filthy way, as we might imagine. The Bible shows us that sins began with something very simple. But actually the first sin was the most serious one—a problem between man and God.

When we look into the New Testament, we see the Lord Jesus saying many times that he who believes has eternal life (John 3:15-16, 36; 5:24; 6:40, 47; 11:25). There are probably fifty or more times that the Lord indicates that he who believes has eternal life. Who then are those who will perish? Is it the murderers who will go to hell? Is it the fornicators who will perish? Is it those who have filthy thoughts and improper behavior who will go into perdition? Not necessarily. The Gospel of John tells us again and again that it is those who do not believe who are condemned (John 3:16, 18). Those who do not believe have the wrath of God upon them always (John 3:36). The Lord Jesus said that the Holy Spirit came that the world would be convicted concerning sin, righteousness, and judgment (John 16:8). Why concerning sin? Is it because you have gone to the movies lately? Is it because you have gambled lately? Is it because you have murdered someone or have committed arson? No. "Concerning sin, because they do not believe into Me" (John 16:9).

The greatest difficulty we have today is that we consider filthiness sin, but we do not pay much attention to the Lord's word to see what God considers sin. The Lord said that he who does not believe has been condemned. The reason man commits all his sins is that he does not have a proper relationship with the Lord Jesus. In the Old Testament, it was when man lost his proper relationship with God that all kinds of sins were committed. In the New Testament, it is when man loses the proper relationship with the Lord Jesus that all kinds of sins are committed. Here lie all the problems. While you are sitting here tonight, you may think that even though I have proven that you are a sinner, you really have not committed very many sins. But no one in the whole world can say that he has not committed the sin of not loving God. Neither is there anyone in the whole world who can say that he has not committed the sin of not believing in the Lord. For this reason, no one can say that he is not a sinner.

Do you remember Luke 15? There you have a prodigal son and his father. The prodigal son left his father and squandered his estate. But when did the prodigal son become prodigal? Was he a prodigal son when he had a lot of money in his pocket and was living lavishly in a distant country? Or did he become a prodigal only after he had spent all that he had and was hungry while he fed the hogs? Actually, he was a prodigal the day he left his father's house. Before he even spent a dime, he was already a prodigal. He did not become a prodigal only after he had spent all that he had and was feeding the hogs and eating the carob pods and while his garments were torn and his stomach was empty. He became a prodigal when he left his father's house. Let me ask you a question. Suppose the younger son had not spent any money when he was in the distant country. Suppose instead that he had earned a lot of money, that he had gone into business, made a fortune, and became even richer than his father. Would he still have been a prodigal? Indeed he would have. In the eyes of his father, he would have still been a prodigal.

Today there is a very wrong concept that must be rooted out of our mind. We think that because a man has failed to do good, he becomes a sinner. This is absolutely wrong. As long as a man has departed from God, he is a sinner. Even if he is ten times more moral than others, as long as he is away from

God, he is a sinner. You must remember therefore that as Christians, we may perform all the outward services that there are to perform, and we may fulfill all the outward duties that there are to fulfill; we may pray as we always have, and we may read the Bible and attend church meetings as we always have; we may do everything as we always have, and may even do them more. Yet if there is a problem between us and God, we have sinned. When the first love is gone, there is a problem. Who is a prodigal? It is not simply one who has squandered his father's estate, but rather one who has just left his father's house. The moment that a person leaves his father's house he becomes a prodigal. Even if he makes a fortune while he is away, he is still a prodigal. Of course, there will never be a prodigal who makes a fortune in the world. A prodigal will never prosper. A prodigal will always squander away all the money he has. God allows the "money" to be squandered, so that man will know that it is not a good thing to depart from God and will realize that he is a sinner after all.

We now see how we have received the qualification of a sinner and how we have become sinners. We become sinners by developing a relationship with sin, and we commit sins by developing a relationship with sins. There is a difference between the two. Since I was born in Adam and am under sin's dominion, sin has become the principle of my life and my living, and I have become a sinner. In the same way, the many individual sins outside of me have made me one who commits sins. Committing sins has to do with sins, and being a sinner has to do with sin.

### THE OTHER SINS

This does not mean that the other sins are unimportant. All sins carry punishment with them. In the Old Testament, those who did not love God committed many other sins spontaneously. In the New Testament, those who do not believe in the Lord also commit many sins spontaneously. The failure to love God and the refusal to believe in the Lord are the two main sins. From these many other sins are produced, such as unrighteous acts, evil deeds, expressions of greed, wickedness, jealousy, murder, strife, deceit, displays of hatred, slander, backbiting, blasphemy, insolence, pride, arrogance, false accusations, disobedience to parents, unfaithfulness, a lack of natural affection and mercy, self-love, the love of money, ingratitude, unholiness, ferociousness, the despising of good, betraying others, recklessness, loving pleasure rather than God, giving the appearance of godliness without having its reality, and so on. But none of these are the most serious sin that man has ever committed, even though they are sins before God. Unfortunately, man does not realize that these sins are produced through one main sin. Both the sinners in the world and the believers in the church try to deal only with these sins. It seems as if the removal of all these sins would rid us of the problem of sin altogether. But man has not realized that these sins occupy only a secondary place in the Bible.

Though impossible, what if someone had received enough grace to deal with all the other sins? If he had been a person in the Old Testament age, he would have realized that there was still the sin of not loving God. Although he would no longer have the other sins, his conscience would still bother him. If he were a person in the New Testament age, he would realize that there is still the sin of not believing in the Lord. Although he would no longer be condemned by the other sins, he would not feel satisfied in the deepest part of his heart, because the Spirit of God would convict him of his sin of unbelief.

Man perishes because of his unbelief. Unbelief causes the punishment for all the other sins to fall upon an unbelieving one. The immediate reason for man's perdition is his many sins. The ultimate reason is man's sin of unbelief. Because of this, we have to be concerned with the sin of unbelief. Of course, we cannot overlook the other sins either.

### THE RESULT OF SIN AND SINS

Once a man succumbs to the power of sin, he commits a variety of sins. Once a man commits these many sins, he brings upon himself the guilt or condemnation for sins, the verdict or judgment for sins. As soon as we have sinned, there is the problem of guiltiness. Being guilty is not used merely to imply one's act of transgression. It is like a verdict in court that pronounces one either guilty or not guilty. It is a description of whether or not one is legally sinful. According to the Bible, it is not our sin that we are responsible for, but our sins. Our sin does not bring in the problem of guiltiness before God. Rather, the sins we have committed bring in this problem. The Bible says that if we say that we do not have sin, we deceive ourselves (1 John 1:8). Yet at the same time, it does not require us to bear the guilt for our sin. If we confess our sins, God will forgive us of our sins (1 John 1:9). This shows us that we do have to bear the responsibility for our sins.

Because there are the sins, there is guilt. Once a person is guilty, there is the problem of punishment. Because there is punishment, there is unrest in the conscience and the consciousness of being apart from God. Sins make us condemned persons before God. They leave us waiting for God's wrath to appear. Only after one is forgiven is his conscience at peace; only then will he have the boldness to come to God. But even if the many sins are forgiven, as long as the problem of sin remains, the many sins will continue to come, and the problem of guilt will recur. This is why after God has forgiven our sins, He must go on to free us from sin.

## MAN'S UNDERSTANDING OF SIN AND SINS

Before we were saved, we did not feel the evil of sin. Before we became Christians, all that we felt was the evil of the many sins. Even after we became Christians, what saddened us were our many sins, not sin itself. The many sins made us feel terrible, not sin itself. Even though we are saved now, we may still lie or lose our temper, and we may be jealous and proud, or be inadvertently loose with others' possessions. Hence, these individual sins bother us. What do we do? We go before God and ask for forgiveness for each of these items. We may say, "O God, I have been bad today. I have sinned again. Please forgive me." If you did twelve wrong things yesterday, you felt sorry inside. But if you have done only two wrong things today, you feel happy within. You feel that you have committed far fewer sins today, that there are fewer sins in you now. But let me remind you that this is only the initial stage of a Christian life. During this period of time, we feel sorry only for the many sins that we commit.

After we have been Christians for many years, we realize that what saddens and bothers us are not the many sins, but sin itself. In the end, we find out that it is not the things that we do that are wrong, but our person that is wrong. It is not the things that we do that are evil; it is our person itself that is evil. One comes to realize that all the things that he has done are but outward matters and that the real evil thing is his person. There is a natural principle inside us that causes us to sin. The outward things can be of many categories. We can call them pride, jealousy, filthiness, or any other names. There can be all kinds of sins outside of us. But within us there is only one principle, and it is something that craves sins. There is an inclination within us toward sins. There is something in our being that craves these outward things. This is why the Bible makes these outward sins plural in number; they are realized item by item. Pride is one, lying is another, and fornication is yet another. Pride is different from murder, and lying is different from fornication. But there is only one thing which inclines us to sin, which controls and entices us. The reason that we sin is that there is a law within us. It constantly directs us toward the outward sins. This sin is singular in the Bible. It does not denote our conduct; rather, it denotes our nature. This sin is in our nature, and we need to be freed from it.

Since God's salvation for man is complete, He must deliver us from the many sins and He must also deliver us from sin itself. If God only delivers us from the many sins, without delivering us from sin, then God's salvation cannot be said to be complete. Since there are two things with us, the sins and the sin, we need a twofold salvation. On the one hand, we need to be delivered from the many sins. On the other hand, we need to be delivered from sin. In the following pages we will see how in accomplishing His complete salvation through the redemption of Christ, God delivers us both from sins and from sin.

I can clarify my point with an illustration. The many sins are like the fruit of a tree. They exist individually, and a tree can bear one or two hundred of them. This is how sins are. Sin, on the other hand, is like the tree itself. What we the sinners see with our eyes is the fruit. We realize that the fruits are bad, but we do not see that the tree is just as bad. The fruits are bad because the tree is bad. This is how God teaches us to understand the problem of sin. At the beginning He shows us the individual sins. In the end, He shows us ourselves. At the beginning we need forgiveness because we have committed sins. But after a while we realize that we need to be freed because we are sinners.

### THE THREE ASPECTS OF SIN

The Bible shows us that there are three aspects of sin. To put it another way, sin is in three places. First, sin is before God. Second, sin is in the conscience. Third, sin is in the flesh. The Bible always shows us sin according to these three lines. It is like one river that is fed by three tributaries. If we want to know sin in a thorough way, we must be clear about these three lines. We must know that our sin is before God, in the conscience, and in the flesh. If we are not clear about these three lines and are not able to distinguish between them, we will not be clear concerning the problem of sin. If we confuse the three lines, we will not realize God's view concerning sin, and we will not comprehend the thoroughness of God's work in dealing with sin. Only when we understand the need will we acknowledge the treatment. If we do not know the need, we will assume that the treatment is unnecessary. Hence, we must know sin first, and then we can know the thoroughness of God's salvation.

God is a righteous God. In the administration of the universe He is the highest authority. He is the Ruler of the universe. He has definite laws and ordinances concerning sins. He rewards man according to what man has done, and He recompenses according to how man has acted. God deals with the world in His position as the sovereign Ruler. At the time of Adam, though there was no such term for it, there was the Adamic law. After Noah, again though there was no such term for it, there was the Noachian law. At the time of Moses, the term *law* specifically began to be used. It was not until then that the law was specifically placed before man. Whether we are talking about the explicit law after the time of Moses or about the implicit law before the time of Moses, God's verdict is that those who sin must die. He demands that those who transgress against the law will be punished with eternal death. While man is alive, though his flesh is living, his spirit is dying. In the end, his flesh will also die. In eternity, his spirit, soul, and body will all die. If man does not sin, God will not execute the punishment. But if man does sin, God will surely execute the punishment. God has enacted ordinances and laws concerning man's sins.

When sins occur in our life, there is first the record of sins before God. Let me illustrate with an example. Recently people were forbidden to park their cars anywhere they pleased. Two months ago you could park your car anywhere. You could even park your car on the wrong side of the street, and you were free to park your car in any direction. But two months ago the traffic department ruled out this practice. Now as you drive, you see all the cars parked in the same direction. There is a new law that says that all cars should be parked in the same direction as the flow of traffic. If you do not do this, you violate the law. If a brother comes to the meeting today by car and parks in the wrong direction, an officer from the police department may see this and record a violation against him at the police department. The violation is recorded not in the street where he parked, but in the police department, even though the brother may not be aware of the fact. The violation may have happened on Ha-tung Road, but the place where the violation is recorded is the Tsin-an-tsu district police department.

The incidents of sin occur in man. But as soon as man sins, there is the record of it before God. God is the sovereign Ruler of the world. He is in control of everything. If in the course of our lives we have transgressed the law, there is a record of our sin before God. This is why the Old Testament frequently speaks of sinning against Jehovah. The reason an act of sin is evil and terrifying is that once a sin is committed, there is the record of sin before God. Since God says that he who sins must die, He has to execute His judgment on sins. There is no way for us to escape, for the record of sin is there already.

Second, there is the knowledge of the sin in our conscience. Though there is a record of the sin before God, until you know about it, you may still be able to smile and rejoice in your seat, and you may be able to act as if nothing has happened. But once you have the knowledge of a sin, the sin that is before God has come into your conscience. Originally, this sin was only before God; now it is identified in your conscience. What is the conscience? It is a "window." God's light shines into you through the window of your conscience. Whenever God's light shines into you, you feel uncomfortable and you know that you have done something wrong.

There may be someone here tonight who has parked his car in the wrong direction. Perhaps he was not aware of his mistake and may have been quite unconcerned. But since I have mentioned it, he will now feel uneasy within. My words have moved the record of his sin from the police department into him. Hence, the conscience is turned by knowledge. Without knowledge, you are ignorant of your sins; and since your conscience does not bother you, you will feel peaceful. But as soon as you have the knowledge and begin to realize God's view and the view of the law concerning you, your conscience will not let you go.

Is it true that everyone has a conscience? Surely everyone has a conscience. But some consciences are closed up and light cannot get in. Some consciences are like a kitchen window that has a thick layer of grime on it. Through it you may be able to see the shadow of a man moving, but you cannot see the man clearly. If a person's conscience cannot take in God's light, he will be unconcerned and happy. But the moment he hears the gospel and sees his own sins, his place before God, and the record of his sins before God, his conscience has a problem. It will be bothered. It will not be at peace, but will condemn him. He will ask what he should do to be able to stand before the righteous God, and how he can become justified before such a righteous God.

The amazing thing about the conscience is that it may at

worst go to sleep, but it will never die. Never think that the conscience has died. It will never die, but it will go to sleep. However, when the consciences of many wake up, they find that it is too late, that they do not have the opportunity anymore to believe or to be saved. Do not think that our conscience will let us go. One day it will catch up with us. One day it will speak. I have seen many who thought this way, who did much evil and thought that they would get by. But when their conscience finally woke up, they were caught by it.

What do people do when their conscience wakes up and they realize that they have sinned? As soon as their conscience catches up with them, they try to do good by performing good works. What is the purpose of man's trying to do good works? The purpose is to bribe the conscience. The conscience shows man that he has sinned. So now he performs more charitable acts and does more good deeds to tell his conscience that although he has done so much wrong, he has also done all these good things. What does it mean to do good works? To do good works means to bribe the conscience when it starts accusing, in order to quell its condemnation. This is a way of salvation invented by man.

But please remember that this is basically the wrong way. Where is the basic error? The error lies in our assumption that sin exists only in our conscience. We forget that sin also exists before God. If sin were only in our conscience, then we would need to perform at most ten good works to more than compensate for our one mistake. But the problem now is not with our conscience. The problem now is what is before God. I cannot be absolved from judgment for one violation of illegal parking just because I park the car legally a hundred times. Sin is something before God. It is not merely something in our conscience. Not only do we have to deal with the sin in our conscience; we also have to deal with our sin before God. Only when we have dealt with the record of sin before God can the sin in our conscience be dealt with. We cannot deal with the problem in the conscience first, for the conscience can be pacified by self-deception. But remember that the conscience will never die.

Perhaps you have not seen the conscience at work yet. I

have often seen people who are troubled in their conscience. When the light of God comes, the conscience is ill at ease. A person in such a condition would crawl into a hole in the floor if there were one. He would do anything to pacify his conscience. He would even forsake his life to redeem himself from sin. Why did Judas hang himself? It was because his conscience would not let him go. He had betrayed Jesus, and his conscience would not let him go.

Why is there no need for God to send many angels to throw men into the lake of fire as though they were throwing stones? Why is there no need for God to have many angels guarding the lake of fire? Is not God afraid of a revolt in hell? I am sure that for a man who has sinned hell is a blessing rather than a curse. When the conscience rises up to condemn a man, it demands that the man be punished. Punishment is not just a demand of God, it is also a demand of man. Before you see what sin is, you are afraid of punishment. But after you see what sin is, you will take punishment as a blessing. Have you ever seen murderers or assassinators at the time of their execution? Before a man sees his sin, he may rejoice in murder. But after he sees his sin, he will rejoice in his own execution. Hence, hell is not only a place of punishment. It is also a place of escape. It is the ultimate place of escape. Sin in the conscience causes pain today and cries out for punishment in the coming age. Hence, for God to save us, He must deal with our sins before Him, and He must also deal with our sins in our conscience.

There is a third aspect to sin. Sin is not only before God and in man's conscience; sin is also in man's flesh. This is what Romans 7 and 8 tell us. What is the sin in the flesh? We have seen that, on the one hand, there is the record of sins before God and that, on the other hand, there is the condemnation of sins in man's conscience. Now we see the third aspect: the power of sin and the activities of sin in man's flesh. Sin has its place. Sin is presiding. Sin is in man's flesh as the chairman. Please remember that sin is the chairman presiding in the flesh.

What do I mean by this? Sins before God and in man's own conscience are objective. For me the record of sins before God and the condemnation of sins in my conscience are matters of my feeling with respect to sin. But sin in the flesh is subjective. This means that the sin that is dwelling in me has the power to force me to sin; it has the power to incite and arouse me to sin. This is what the Bible calls the sin in the flesh.

For example, there may be a brother who earns a hundred dollars a month, but spends a hundred and fifty dollars a month. He likes to borrow money. It is his disposition. If he does not borrow, his hands will itch; even his head and his body will itch. After using up all of his salary, he must borrow some and spend it before he can feel comfortable. In him we can see the three aspects. First, he has many creditors, who have the records of his debts. Second, unless he has no knowledge of the consequences of borrowing, in which case he may still go on borrowing peacefully, he realizes that he is in danger and thus is burdened not only with the record of debt before his creditors, but also with the exposing by his conscience. Yet in addition, there is the sin in his flesh. He knows that it is wrong to borrow, yet he feels restless unless he continues to borrow. Something is prompting him and arousing him, telling him that he has not borrowed for months and that he should do it one more time. What is this? This is the sin in his flesh. On the one hand, sin is a fact with him; it results in a record of sin before God and sin in his conscience. On the other hand, sin is a power in his flesh; it incites and compels him, even drags and pulls him, to sin.

If you have never resisted sin, you have not felt its power. But if you try to resist sin, you will sense its power. When water is flowing, you do not feel its power if you flow along with it. But if you try to go against the flow, you will feel its power. Most rivers in China flow from the west to the east; so if you try to travel from the east to the west, you will feel how powerful China's rivers are. Those who know the power of sin the most are those who are the holiest, for they are the ones who try to oppose and to stand against sin. If you are joined to sin and are going along with it, surely you will not know its power. The sin in your flesh is all the time arousing and compelling you to sin, but only when you wake up to deal with sin will you realize that you are a lost and perishing sinner. Only

then will you know that you are helpless and that you have
no way to solve the problem of sin in your flesh, not to mention the presence of sins in your conscience and the record of
sins before God.

Therefore, we have to see that when God saves us, He
deals with all three aspects. The inward sin is dealt with by
the cross and the crucifixion of the old man. We have mentioned this many times before, so we will not repeat it now.
Our Bible study this time covers God's way of dealing with
our sins before Him and the condemnation of sins in our conscience. Earlier I mentioned the problem of sin and sins. Sins
refer to the sinful acts before God and in our conscience.
Every time the Bible mentions sins, it is referring to the
sinful acts before God and in our conscience. But every time
the Bible mentions the sin in the flesh, it uses the word *sin,*
not *sins.* If you remember this, you will have no trouble later
on.

We thank God that His salvation is complete. He has dealt
with our sins before Him. He has also judged our sins in the
person of the Lord Jesus. Furthermore, the Holy Spirit has
applied Christ's work to us, so that we could receive the Lord
Jesus and have peace in our conscience. Once the conscience
is cleansed, there is no more consciousness of sin. Many times
I have heard Christians say that the blood of the Lord Jesus
washes away their sins. When I ask if they feel peaceful and
happy, they say that at times they still feel the presence of
their sins. This is inconceivable. I am happy because when
the conscience is cleansed, there is no more consciousness of
sins. Our conscience has the consciousness of sins because
there is the record of sins before God. But if the sins are gone
before God, how can we still have the consciousness of them?
Since the sins before God have been dealt with, the sins in our
conscience should be dealt with as well. Hence, we should not
have the consciousness of our sins any longer.

# CHAPTER TWO

## GOD'S LOVE, GRACE, AND MERCY

Tonight we will consider God's love and grace, and we will also touch the subject of God's mercy.

Many times the Old Testament says that salvation is of Jehovah. This indicates that salvation does not originate with us. Since sin is committed by man we would naturally think that salvation also originates in man. But even the thought of our salvation did not originate with us; rather, it originated with God. Although man has sinned and is destined for perdition, it is not his intention to seek salvation. Though he has sinned and ought to perish, it was God who took up the thought of saving him. Hence, the Old Testament mentions again and again that salvation is of Jehovah. The reason for this is that it is God who wants to save us. Man has never wanted to save himself.

Why is salvation of Jehovah? Why is God interested in man? In a general way, we can say that it is because God is love. But more specifically, it is because God loves man. If God did not love man, He would not need to save him. Salvation is accomplished because, on the one hand, man has sinned and, on the other hand, God has loved. If man had not sinned, there would be no place and no way for the love of God to be manifested. And if man had sinned but God had not loved, nothing would have been achieved either. Salvation is accomplished and the gospel is preached because on the one hand God has loved and on the other hand man has sinned.

Man's sin shows us man's need. God's love shows us God's provision. If there is only the need without the provision, nothing can be done. But if there is the provision without the need, the provision will be wasted. Salvation is accomplished and the gospel is preached due to the two greatest facts in the universe. The first is that man has sinned and the second is that God loves man. These are two immutable facts. They are two facts that the Bible emphasizes. If you drop either of these two ends, salvation will be lost. You do not need to drop both ends. As long as one end is gone, there will be no possibility for salvation to be accomplished. God has love and man has sin. Because of these two facts, there is salvation and there is the gospel.

## GOD'S LOVE

The Bible never fails to point out the love of God. In our Bible study this time, we will cover the truth of the gospel only in a sketchy way. We will mention a lot of things, but will not consider them in detail. Tonight I cannot cover every aspect concerning the love of God found in the Bible. I can mention this matter only briefly. We must consider three aspects of the love of God. First, God is love. Second, God loves man. And third, the expression of God's love is in the death of Christ.

### God Is Love

Let us come to the first point: God is love. This is recorded in 1 John 4:16. Here it does not say that God loves. Nor does it say that God may love, or that God can love, or that God has loved or will love. Rather, it says that God is love. What does it mean to say that God is love? It means that God Himself, His nature and His being, is love. If we can say that God has a substance, then God's substance is love.

The greatest revelation of the Bible is that God is love. This revelation is what man needs the most. Man has many conjectures and theories about God. We ponder all the time about what kind of God our God is, what kind of heart our God has, what intentions God has toward man, what God Himself is like. You can ask anyone about his idea of God, and he will give you his concept. He will think that God is this kind of God or that kind of God. All the idols in the world and all the images made by man are products of man's imagination. Man thinks that God is a fierce God or a severe God. He pictures God this way and that way. Man is always trying to reason and to explore what God is like. In order to correct the different conjectures man has concerning God, He manifests

Himself in the light of the gospel and shows man that He is not an unapproachable or unfathomable God.

What is God then? God is love. This statement will not be clear to you unless I give an illustration. Suppose that there is a patient person. He has patience no matter what he encounters and no matter how difficult or bad the conditions are. For such a person, we cannot say that he has acted patiently. The adverb *patiently* cannot be used to describe him. Nor can we say that he is patient, using an adjective. We must say that he is patience itself. Perhaps we would not refer to him by his name. Instead, behind his back we would say that Patience has come or that Patience has spoken. When we say that God is love, we mean that love is the nature of God. He is love from inside to outside. Therefore, we would not say that God is loving, using an adjective, or that God loves, using a verb. Rather, we would say that God is love, applying the noun to Him.

In our friend Patience we cannot find rashness. The man is patience itself; he is not simply patient. He is just a lump of patience. Would you think that with such a person there could be rashness? Could he lose his temper? Could he exchange sharp words with others? It is impossible for him to do such things because there is no element in his nature to do such things. There is no such thing as temper in his nature. There is no such thing as rashness in his nature. He is simply patience.

The same is true with God, who is love. God as love is the greatest revelation in the Bible. For every Christian, the greatest thing to know in the Bible is that God is love. It is impossible for God to hate. If God hates, He will not only have a conflict with whomever He hates, but will also have a conflict with Himself. If God hated any one of us here today, He would not have a problem with that one alone; He would have a problem with Himself. God must develop a problem with Himself before He can hate or do anything in a way that is not in love. God is love. Although these three words are most simple, they give us the greatest revelation. The nature of God, the life-essence of God, is just love. He cannot do anything otherwise. He loves, and at the same time, He is love.

If you are a sinner today, you may wonder what you must do before God will love you. Many people do not know God's mind toward them. They do not know what God is thinking or what intentions God has. Many think that they should do something or that they should suffer or should be very conscientious before they can please God. However, only those who are in darkness and do not know God will think this way. If there were no gospel today, you would be able to think this way. But now that the gospel is here, you cannot think this way anymore, for the gospel tells us that God is love.

We human beings are nothing but hatred. For us to love is extremely difficult. Likewise, it is equally difficult for God to hate. You may think that it is difficult to love and that you do not know how to love others. But it is impossible for God to hate. You have no way to love, and God has no way to hate. God is love, and for Him to hate is for Him to act contrary to His nature, which is impossible for Him to do.

## God So Loved the World

This is not all. God Himself is love, but when this love is applied to us, we find that "God so loved the world" (John 3:16). "God is love" speaks of His nature, and "God so loved the world" speaks of His action. God Himself is love; hence, that which issues out from Him must be love. Where there is love, there must also be the object of that love. After showing us that He is love, God immediately shows us that He loves the world. God has not only loved us, but has also sent forth His love. God could not help but send forth His love. He could not help but love the world. Hallelujah!

The greatest problem the world has is that it thinks that God always harbors evil intentions for man. Man thinks that God makes severe demands, and that He is strict and mean. Since man has doubts about the love of God, he also doubts that God loves the world. But as long as God is love, He loves the world. If love is His nature, He can conduct Himself toward man in no other way except in love. It would make Him uncomfortable if He did not love. Hallelujah! This is a fact! God is love. He cannot help but love. God is love, and what spontaneously follows is that God loves the world.

We can blame ourselves for our sins, for being susceptible to Satan's temptation, for being entangled by sin. But we cannot doubt God Himself. You can blame yourself for committing a sin, for having failed, for succumbing to temptation. But if you doubt God's heart toward you, you are not acting like a Christian, for to doubt God's heart toward you is to contradict the revelation in the gospel.

I cannot say that you will never fail again. Nor can I say that you will never sin again. Perhaps you will fail and you will sin again. But please remember that for you to fail or sin is one thing, but God's heart towards you is another. You must never doubt God's feeling toward you simply because you have failed or sinned. Although you may sin and fail, God does not change His attitude toward you, for God is love and He loves the world. This is an unchangeable fact in the Bible.

On our side, we change and turn. But on the side of the love of God, there is no change or turn. Many times your love can change or become cold. But this does not mean that God's love is affected. If God is love, no matter how you test Him, what comes forth from Him is always love. If there is a piece of wood here, no matter how you hit it, you will always get the sound of wood. If you hit it with a book, it will give you the sound of wood. If you hit it with your palm, it will still give you the sound of wood. If you hit it with another piece of wood, it will again give you the sound of wood. If God is love, no matter how you "hit" Him—if you reject Him, deny Him, or cast Him aside—He is still love. One thing is sure: God cannot deny Himself; He cannot contradict Himself. Since we are just hatred itself, it is altogether natural for us to hate. Since God is love, it is altogether natural for God to love. God cannot change His own nature. Since God's nature cannot be changed, His attitude toward you cannot be changed. So we see that God loves the world.

## God's Expression of Love

Does the whole matter stop with God loving the world? "God is love" speaks of God's nature; it speaks of God Himself. "God so loved the world" speaks of God's action. But God's love toward us has an expression. What is this expression of His love? Romans 5:8 says, "But God commends His own love to us in that while we were yet sinners, Christ died for us." God's love has an expression. If I love a person and merely tell him that I love him, that love has not yet been consummated. Unless love is expressed, it is not consummated. There is no love in the world that is without an expression. If there is love, it must be expressed. If a love is not expressed, such a love cannot be considered love. Love is most practical. It is not vain and is not merely a verbal matter. Love is expressed through actions. If you put a ball on a surface that is not level, you can be sure that something will happen; it will end up rolling down. The same is true with love. You can be sure that it will have an expression.

Since God loves the world, He has to be concerned about man's need. Hence, He must do something for man. We are sinners. We have no other choice but to go to hell, and no other place to be except in the place of perdition. But God loves us, and He will not be satisfied until He has saved us. When God says, "I love you," His love will step up to bear all our burdens and remove all our problems. Since God loves us, He must provide a solution to the problem of sins; He must provide the salvation that we sinners need. For this reason, the Bible has shown us this one great fact: the love of God is manifested in the death of Christ. Since we are sinners and are unable to save ourselves, Christ came to die in order to solve the problem of sin for us. His love has accomplished something substantial, and this has been put before us. Now we can see His love in a substantial way. His love is no longer merely a feeling. It has become a thoroughly manifested act.

In this great matter of God's love, we must take note of three things: the nature of God's love, the action of God's love, and the expression of God's love. Thank and praise God! His love is not only a feeling within Him. It is also an action, and even an expression and manifestation. His love made Him do what we cannot do by ourselves. Since He is love and since He has loved the world, salvation has been produced. Since man has sin and since God is love, a lot of things follow. If you are not poor, you will have no need of me. But if I do not love you, even if you are extremely poor, I will not be concerned at all. The situation today is that man has sinned and God has loved; therefore, things begin to happen. Hallelujah, a lot is happening because man has sinned and God has loved. When you put the two things together, the gospel comes into being.

## GOD'S GRACE

But, brothers and sisters, God's love does not stop here. Since God is love, the matter of grace comes up. It is true that love is precious, but love must have its expression. When love is expressed, it becomes grace. Grace is love expressed. Love is something in God. But when this love comes to you, it becomes grace. If God is only love, He is very abstract. But thank the Lord that although love is something abstract, with God it is immediately turned into something substantial. The inward love is abstract, but the outward grace has given it substance.

For example, you may have pity on a pauper, and you may love him and have sympathy for him. But if you would not give him food and clothing, the most you could say is that you love him. You could not say that you are grace to him. When can you say that you have grace toward him? When you give him a bowl of rice or a piece of clothing or some money, and when the food, clothing, or money reach him, your love becomes grace. The difference between love and grace lies in the fact that love is within and grace is without. Love is primarily an inward feeling, while grace is an outward act. When love is turned into action, it becomes grace. When grace is traced back to its feeling, it is love. Without love, grace cannot come into being. Grace exists because love exists.

The definition of grace is not just the act of love. We must add something else to this. Grace is the act of love upon the destitute. God loves His only begotten Son. But there is no element of grace in this love. One cannot say that God deals with His Son in grace. God also loves the angels, but that cannot be considered as grace either. Why is not the Father's love toward the Son and God's love toward the angels grace? The reason is that there is no destitution and deprivation involved. There is only love; there is no thought of grace. Only when there is deprivation and destitution, when there is no way for one to solve his problems on his own, is love realized as grace. Since we are sinners, we are those with problems; and we have no way to solve our problems. But God is love, and His love is manifested to us as grace.

Hence, when love flows on the same level, it is simply love. But when it flows down, it is grace. Therefore, those who have never been on the low end can never receive grace. Love can also flow up. But when it does, it is not grace. Love can also flow between equal heights. When it does, it is not grace either. Only when love flows downward is it grace. If you want to be above God, or if you want to be equal with God, you will never see the day of grace. Only those who are below God can see the day of grace. This is what the Bible shows us about the difference between love and grace.

Although the Bible mentions the love of the Lord Jesus, it pays more attention to the grace of the Lord Jesus. The Bible also speaks of the grace of God, but it pays more attention to the love of God. I am not saying that there is no mention of the love of the Lord Jesus and the grace of God in the Bible. But the emphasis in the Bible is on the love of God and the grace of the Lord Jesus. How did Paul greet the church in Corinth? "The grace of the Lord Jesus Christ and the love of God and the fellowship of the Holy Spirit be with you all" (2 Cor. 13:14). You cannot change the sentence to read, "the grace of God and the love of the Lord Jesus Christ and the fellowship of the Holy Spirit be with you all." You cannot do this, because the emphasis of the Bible is on the love of God and the grace of the Lord Jesus. Why is this so? Because it was the Lord Jesus who accomplished salvation. It was He who substantiated love and accomplished grace. The love of God became grace through the work of the Lord Jesus. Therefore, the Bible tells us that the law was given through Moses, but grace came through Jesus Christ (John 1:17).

## GOD'S MERCY

Thank the Lord that in the love of God, there is not only grace, but another great item as well, God's mercy. The Bible puts much emphasis on mercy also. But we have to admit that *mercy* is more particularly an Old Testament word, in the same way that *grace* is more particularly a New Testament word. This does not mean that you will not find *mercy* in the New Testament. But if you have a cross-reference Bible or a concordance, you will find *mercy* in the Old Testament far more frequently. Mercy is something of the Old Testament, in the same way that grace is something of the New Testament.

The outlet of love is either grace or mercy. Mercy is negative, and grace is positive. Mercy is related to the present condition, and grace is related to the future condition. Mercy speaks of the poverty of your present condition, and grace speaks of the bright condition that you will be saved into in the future. The feeling that God has toward us when we are sinners is mercy. The work that God does upon us to make us the children of God is grace. Mercy arises from our existing condition; grace arises from the work that we will receive.

I do not know if you are clear about this or not. Suppose there is a destitute person here with us. You love him and have pity upon him. You feel sorry for his difficult situation. If you did not love him, you would not suffer and grieve for him. But by doing so, you are having mercy on him. But such mercy is negative. Your mercy on him is in sympathy for his present condition. But when is grace accomplished? It is accomplished when this person is rescued today out of his poor condition to a new position, to a new realm and a new environment. Only then does your love to him become grace. This is why I say that mercy is negative and for today, while grace is positive and for the future. The future I am talking about is the future in this age, rather than the future in the coming age. I do not mean that the Old Testament speaks only about mercy. The Old Testament speaks about grace, too. It is not true that we no longer need mercy. No, we still need mercy. God was merciful in the time of the Old Testament, because His work was not yet completed. Therefore, the Old Testament was full of mercy. God showed mercy for four thousand years. But today, in the New Testament age, we have grace because the Lord Jesus has accomplished His work. He has come to bear our sins. Hence, what we have received today is not mercy, but grace. Hallelujah! Today is not a day of mercy, but a day of grace.

If there were only mercy, we could only have hope. In the Old Testament, there was only hope; hence, the Old Testament speaks of mercy. But thank the Lord, today we have obtained what was hoped for. There is no need to hope for it anymore.

Mercy comes from love and issues in grace. If mercy has not come from love, it will not issue in grace. Since it originates in love, it arrives at grace. In the Gospels there is the account of a blind man receiving his sight (Mark 10:46-52). When he met the Lord, he did not say, "Lord, love me!" or "Lord, be gracious to me!" Rather, he said, "Son of David, have mercy on me!" (v. 48). He asked for mercy because of his present condition, his present difficulty, and his present pain. He knew that if the Lord Jesus were to sympathize with him, He would not stop at showing mercy to him; He would surely do something.

In the New Testament there are also a few places where mercy is mentioned. In most cases, mercy is mentioned in reference to the situation at the time. Some may ask, "Since the love of God is so precious, why must there be mercy? Love is very good as the source, and grace is also very good as the result. Why then is there the need for mercy?" It is because man is destitute. We have no courage to go to God and ask for His love. We are of the flesh and do not know God well enough. Although God has revealed Himself to us in the light, we still do not dare come close to Him. We feel that it is impossible for us to go to God and ask for love. At the same time, we do not have the adequate faith to go to Him and ask for grace, telling Him that we need such and such a blessing. We have no way to ask for God's love, and we do not have enough faith to ask for God's grace.

But thank the Lord. Not only do we have love and grace; we also have mercy. Love is manifested in this mercy. Because God is merciful, if you hear the gospel and are still unable to believe, you can cry, "Son of David, have mercy on me!" You may be afraid to ask about other things, but you need not be afraid to ask this one thing. I dare not ask the Lord to be gracious to me. I dare not ask Him to love me. But I can ask Him to be merciful to me. For other things we dare not ask. But we can be bold to ask for mercy. God is pleased with this. God has placed His love among us so that we would have the right to come to Him. But if there were only love, we would still be afraid to come to God. Since God is also merciful, we are able to come to Him. I dare not ask God to love me, nor do I dare ask Him to show grace. But I can ask God for mercy. I can at least ask for that.

Last year I met a man who was very old and was suffering from a serious illness. When he saw me he cried. He told me that he was not bitter toward God, but that he was indeed in much pain. I told him that he should ask God to love him and be gracious to him. He said that he could not do this. When I asked him why not, he answered that for sixty years he had been living for himself and not for God. Now that he was dying, he would be ashamed to ask God to love him and be gracious to him. Had he not been so far away from God, had he drawn closer to God during the past few decades, had he developed some affection for God, it would have been easier for him to ask for love and grace. But such as he was, away from God his whole life, how could he ask God to love him as he lay on his deathbed? In spite of my persuasion, he would not believe my words. I told him that God could grant grace to him, that He could be gracious to him and could love him. But he simply could not believe it. I went to see him many times, but I could not get through. Then I prayed, "O God, here is a man who will not believe in You. Nor will he believe in Your love. I have no way to help him. Please open up a way for him in his last hour." Later I felt that I should not speak to him about grace, nor about love, but only about mercy. I went to him again rejoicingly. I said to him, "You should forget about everything now. Forget about the love of God or the grace of God. You should go to God and say to Him, 'God! I am suffering. I have no way to go on. Have mercy on me.'" Immediately he agreed. And as soon as he agreed, his faith came and he prayed, "God, I thank You that You are a merciful God. I am weak and suffering. Have mercy on me." Here you see a person being brought to the presence of the Lord. He realized his destitute situation and asked for mercy. In his present condition, he asked God to be merciful to him.

Now let us look at a few verses. Ephesians 2:4-5 says, "But God, being rich in mercy, because of His great love with which He loved us, even when we were dead in offenses." Paul said that God was rich in mercy because of something. That something is His great love with which He loved us. Without love, there would be no mercy. In what situation was He merciful to us? He was merciful to us when we were dead in offenses. His mercy had to do with our present distressing situation. Because we were dead in sins, He had mercy on us. He had mercy on us based on His love toward us. What happens after mercy? Verse 8 goes on to tell us that He saved us by grace. Hence, mercy was shown to us because we were in a situation of being dead in offenses; then, grace was given to us for our salvation, indicating that we received a new position and entered a new realm. Thank God that there is not only love and grace, but great mercy as well.

In 1 Timothy 1:13 Paul says, "Who formerly was a blasphemer and a persecutor and an insulting person; but I was shown mercy because, being ignorant, I acted in unbelief." Paul explains here how he obtained mercy. His obtaining mercy had to do with his life history. It had to do with his being a blasphemer, a persecutor, and an insulting person. Before he was saved, he was in a condition of being a blasphemer, a persecutor, an insulting person, and an ignorant and unbelieving person. While he was in such a condition, God had mercy on him. So you can see that mercy is negative and has to do with the hard and difficult situations of our past. Grace, on the other hand, has to do with the positive aspects related to us. The two must be distinguished and should not be considered the same.

Titus 3:5 says, "Not out of works in righteousness which we did but according to His mercy He saved us...." There is no righteousness in ourselves. While we were without righteousness and were in a suffering and helpless situation, God had mercy on us. Thank the Lord that there is mercy! We saw earlier that mercy originates in love and terminates in grace. When mercy extends itself, we are saved. He had mercy upon us in the condition that we were in, and as a result we were saved.

Romans 11:32 says, "For God has shut up all in disobedience that He might show mercy to all." Why did God shut up all in disobedience? It was so that He might show mercy to all. God allowed all to become disobedient and has shut up all in disobedience, not for the purpose of making them disobedient, but for the purpose of showing mercy to all. After He has shown mercy, His next action is to save them. Therefore, mercy has to do with your condition, not the condition after you became a Christian, but the condition before you were saved. But thank God that He did not stop with mercy. With Him there is also grace.

There is one place in the Bible that shows us clearly that our regeneration is of mercy. First Peter 1:3 says, "Blessed be the God and Father of our Lord Jesus Christ, who according to His great mercy has regenerated us unto a living hope through the resurrection of Jesus Christ from the dead." All of God's work in grace was planned according to His mercy in love. His grace is directed by His mercy, and His mercy is directed by His love. It was according to His great mercy that God regenerated us unto a living hope through the resurrection of Jesus Christ from the dead. Hence, both regeneration and the living hope are related to mercy. Because there is mercy, there is grace.

Jude 21 says, "Keep yourselves in the love of God, awaiting the mercy of our Lord Jesus Christ unto eternal life." This verse shows us that today we should keep ourselves in the love of God. Until the Lord comes again, that is, until He appears to us, we should await His mercy unto eternal life. Before we are raptured, we should await His mercy. Today while living on this earth, we receive not only mercy, but also grace. Thank the Lord that we have been saved and belong to God, but there is still one problem. Our bodies are not yet redeemed. Although we are no longer of the world, we are still in the world. It is good not to belong to the world, but this is not enough. Sooner or later the Israelites had to leave Egypt. Sooner or later Noah had to leave the ark to enter into the new age. Sooner or later Lot had to leave Sodom. And the day must come when the Christians must leave the world. While I am being attacked in this world, I await the mercy of the Lord Jesus. While I am being entangled by sin in this world, I await the mercy of the Lord Jesus. While I am being buffeted by Satan in this world, I await the Lord's salvation. Hence, while we are living on earth and keeping ourselves in the love of God, we await the day when the Lord will show mercy to us. Therefore, it is still necessary for His mercy to be upon us. We have to await His mercy until the day that we are raptured.

The Bible shows us one thing more concerning mercy and grace. Both in the Old Testament as well as in the New Testament, the word *mercy* is always preceded by either *show* or *have*. Mercy is something that is shown, and those who are shown mercy are said to have received mercy. Why does the Bible say "to show mercy" instead of "to give mercy"? It is because mercy does not require our doing. Grace, on the other hand, requires some doing. When we obtain grace we obtain something definite. But when we receive mercy, it is only a receiving; all that we have to do is to receive.

Hebrews 4:16 exhorts us to come often to the Lord to pray. When we come to pray before the Lord, we will receive mercy and find grace for timely help. Some versions use the expression *obtain mercy*. But actually, in the original language, the word is not *obtain*. *Obtain* is something too active. The word is more passive in Greek. It should be translated "receive." We are to receive mercy and to find grace. What is to receive? To receive means that everything is here; it is always ready for use anytime. What is grace? Grace is something that you have to "find," because it is something that God will do. Grace is something positive; it is something to be worked out. That is why it says to "receive" mercy and to "find" grace. The Bible is very clear about mercy and grace. There is no confusion between the two.

# CHAPTER THREE

## THE NATURE OF GRACE

On the first evening we discussed the problem of sin. Last night we spoke about God's grace. However, we did not finish these matters. Therefore, we will continue the two previous messages and cover the matters of grace and sin further.

First, we have to see what is the nature of grace. What characteristics does grace have? We treasure the love of God, for without God's love as the source, there would not be the flow of salvation. The flow of salvation issues from the love of God. At the same time, without God's mercy there would be no possibility of salvation. Because God has shown mercy on us, He has given us His salvation. God's salvation is the concrete expression of God's love. Hence, we treasure love, and we also treasure mercy. But the most precious of all that reaches us is grace. Love is indeed good, but it does not give any concrete benefit to us. Mercy is also very good, but it also does not bring us any direct benefit; however with grace there is a direct benefit. Hence, grace is more precious. The New Testament is filled, not with the love of God, nor with the mercy of God, but with the grace of God. Grace is God's love coming forth to accomplish something for the fallen, lost, and perishing sinner. Now we not only have an abstract love and a sentimental mercy, but we have grace to meet our needs in a concrete way.

We may think that it is wonderful enough if God is merciful to us. A fleshly or fleshy person will think that mercy is good enough. The Old Testament is filled with words of mercy. There are not many words on grace. When man is in the flesh, he thinks that mercy is enough, that there is no need for grace. He thinks this way because he does not consider sin to be something serious. If man were without food or clothing or housing, mercy would not be adequate; there would also be the need of grace. But the problem with sin is not a lack of food, clothing, or housing. The problem with sin is unrest in man's conscience and judgment before God. For this, man thinks that if only God would be merciful to us and be a bit more lenient, everything would be fine. If God would overlook our sins, it would be good enough for us. In our hearts we hope that God would be merciful to us and let us go. Man's concept is to let go and to overlook. But God cannot mercifully overlook our sins. He cannot let us get by loosely. He must deal thoroughly with our sins.

Not only does God have to show mercy on us; He has to give us grace as well. What issues out from God's love is grace. God is not satisfied with mercy alone. We think that if there were mercy and that if God would let us go and not reckon with us, everything would be fine. But God did not say that since He has pity on us He would let us go. This is not the way God works. When God works, He must do so in harmony with Himself. Therefore, God's love cannot stop with mercy. His love must extend into grace. He must deal thoroughly with the problem of our sins. If the problem of sins were something that could be overlooked, God's mercy would be sufficient. But to Him, letting us go and overlooking our sins are not sufficient. Thus to have mercy alone is not sufficient. He must settle the matter of sins thoroughly. Here we see the grace of God. This is why the New Testament, though not void of mercy, is full of grace. In it we see how the Son of God, Jesus Christ, has come to the world to show forth grace and to become grace so that we might receive grace.

What is grace? Grace is nothing other than God's great work accomplished freely in His unconditional and boundless love for helpless, unworthy, and sinful man. God's grace is just God working for man. How does this contrast with the law? The law is God requiring man to work for Him, while grace is God working for man. What is the law? The law is God's demand for man to do something for Him. What is work? Work is man's effort to do something for God. What is grace? Grace is neither God requiring something nor God receiving man's work, but grace is God doing His own work. When God comes forth to do something for and on behalf of man, that is grace.

The emphasis in the New Testament is not on the principle of the law. In fact, the New Testament opposes the principle of the law because law and grace can never mix. Is it God who is working or is it man who is working? Is God giving something to man or is He asking for something from man? If God is asking for something from man, we are still in the age of the law. But if God is giving something to man, we are in the age of grace. You would not go to someone's home to give him money while you are there to collect money. Likewise, law and grace are opposite principles; they cannot be put together. If man is to receive grace, he must put the law aside. On the other hand, if he follows the law, he will fall from grace.

If man is to follow the law, he must have God accept his works. If there is the principle of the law and of works and if man is to give something to God, he must give God what He demands. The Bible indicates that man's works should be a response to God's law. God's law demands that I do something. When I do it, I am responding to God's law. This is what the Bible calls works. But when grace is here, the principle of law and of works is set aside. Here we see that it is God working for man instead of man working for God.

Grace, which is God working for helpless, poor, and troubled man, has three characteristics or natures. Everyone who wants to understand God's grace must remember these three characteristics or natures. If we forget these three characteristics, we as sinners will not be saved, and we as Christians will fail and fall. If we see the characteristics and nature of God's grace, we will receive more grace from God for timely help. Let us consider briefly these three characteristics from the Bible.

What are man's works? Generally speaking, there are three things to man's work: (1) his wrongdoings, (2) his achievements, and (3) his responsibilities. The works of man that are evil are his wrongdoings, those that are good are his achievements, and those that he is willing to bear are his responsibilities. Here we have three things: of the things that man does, those that are not done well become his wrongdoings, those that are done well become his achievements, and those that he promises to do for God are his responsibilities. In terms of time, wrongdoings and achievements are things of the past, and responsibilities are things of the future; they are things that a man is responsible for. If God's grace is God working for sinful, weak, ungodly, and helpless man, right away we see that God's grace and man's wrongdoing cannot be joined together. Neither can God's grace be joined with man's achievements and responsibilities. Where the question of wrongdoing comes into play, grace does not exist. Where the question of achievement comes into play, grace also does not exist. Likewise, where responsibility is, grace does not exist. If God's grace is indeed grace, wrong-doings, achievements, and responsibilities cannot be mixed in. Whenever wrongdoings, achievements, and responsibilities are mixed in, God's grace loses its characteristics.

## GOD'S GRACE NOT RELATED TO MAN'S WRONGDOINGS

The first characteristic of God's grace is that it is not related to man's wrongdoings. God's grace is given to sinful man, to helpless, low, weak, and ungodly sinners. If the question of wrongdoing comes up and if it is stipulated that those with sin shall not have grace, then grace is basically annulled. God's grace can never be held back just because man has sinned. God's grace cannot even be reduced when man's sins increase. There can never be such a thing.

Man's mind, being fully of the flesh, is filled with the thought of the law. We may think that the ones who have achieved may receive grace but we, the sinners, as those without achievements, are unqualified to receive grace. In man's thought, wrongdoing and grace are at opposite poles. In man's thought, grace only comes where there is no wrongdoing. If you told anyone who has some consideration about God that God loved him and has given him grace, he would immediately wonder how this could be since he has committed so many sins. Man's thought is that grace can be received only when there is no wrongdoing. He fails to realize that this is absolutely wrong. Why? Because wrongdoing provides the best opportunity for grace to operate. Without wrongdoing, grace has no opportunity to manifest itself. Not only is wrong-doing unable to stop grace; it is the necessary condition for grace to be manifested.

In the same way, our poverty before the Lord is not a deterrent to grace. On the contrary, our poverty is a condition for receiving grace. Without being so poor, we would not be willing to receive grace. Every Lord's Day morning there are eight or nine beggars here in our meeting hall. They come every Lord's Day morning, and they are very punctual. When they come to you and you give them a coin or two, they smile and take it. But what would happen if you offered a coin to any brother or sister among us who is well groomed and who has a good upbringing, saying, "Here, take this. Find yourself two more coins and you will be able to buy some fritters on the street"? Surely he or she would not accept it. He or she would not only refuse it, but would consider it an insult. Therefore, being poor is a condition for receiving grace; in fact, it is the most necessary condition.

Man is very illogical. He says that he cannot receive grace because his sins are too numerous. No statement is more contradictory than this. No statement is more senseless. Because the sick are sick, they need a doctor; because the poor are poor, they need relief; and likewise, because man is a sinner, he needs grace. Hence, sin is not a deterrent. On the contrary, it is an opportunity. Our problem today is that we always think that we have to be in a condition that is different from where we are today. We think that we must be holier and better people today than yesterday if we are to receive grace.

My friends, if you want to be a magistrate, there is the matter of qualifications. If you want to enter a school, there is the matter of standards. If you want to be a doctor in a hospital, there is the matter of capability. If you want to do business, there is the matter of skill. Qualifications, standards, capabilities, and skills are indeed useful in certain things. But if man wishes to come to God, qualifications, standards, capabilities, and skills are out of the question. Only when I am a helpless sinner, standing on the lowest ground, can I receive grace. Man misses grace not because he

is too sinful, but because he is not low enough. He is too proud
and too moral. This is precisely where the greatest problem
lies. We are great in all kinds of sins. At the same time, we are
very great in the sin of pride. On the one hand, we have an
absolute need; on the other hand, the ground we stand on is
one on which we cannot receive the grace we need. This is due
to nothing other than our pride.

Romans 5:20 tells us that "Where sin abounded, grace
has super-abounded." The Word of God shows us that where
sin is, grace is also. Where sin abounds—not that it has really
abounded, for all men sin alike, but that sin has manifested
itself more abundantly—the grace of God abounds even more.
The word *abound* in the original language has to do with the
idea of overflowing. I do not know if you have ever been to
the seashore or riverside. When high tide comes, a water line
is left on the shore or bank. But if a flood comes, it overflows
the water line. When the water is at the water line, we say
that there is only a normal rise of the tide, but if the water
rises above the line, there is a flood. This is what *abound*
means here. Sin is so high, but grace is higher and even
covers sin. Hallelujah! Sin is high, but grace is even higher
and has covered sin. This is God's grace. Man has the strange
thought that to receive grace, he must be without sin or
wrongdoing. But there is no such thing. Although our
wrongdoings are quite serious and can rise quite high, God's
grace rises even higher. Since the grace of God is here to deal
with the problem of wrongdoings, they are no longer a
problem.

What is the nature of God's grace? God's grace is just God
coming in the sinner's position to take upon Himself the consequence of his sins. Please remember the definition that we
gave earlier, that grace is God working for man. If we do not
have any wrongdoings, we do not need God to do anything for
us, and as a result, we do not need God's grace. But because
we have sinned and because we have problems, He has to
come and solve our problems. Hence, we need grace. If I say,
"Since I have sinned, I cannot receive grace," it is like saying,
"Because I am too sick, I am too shy to see the doctor. I will
see the doctor when my temperature is down a little." Since

there is no such patient in the world, there should be no such sinner in the world either. Thus our wrongdoings are the condition for us to receive God's grace.

Since the problem of sin is taken care of by God and since He takes the responsibility to deal with our wrongdoings, any sin we have, whether great or small, is no problem before God. Both great sins and small sins pose no problem, for both can be solved by God's work and by God's work alone. The great sin is taken care of by God's work. The small sin likewise requires God's work. If it were up to us to deal with our sins, we would distinguish between great sins and small sins. But if our sins are taken care of by God, they will be taken care of regardless of whether they are great or small. Since they are taken care of by God, it makes no difference at all to us. All that we are doing is receiving grace.

Earlier we saw why man cannot receive grace. Recall Peter's words in 1 Peter 5:5: "In like manner, younger men, be subject to elders; and all of you gird yourselves with humility toward one another, because God resists the proud but gives grace to the humble." God gives grace to the humble. If you humbly confess that you are a sinner, your wrongdoings will not deter you from receiving God's grace; rather, they will cause you to receive His grace. As long as you humble yourself before God, God's grace will flow to you. Thank God that the grace of God flows down to us; it is not pumped up to us. No one can ever pump God's grace up to himself. Therefore, all those who are high have to come down.

Who are the sinners and who can receive grace? The Bible shows us clearly in Romans 3:23-24 that "all have sinned," but the all who have sinned are "justified freely by His grace." The Bible shows us that once man sins, spontaneously he can receive grace. Without being a sinner, he cannot receive grace. Man thinks that those who have sinned cannot receive grace. But God says that because man sins, he can receive grace. It is so obvious: since man has sinned grace comes. Never think that when sin comes, grace goes away. Sin is one of man's great mistakes, but to think that sin blocks man from receiving grace is a greater mistake.

Therefore, the first thing we must see is that man's

wrongdoings cannot stand in the way of God's grace. With God's grace, there is no problem because of wrongdoings. On the contrary, God's grace is there to deal with man's wrongdoings. God is giving grace because man has sinned.

### GOD'S GRACE NOT RELATED
### TO MAN'S ACHIEVEMENTS

Now the second issue arises. Not everything that man does is sin. In God's eyes, all of man's acts are sins, but in man's eyes, many things he does are achievements. Some consider that since they are such extreme sinners, they cannot receive grace. Others think that because they sin, they have to improve themselves before they can receive grace. Please notice that there is a difference here. The first group says that they have sinned and are therefore unqualified to receive grace. This group is absolutely in the negative realm. The second group is a little more positive. They say that they are sinners and will only receive grace if they act better. They think that they have to attain a certain standard of conduct and certain achievements before they can receive grace. In the mind of the first group, the problem is hindrance from grace. In the mind of the second group, the problem is how to obtain grace. Some think that wrongdoings will hinder us from receiving God's grace. Others think that achievements will enable us to obtain God's grace.

Friend, do you know what grace is? Grace is unconditional. It is free, and it is not given based on any reason. It is God's work of love which He bestows on us, the sinners. If God's grace were related to man's achievements, the nature of grace would immediately be lost. As long as a trace of achievement is allowed to remain in us, God must reward us according to our achievement. God is righteous. And since He is righteous, He is just. He has to reward and recompense man according to his achievements. But if God's giving is a recompense or reward, it is not grace. As soon as achievements come in, recompense must also come in and grace is out. If a man gives you a month's labor and you give him a month's wages, the payment cannot be considered a gift; it is a recompense. He has done something for you; it is his achievement. If it is an achievement, the payment is not grace, but recompense. Once recompense comes in, grace goes out.

Romans 4:4 makes the matter very clear: "Now to the one who works, his wages are not accounted according to grace, but according to what is due." Wrongdoings do not stop us from receiving grace; on the contrary, they afford us the opportunity to receive God's grace. Achievements do not help us to receive God's grace; on the contrary, they annul the nature of God's grace. Unless it is free, it is not grace. Unless it is given without reason and cause and unless it is a gift, it is not grace. If there is some reason or some cause involved, if there is a price involved, or if there is some work involved, the matter of recompense immediately comes in because God is righteous. Once recompense comes in, the nature of grace is lost.

If you are standing on a position that is above God, or even one that is equal with God, you cannot receive grace. That is why Romans 4 says clearly that no one can come before God and say that he has done this or that and, therefore, unashamedly ask for grace. If a person says that he is not like others who have extorted money or who are so unrighteous, that he fasts at least twice a week, that even though he may not have tithed, he at least offered up one-twentieth of what he has, he cannot receive God's grace. What is grace? Let me say this in an emphatic way—grace is receiving without having a reason to receive. Once there is a reason, it becomes recompense. If you have any achievements, the matter of recompense comes in and grace is out. We must pay much attention to this matter.

There is still another sentence in Romans which is very clear on this point: "But if by grace, it is no longer out of works; otherwise grace is no longer grace" (11:6). Someone in my family once said that we should give a gift to a certain doctor at the end of the year. When I asked why, I was told that two months earlier my two younger brothers were sick, and they were cared for by that doctor. Because the doctor was a friend, he would not accept any money for his services. Therefore, we were to buy him something. "In that case," I said, "we are not giving him something, but returning something." Why? Because there was a work and a debt. Strictly speaking, our giving was a returning of what we owed.

My friends, if we had any achievements before God, whether these achievements were great or small, God's salvation to us would become a payment of debt and would no longer be grace. Thank God that there is no one who can claim any achievements before God. Thank the Lord that we are saved by grace. If I, Watchman Nee, were saved by my achievements, I would never say, "God, I thank You for giving me grace." Instead I would say, "God, I am saved because You have paid back Your debt." I could proudly claim that I am saved by achievements. Why is it that no one can save himself by achievements? It is because God wants to remove all pride from man, that man may do nothing other than thank and praise Him. Once the matter of achievements arises, grace is no longer grace.

Please remember that God cannot withhold grace from man because of his wrongdoings. Nor can He reduce His grace to man because of his wrongdoings. He has to give, and He cannot reduce His giving. Grace is not related to wrongdoings. What about achievements? In grace there is no possibility of mixture with anything, even in the nature of achievements. Grace is not God's payment of debt to us. It is not that God owed us and that now He is paying us back. Some may say, "Mr. Nee, we are not so extreme. Even though we dare not say that we come to God only by our achievements, you have to believe that we need some achievements before God. It is impossible to have nothing at all. We should do a little work, and then God can make up our lack. We will do our best, and God will make up the rest." My friends, we cannot say this. Grace is not God's payment of a debt. In the same way, neither is grace God's overpayment of a debt, as if God owed you five dollars, but is now returning ten to you. Grace is like someone giving you a new garment. It is not like someone patching up your torn garment. If grace is a patching up, it has lost its standing, and its nature is annulled.

Let me repeat again, grace has nothing to do with achievements. Man naturally sees that some people are better and others are worse. Therefore, he thinks that the better ones require less of God's grace and the worse ones require more of God's grace—a bigger patch for a bigger hole and a smaller patch for a smaller hole. But such a concept does not exist in the Bible.

Who has sinned? I believe all of us know the phrase by heart: "For all have sinned." Why is it that all have sinned? It is because they "fall short of the glory of God" (Rom. 3:23). If the Bible were to say that all have sinned because all have broken the Ten Commandments, there would be a difference between great sinners and small sinners, for some may have transgressed nine commandments, while others may have transgressed only one. If the Bible were to say that all have sinned because all have fallen short of society's customs or the law of the land, there would still be some who are good and some who are not so good. But strangely enough, the Bible says that all have sinned because all have fallen short of the glory of God. What then is the glory of God? If you want to understand what the glory of God is, you have to understand Romans 1 through 8. God's grace is linked to God's glory. Grace seeks out man on the lowest level, and glory brings man to the highest level. Romans 1 through 3 tells us how man has sinned. Then after giving the way of salvation by the Lord Jesus in chapters three through five, the crucifixion with Christ in chapters six and seven, and the work of the Holy Spirit at the beginning of chapter eight, Romans tells us the following at the end of chapter eight, "Whom He foreknew, He also predestinated...whom He predestinated, these He also called; and those whom He called, these He also justified; and those whom He justified, these He also glorified" (vv. 29-30). Salvation is God pulling a sinner from the mud of sin and taking him all the way to glory. Although we are justified, we know that justification is not enough. Justification is not the goal of God's salvation for us. God will not stop until we are in glory. Hence, Romans 1 through 8 begins with sins and ends with glory.

What does it mean to fall short of the glory of God? It means that one cannot enter into glory. All have sinned because they cannot enter into glory. If all have sinned because they have not honored their parents, you could find some "great" dishonoring ones, some "mild" dishonoring ones, and some "little" dishonoring ones. Perhaps for the 400 million Chinese, there are 400 million classes of dishonoring ones. But in falling short of the glory of God, that is, in failing to enter into glory, you and I are exactly the same. You may be a moralist, and I may be a criminal. As a criminal I cannot enter into glory, but neither can you as a moralist. Hence, before God all have fallen short of His glory, and no one is qualified to enter in.

You can go to the street and tell anyone that he has sinned. If he says that he has not sinned, you can ask if he thinks he can enter into glory. Of course, he will not know what glory is. If we are in God's light, and if we have a little knowledge of the Scripture, we will know that we are not qualified to enter in. None of us can enter in.

Two months ago, while I was in Hong Kong, the world tennis championship was there. The tennis pavilion where the match was held could hold only five to six hundred spectators. Another eight hundred people could not get in and had to stand outside. The problem was not whether they had money or not, whether they were male or female, or whether they were masters or slaves. None of them could go in. Whether one was rich or poor, educated or illiterate, male or female, made no difference. The difference between them and those inside did not lie in their being rich or poor, male or female, educated or illiterate. The problem was that they could not get in.

In the same way, whether or not you are moral or whether or not you are gentle is not the question. The question is whether or not you can enter into glory. All those who cannot enter into glory are sinners and are disqualified before God. God has leveled everyone before Him. We have a plot of land in Jen-ru. Recently we needed to put some grass on it. To do that I had to hire some workers to level the ground. The question today is whether or not we can enter in. Regardless of whether or not you are moral, you cannot enter into glory. God has leveled everyone. Why has God leveled everyone? Galatians 3:22 tells us that "the Scripture has shut up all under sin in order that the promise out of faith in Jesus

Christ might be given to those who believe." God has shut up all under sin. Everyone has become a sinner, so that all who believe in Jesus Christ may receive the grace of God. God has leveled everyone so that He might bestow grace on everyone.

Romans 11:32 says, "For God has shut up all in disobedience that He might show mercy to all." God has shut up all in disobedience. He has leveled them all. For what goal? The goal is that He might show mercy to all. Hence, before God achievements can have no place at all. Everyone stands on the same ground.

Romans 3:9 says, "What then? Are we better? Not at all! For we have previously charged both Jews and Greeks that they are all under sin." God's verdict is that both the Jews and the Gentiles are all under sin. There is absolutely no chance for achievements to have a place. In the portions of the Scriptures that we have just read, we see that all have been shut up in sin and disobedience in order that we may go to God to receive grace and mercy. What is God's grace? God's grace is His giving to man not according to what he deserves. God's grace does not give to man more than what he deserves or better than what he deserves. Grace is simply God giving to man what he should not have and does not deserve.

## GOD'S GRACE NOT RELATED TO
## MAN'S RESPONSIBILITIES

Now we come to the third matter, man's responsibilities. God's grace can never be tied to man's responsibilities. What are man's responsibilities? Suppose I give a brother ten thousand dollars to send to a certain place, but because I am afraid that he will lose the money, I charge him, saying, "You are responsible for this money." What do I mean? I mean that if he loses the money, he has to pay it back. This is the meaning of responsibility. Wrongdoings are matters of the past. Achievements are also matters of the past. But responsibilities are matters of the future. If God is to give us grace, it cannot be tied to responsibility. When I ask a brother to take ten thousand dollars to the bank, that money is not his, so I tell him that he is responsible for the money. But if this money is a free gift to him, can I say, "You are responsible for it"? Surely not. Once I give the money away to him, the money is his. What he does with the money is up to him even if he throws it into a river or a trash can.

Some have said that prior to our salvation we did not have good works and were unable to save ourselves. There was no other way to be saved except to have God's grace save us. But now that we are saved, they say, we should do good works, for if we do not do good works now, we are again doomed to perish. Many think that salvation is of grace, but that maintaining salvation is of our merit and work. This is what I mean by responsibility. Many think that if we behave properly after we are saved, our salvation will be preserved, and if we do not behave properly, God will take back His salvation. If salvation can be taken back, is it grace anymore? If it is grace, there is no question of past merit, present work, or future responsibility. If we bring in future responsibility, then again it is no longer grace.

Once a preacher came to talk to me who did not believe that once a person is saved, he is forever saved. I asked him why he thought so. He said that he believed that man is saved by grace, but if man does not behave properly after salvation, he will perish. "Is this then grace?" I asked. Then I gave him an illustration. Suppose we go to a bookstore together and each of us pick out the same book to buy. When you ask the salesman the price, he tells you that it costs sixty cents. You give him sixty cents and take the book home. But I dig into my pockets and realize that I do not have any money. I want the same book also, so I tell the salesman that I have not brought any money with me, and ask if I can take the book now and send him the money later. He says that it is fine to do so because we know each other well. Thus, I take the same book home also. You have paid cash, but I have postponed the payment. Let me ask you, was the cash transaction grace? Surely it was not, because the book was paid for with sixty cents. For man to be saved through good works is like a cash transaction. If you have done good works, you can go to God and He will say, "Fine, you can be saved." If a man is saved this way, his salvation is not through grace. Thank the Lord that no one is saved this way. How about my case of postponing the payment? This is like God advancing salvation to man. If man would not do good after salvation, his salvation will be claimed back from him. One would have to do good in order to keep his salvation. But this is not grace either. Grace is not a cash transaction nor is it like a postponed payment. In a cash transaction one pays now; with a postponed payment one pays later. But both have to pay. We do not purchase our salvation on credit. I told the preacher that if salvation is of grace, there is no need for good works. Then he asked, "Does this mean that we do not need good works anymore?" I said, "No. Christians need to do good works. But the good works that I am talking about have nothing to do with salvation. The good works that I am talking about have to do with the kingdom, with the reward and the crown. Salvation is not bought, nor is it purchased on credit. Salvation is given freely."

What does it mean to give freely? The Lord Jesus said, "And I give to them eternal life" (John 10:28). Eternal life is given to us by God. Once I went to buy something at a friend's shop. He and I know each other very well, so he would not take money from me. He said that he would give me the item I wanted. I could not persuade him to take the money, yet he insisted that I take the item. In the same way, God says that He will give us eternal life. He did not say it only to come back and check on it. He did not say that it would be ours if we do good and that He would take it back if we do not do good. I do not mean that Christians should not have good works. I hate loose living, but this has nothing to do with my salvation. Hallelujah! Salvation is given to us; it is not bought by us. However, we should not despise good works. Good works are related to the kingdom reward, to the crown or punishment, but they have nothing to do with salvation. If salvation is of grace, the question of the future is out.

Romans 6:23 says, "For the wages of sin is death, but the free gift of God is eternal life in Christ Jesus our Lord." What is a free gift? A free gift is a present. I cannot send a present to your house, and then later send you a bill for it. If it is a present, it is given absolutely free and cannot be changed.

Therefore, grace is not related to your past wrongdoings, your present achievements, or your future responsibility. If it is related to your future responsibility, it is not grace; it is a purchase on credit instead. Thank God that eternal life is not a purchase on credit. It is a gift. Thank the Lord that eternal life is God's gift in His Son Jesus Christ.

Since salvation is given to us by God, we must remember one thing after we are saved: salvation is obtained strictly through believing, and it is preserved apart from our faithfulness. Therefore, the condition for preserving our salvation is the same as the condition for obtaining salvation. Since salvation is obtained freely it is also preserved freely. Thank God that because the obtaining of salvation is free the preserving of salvation is likewise eternally free.

At the end of the book of Revelation, after the new heaven, the new earth, the kingdom, the lake of fire, Satan's end, and the great white throne have all been covered, the Bible says, "Let him who wills take the water of life freely" (22:17b). Thank the Lord that He has purposely put taking freely of the water of life at the end of chapter twenty-two. After we have seen the lake of fire, the second death, Satan's end, the kingdom, the new heaven and the new earth, we may fear that God would harden His heart again; but after all these things, God purposely stated that the water of life is free. There is no charge for it. Thank the Lord that we have grace through Jesus Christ, and that this grace is free. It is not related to our responsibility.

I have heard many times that we have to do good and repay God's grace. These are common sayings in the church today. But I have to ask where in the Bible is there a verse that says that we have to repay God's grace? This word is too contradictory. If there is repayment, there is no grace. And if there is grace, there is no need of repayment. Thank the Lord that in the whole New Testament we are never told to repay anything. It is true that we Christians ought to have good works. But why should we have good works? Why do we have to suffer for the Lord? Why do we have to bear the shame? Why do we serve the Lord? As the Lord has dealt with us in love, so we deal with the Lord in love; but there is no thought of a trade here. It is not that God gives me so much and I give back so much in return. Because He has loved me, I cannot help but love Him; because He loved me, He was crucified for me; and because I love Him, for Him I bear the cross willingly. What He has given me has been given freely, and what I am giving Him is also given freely. The difficulty lies in man's legal mind. In everything he has the thought of bargain and law. Even the matter of salvation is seen from a bargaining perspective. Today if we work, serve the Lord, suffer reproach, or bear the cross, it is not because we want to pay back His grace—it is because we love Him. The love with which He has loved us has taken hold of us, captured our hearts, and constrained us to serve Him.

If you speak of repayment, you are ignorant of the value of the grace you have received. If you borrow ten dollars from a friend today, you will want to repay him. If you borrow a hundred dollars, you will want to repay him as well. If you borrow a thousand dollars, or even ten thousand dollars, you might still want to repay him. But if you borrow a million dollars, you may not have the thought of repaying him. And if you borrow ten million dollars or a hundred million dollars from him, you cannot imagine repaying him. If you are going to borrow a trillion dollars from him, you do not even know how to think about repayment anymore, for repayment has become impossible. If you want to repay God today, it simply means that you do not know how much God has given you. You do not know the depth, length, height, and breadth of God's grace to you. If you realized just a little of the length, breadth, height, and depth of the grace that you have received, you would quiet down and give up the idea of repayment. You would owe the Lord willingly, saying, "I am a willing debtor forever." The grace that He has given us is too great. Even if we want to repay, there is no possibility to do so.

My friends, if you owe someone a hundred million dollars, would you have the audacity to buy him a ten-cent cookie and call it your "little token of appreciation"? Can this be even a "little token"? Our God has done so much for us. Dare we say that we are giving Him "a little token" as repayment? No! We can only say that God has freely given us so much. I am happy to be an eternal debtor. God has loved us with an eternal love. There is no limit to the length, breadth, height, and depth of His love to us. Are we going to repay God with a "ten-cent cookie"? We can only say that we accept His love willingly. I hate to hear men talk about repaying! I hate the thought of the law! I only wish that God's children would see that as God is grace to us, we may be grace to Him. As God has dealt with us generously, let us deal with God generously.

Hallelujah! There is no question of wrongdoings, achievements, or responsibilities. Salvation is nothing other than God for me. It is not I for God. Grace is what God has done for me. It is not what I have done for God. Please remember the peace and joy of a sinner and the peace and joy of a Christian do not lie in how much they love the Lord, but in how much the Lord loves them. Our peace and joy do not lie in how much we have done for the Lord, but in how much the Lord has done for us. We are not resting daily on what we have, but on what God is. We must be delivered from ourselves. We must see God in the light of the gospel. We have to see that we are resting on what God is and what He has. We are resting on the grace and mercy of God. If we see this, we will not fail or be sorrowful. If we rest on ourselves, considering that we are quite good and that we love the Lord quite much, we will be like drifting sand; we will not be able to build a house on it. We cannot find any peace and joy in ourselves. We can only find them in the Lord, in God.

It is wonderful to realize that while we live on this earth, God is for us. Do you remember the words of Romans 8:31? "If God is for us, who can be against us?" I do not believe there is a better word for us than this. When I come to break bread on the Lord's Day, I do not ask myself whether or not I have behaved properly for the last few days. Rather, I ask if the Lord has loved me the last few days. Perhaps your condition for the last few days has been very poor. Perhaps you have been very cold in your emotions for the last few days. But you only need to ask if the Lord still loves you. If the Lord does not love you anymore, you can withhold your praise. But if the Lord still loves you, you have to praise Him. Have you noticed how the disciples were with the Lord for three and a half years and yet were so foolish in the end as to argue about who was greater among them? Yet the Bible says that the Lord, having loved His own, loved them to the uttermost (John 13:1). Thank the Lord that everything depends on Him. If it were up to your love, if you had to trust in yourself, it would be like putting a candle in a boat, launching the boat to sea, and sailing it in stormy weather. You can imagine how shaky that would be. Thank God that everything is grace. Everything depends on Him. May God grant us to truly know the characteristics of the grace of the Lord Jesus.

CHAPTER FOUR

# THE FUNCTION OF THE LAW

We realize that man's position before God is that of a sinner. Now, let us consider why God set up the law. Once we understand the law, we will be able to understand God's work.

God has always known man's condition, but does man know his own condition? Since sin has been manifested before God, it should also be felt in man's conscience. But is man's conscience aware of sin? Unfortunately, it is not. Because man is unaware of sin, we need the functioning of the law. Tonight we will study this matter.

What is the law? The law is nothing other than God's demand on man that man work for God. In Romans, Ephesians, and Galatians, the apostle Paul shows repeatedly that man is saved by grace, not by the law. In other words, man is saved because God works for man, not because man works for God. It is not a matter of being something before God or doing something for God, but a matter of God Himself coming into our midst to become something and do something for us. This is why the apostle, under the revelation of the Holy Spirit, constantly emphasized that, both for the Gentile and the Jew, salvation is absolutely of grace and not of the law. We want to spend some time to see that it is impossible for man to be saved by the law. I am not using the term *law* in reference to the law mentioned in the Old Testament. *Law,* as I use it here, refers to a principle, that is, the principle of man working for God. We will see whether or not our salvation is due to our working for God.

The way I use the word *law* is not without a biblical basis. The apostle Paul used words in a very precise and meaningful way. In the Bible the word *Christ* is often used. In the original language, sometimes there is no definite article before the word *Christ*. At other times there is a definite article, and thus we should understand it as *the Christ*. Unfortunately, not many versions translate this accurately. Another word that is often used is *faith*. Sometimes there is a definite article; in these places it is *the faith*. Similarly, there are places in the Bible where the word *law* has a definite article, and we should read *the law*.

The meanings of these words with the definite article is quite different from their meanings without the definite article. For example, when *Christ* is mentioned, it refers to the Lord Jesus Christ; but when *the Christ* is mentioned, you and I are also included. When the Bible speaks of the individual Christ, there is no definite article; but when it speaks of the Christ who includes us, we find *the Christ*. When the Bible speaks of our individual believing, it uses *faith,* without the article. But when it speaks of what we believe in, that is, our faith, it uses *the faith*. Bible translators all know that whenever the Bible mentions *the faith,* it is not referring to our individual believing, but to that which we believe in. What then is *the law*? In the Bible, *the law* always refers to the Mosaic law, the law in the Old Testament. But if there is no definite article before *law,* it refers to the requirement God places upon man.

Therefore, let us keep in mind that *law* in the Bible does not merely refer to the law given to us by God through Moses. In many places in the Bible, *law* refers to the principle God applies toward us, or the principle of God's requirement of us. The law does not only mean the Mosaic law, the law given on Mount Sinai, or the Old Testament law. It also means the condition for fellowship between God and man. The condition for fellowship between God and man is God's requirement upon man, what God wants man to do for Him, to accomplish for Him.

Is man saved by the works of the law? Does God save man because man has done things for God? The whole world says we must do good before God will save us. If we put this in biblical terms, it means that we must have the works of the law in order to be saved. Those who talk this way have made two great mistakes. The first is that they do not know who man is. The second is that they do not know what God's intention was when He gave man the law. If we know what we are, surely we will not say that man needs to have works of the law in order to be saved. If we know the purpose of God's giving the law, neither will we say that man can be saved through the works of the law. Because man has made these two great mistakes, he bears the wrong concept and says wrong things.

### THE FIRST GREAT MISTAKE— NOT KNOWING WHAT MAN IS

Why would man say that he can be saved by the works of the law when he does not even know what he is? It is because man does not know how evil he is; he does not know that he is fleshly. Since man has become fleshly, there are three things in him that are unchangeable: his conduct, his lust, and his will. Because man is fleshly, whatever he does is sin and evil. At the same time, his lust within is actively tempting him, provoking him to sin all the time. In addition, man's will and desire reject God. Since man's conduct is against God, his lust is provoking him to sin, and his will is rebellious against God, there is no possibility for him to have the works of the law and be obedient to God. Therefore, it is impossible for man to satisfy God's requirement by the righteousness of the law. Not only do we have our outward conduct, but we also have the lust in our body. Not only do we have the lust in our body, but we also have the will in our soul. You may be able to deal with your conduct, but the lust stirring within you, even if it is not successful in precipitating sinful, outward conduct, exists and provokes you all the time. And even if you hate your lust and do your best to deal with it, your will is altogether not compatible with God. Deep in his heart, man is rebellious against God and wants to crucify the Lord Jesus. On the one hand, the cross signifies God's love; but on the other hand, it signifies man's sin. The cross signifies the great love God has in dealing with man; but it also signifies the tremendous hatred man has toward God. The Lord Jesus was crucified on the cross not only by the Jews, but also by the Gentiles. Man's will toward God has never changed. Man's will is totally at enmity with God.

Romans 8:7-8 says, "Because the mind set on the flesh is enmity against God; for it is not subject to the law of God, for neither can it be. And those who are in the flesh cannot please God." The mind set on the flesh is enmity against God. Those who are in the flesh are not subject to the law of God, neither can they be. We do not understand man enough. We think that man is still curable and useful. Hence, we say that the works of the law can still save man. But man can never be subject to the law of God; it is just not in our nature. In our conduct there is not the power to be subject to the law, and our nature cannot be. Not only are we unable to be subject to the law, we simply are not willing to be. Being unable to be in subjection is a matter of our nature and our lust; being unwilling to be in subjection is a matter of our will. Basically, man is not subject to God in his will.

Therefore, the law will manifest nothing except man's weakness, uncleanness, and sinfulness. It will not manifest man's righteousness. If one says that a person can have life and be justified by the works of the law, he really does not know man. If man were not fleshly or sinful, the law could perhaps give him life. This is why Galatians 3:12 says, "He who does them [the works of the law] shall live because of them." Unfortunately, human beings are all sinners. They are fleshly and powerless in being subject to God, and they have no heart to be subject to God. Man does not have power to do the works of the law, nor does he have the heart to do the works of the law. The law is good but the person who does the works of the law is not. We all must admit this.

## THE SECOND GREAT MISTAKE—
## NOT KNOWING GOD'S INTENTION
## IN GIVING THE LAW

Man thinks that he can be saved by the works of the law because he has never read the Bible or seen the light or the heavenly revelation. He has never understood God's desire and intention. He has never understood the way of salvation. If you want to know whether or not you can be saved by the works of the law, you need to first ask why God gave the law. Only after you find out God's purpose in giving the law will you know whether or not you can be saved by the works of the law.

Before me is a podium. If I ask you what this is, some may answer that it is a high chair. A small girl may answer that it is a bed short of two legs. Another may say that this is a dresser because there are drawers in it. If I were to ask a brother, he may say that this is a bookshelf, because one can put books on it. If I were to ask ten people, I might get ten different answers. A bookseller, for instance, may tell me that it is a perfect sales counter. Every person would have an answer according to his own experience and concept. But if you want to know what it really is, you need to ask the one who made it in the first place. If he tells you that this is a dresser, then it is a dresser. If he tells you that this is a bookshelf, then it is a bookshelf. If he tells you that this is a podium, then it is a podium. In the same manner, if you ask me or anyone else what the function of the law is, you are asking the wrong person. The law was given by God, so we have to ask God about its function. Once God tells us His intention in giving the law, we will know whether man can be saved by the works of the law or not. Therefore, we must spend some time to look into the Bible concerning this matter. We must see how the law came in, step by step. We have to see historically from the record of the Bible why God gave man the law.

## THE LAW NOT BEING
## GOD'S ORIGINAL THOUGHT

The first thing we must see is that the law was not at all in God's original thought. The law was added in afterwards; it was brought in to meet certain urgent needs. It was produced to take care of certain things that came in along the way. The law was not in God's original thought; grace was in God's original thought. Second Timothy 1:9-10 says, "Who has saved us and called us with a holy calling, not according to our works but according to His own purpose and grace, which was given to us in Christ Jesus before the times of the ages but now has been manifested through the appearing of our Savior Christ Jesus, who nullified death and brought life and incorruption to light through the gospel." Here the apostle Paul tells us that God had a thought, and this thought began before the times of the ages, before the creation of the world. This was God's original thought. And what kind of thought was it? Paul says that this grace was given to us in Christ Jesus before the times of the ages. Before man ever sinned, and even before the creation of the world, God had already made the decision to give us His grace through Christ Jesus. Therefore, grace was God's original thought. It was something that God planned from the very beginning.

Why did God want to give us grace? Paul says that God "has saved us and called us with a holy calling, not according to our works but according to His own purpose and grace." God's will is to dispense His grace, and this grace saves us. He saved us and called us with a holy calling so that we may enjoy His glory. This is what God's grace is doing. He desired to save us and to call us with a holy calling according to His purpose, according to what He plans to do. Here Paul was very careful; he added a phrase to show us whether the law is according to God's purpose. He says, "Not according to our works." God's salvation is not according to how much we can do for God; it is not according to how much responsibility we can bear before Him. Rather, it is God coming to accomplish something for us, and it is God giving us His grace. This grace was always related to His plan. So let us remember that before the times of the ages, God's thought was grace, not works or the law.

Paul continues, "Which was given to us in Christ Jesus before the times of the ages but now has been manifested through the appearing of our Savior Christ Jesus." This grace has not been manifested until now. Hence, you see that though this grace was planned long ago, it was not until the Lord Jesus came that we knew what grace really was. What does this grace do for us? Let us read on: "Who nullified death and brought life and incorruption to light through the gospel." When the Lord Jesus was manifested, He abolished works as well as the result of works. The result of evil works is death. Even if you have done the worst works, the most that the law can do is require your death. After you die, the law cannot do anything else.

You may ask, "What happens if my works have not violated the law? Do I still need to die?" Yes. But the Lord has also nullified death. The Lord has done away with works, and He has done away with death. This is our gospel, which was planned before the times of the ages, even though it was not manifested until the appearing of the Lord Jesus. Hence, the basic thought with God was grace.

After man was created, both Adam and Eve sinned and rebelled. Sin entered into the world through one man. But God did not give man the law at that time. For a period of about 1600 years after man sinned, God did not give man the law. God had no demands on man during that period of time. God allowed history to take its natural course. Then one day, four hundred and thirty years before Moses instituted the law, God spoke to Abraham, the father of faith, and chose him to be the one through whom Christ would come into the world. God chose Abraham and gave him the great promise that all the nations would be blessed through his seed (Gen. 12:3; 22:18). Notice that the seed is singular, not plural; it is one seed, not many seeds. Paul explained in the book of Galatians that this seed refers to the Lord Jesus (Gal. 3:16). When God spoke to Abraham, it was the first time God revealed His purpose that had been planned before the times of the ages. God told him that His purpose, from before the times of the ages, was that through his seed, Jesus Christ, the nations would be blessed. Abraham was an idol worshipper, yet God chose him and gave him a promise. He was the first one to be without works; he was a person of faith. Hence, God unfolded His purpose before him.

You have to pay attention to one particular point here. God's word to Abraham is unconditional. God simply said, "I will save and bless the world through your seed." He gave no conditions. God did not say that Abraham's descendants had to be this or that, or that the kingdom to come forth from him in the future had to be this or that before he would have a seed and the world would be blessed. No. God simply said that he would have a seed who would save the world. It did not matter if Abraham was good or bad; it did not matter if his descendants were good or bad; and it did not matter if his kingdom was good or bad. There was no condition attached. This is the way He wanted it done. He would cause the seed to bring blessing to the people in the world.

After this word was spoken, Christ the Son of God did not immediately come to the world. Abraham begot Isaac, but Isaac did not come to save the world. Isaac was not the Son of God. Four hundred and thirty years later, Moses and Aaron came. And though they were very good people, they were not the Christ of God. Through God's revelation, Paul pointed out to us that the seed of Abraham does not refer to many seeds, but to one seed, who did not come until two thousand years later. There is a great reason why the seed did not come sooner. It is true that God wants to do things for man, that God wants to give man grace. However, will man allow God to do things for him? God sees that we are not doing well, and He wants to help us; but we may still think that we are quite capable. We are evil, but we may still consider ourselves to be good. We are filthy, but we may still consider ourselves to be clean. We are weak, but we may still consider ourselves to be strong in everything. We are useless, but we may still consider ourselves to be useful. We human beings are sinful and completely incapable, but we may still consider ourselves to be good and useful. God's purpose from before the times of the ages was to give grace, and in time He told Abraham that He would indeed give grace to man. But because man was ignorant, weak, useless, sinful, and deserving to die and perish, God had no choice but to give man the law four hundred and thirty years after He gave Abraham the promise. After God gave man the law, man found out that he was sinful. God put the law there to let man find out if he is right or not and if he is able or not. God put the burden of the law there to let man see if he could lift it or not. Let us remember that God's giving of the law was not His original intention. I must emphasize that the law was something added in for meeting a temporary need. It was not something in God's original intention.

Let us take a look at Galatians 3:15-22. We must consider these verses carefully because they are very important. Verse 15 says, "Brothers, I speak according to man, though it is a man's covenant, yet when it has been ratified, no one nullifies it or makes additions to it." Let us lay aside man's covenant with God for a moment and consider the covenants men make among themselves. Suppose someone is selling a house, and a contract has been agreed upon and signed. Can the seller come later and ask for two hundred dollars more? Can he, after signing the contract, go and consider a little more and then tear the contract up? No. Even with contracts between men, once they are signed, it is impossible to add conditions to them or to subtract conditions from them. If a contract between men is like this, how much more a covenant between God and man!

How did God make His covenant with man? The next verse says, "But to Abraham were the promises spoken and to his seed" (v. 16). God covenanted with Abraham through promises because it concerned the future. What is already accomplished is grace; what is not yet accomplished can only be a promise. Because the Lord Jesus had not yet come, we cannot say that God's covenant with Abraham was grace. Its nature was indeed grace, but because it had not been manifested, it was still a promise. This promise was given to Abraham and to his seed. Paul says, "He does not say, 'And to the seeds,' as concerning many, but as concerning one: 'And to your seed,' who is Christ" (v. 16). The seed is singular, not plural; it is one, Christ. God promised Abraham that he would bring forth Christ and that through Christ the nations would be blessed. Verse 14 says, "In order that the blessing of Abraham might come to the Gentiles in Christ Jesus, that we might receive the promise of the Spirit through faith." This is the covenant God made with Abraham.

Since God wants to bless the nations through Christ Jesus, why did He give man the law four hundred and thirty years later? Since the covenant God made with Abraham could not be annulled or supplemented, why would not the Lord Jesus just come to give us grace? Why did the problem of the law intervene? You have to see the argument Paul was making here. Paul was explaining why after four hundred and thirty years the law came in. Verse 17 says, "And I say this: A covenant previously ratified by God, the law, having come four hundred and thirty years after, does not annul so as to make the promise of none effect." Although God gave the law to man, the covenant He made four hundred and thirty years before could not be made of none effect. God could not cancel the covenant formerly made after some further thought four hundred and thirty years later. The law is something absolutely contradictory to promise and grace. What is a promise? It is something given to someone freely. Although he may not have it yet, he will definitely have it later. But what is the law? The law implies that one has to do this or that in order to get something. You can see that these two things are completely opposite. The promise implies that God will do something for man; the law implies that man will do something for God.

Verse 18 says, "For if the inheritance is of law, it is no longer of promise." If what was to be given is according to the principle of the law, it cannot be according to the principle of promise. These two things are completely opposite.

Verse 19 says, "Why then the law?" Now the problem arises; here we have the problem. This is a most difficult problem to solve. The law and the promise are basically contradictory in their natures. If you have the law, you cannot have the promise; if you have the promise, you cannot have the law. These two matters cannot stand together. But now there is the law, and there is also the promise. God gave the promise, and then four hundred and thirty years later He gave the law. What should you do? If the covenant made by God could not be changed, either by subtracting from it or by adding to it, why then was the law given? Since a covenant cannot be changed, a promise will always be a promise, and grace will always be grace. Why then is there the need for the law?

In verse 19 Paul gives us the reason: "It was added because of the transgressions." What does it mean to add something? Recently I went to a certain place to work. During my stay there, I went with a few brothers to a restaurant for dinner one night. Because we do not have a home there, we went to a restaurant and ordered a meal of five dishes. These dishes were eaten very quickly, and so we asked the waiter to add one more dish. The addition of another dish was not our original intention; it was added to meet the immediate need. In a similar way, Paul said that the law was added. Actually, God does not have to give us the law, and neither did He need to give it to the Jews. God gave the law to the Jews because He wanted to show the world through the Jews that He gave the law because of transgressions.

Why was the law added because of transgressions? Let us look now at the last part of Romans 4:15: "But where there is no law, neither is there transgression." And let us also look at Romans 5:20: "And the law entered in alongside that the offense might abound." The purpose of the law is to cause the offense to abound. What does this mean? Sin entered the world through man, and therefore, sin is in the world. Death came from sin and began to reign. From the time of Adam to the time of Moses, sin was in the world. But how can we prove this? It is evidenced by death being in the world. If there were no sin from Adam until Moses, man would not have died. The fact that from Adam until Moses all died proves that sin was there. Although there was sin during that time, there was no law. Hence, there was only sin but no transgression. What is transgression? Sin was real and present in the world, but man did not know that sin was here until the law of God came. Through the law God showed us that we have sinned. Actually, there was sin already within us. We were corrupted already, but we did not know about it until the law came, at which time the sin within was manifested as transgressions.

The law is like a thermometer. A person may be sick with a fever. But if you say to him, "Friend, your complexion does not look very good; you have a temperature," he may not believe you. All you would have to do is get a thermometer and put it in his mouth. After two minutes you could show him definitely that he has a temperature. We were already sinful; we already had a "temperature"; but we did not know about it. So God gave us a standard. Although the law may not be a perfect standard, it is a sufficiently high standard. God uses the law to measure us. By it we see that we have transgressed. Once we see that we have transgressed the law, we know that

we have sinned. Sin was within man already; but without
transgressions, he would never have confessed that he had
sin. It was only after he transgressed that he would confess
that he really had sin.

When I read the Bible, I marvel at the words the apostle
used. In these verses he did not use the word *sin;* rather, he
used the word *transgression* three times. Sin is always within
man, but until it is carried out, sin does not become transgression. There must be something to transgress before there
can be the possibility of transgression. Let me illustrate. Suppose there is a little child who always gets his clothes dirty.
He always uses his sleeves to wipe his nose, and his clothes
get dirty quickly. In his temperament, habit, thought, and
conscience, he never considers that to dirty his clothes is a
sin. His father does not consider it a sin either. The fact of sin
is there even though there is no disobedience. The child's
clothes are very dirty, but he does not mind it at all. His conscience feels fine, because his father has never said that this
is wrong. He can be unconcerned about it. Even when his
clothes are very dirty, he can still eat with his father, sit with
his father, and walk with his father. Everything is fine as far
as he is concerned. In other words, he has not transgressed.
But one day his father tells him that he cannot get his clothes
dirty anymore, and that if he does it again, he will spank him.
If the child has been doing this habitually, his father's speaking will manifest his sins. Originally there was sin only,
no disobedience. But once the child disobeys, there is transgression. In the same way, only when there is the law will
there be the transgression. When the law tells you to do this
or that, transgression will be manifested. Originally this
child could come before his father uprightly and without fear.
But now if he behaves according to his habit and does this
again, he will have no peace within and his conscience will
speak.

All the Bible readers and all those who understand God's
will know that God did not give us the law with the intention that we keep it. The law was not meant for us to keep,
but for us to break. God gave us the law so that we would
transgress against it. This may be the first time for many of

you to hear such a word, and you may feel that it is strange. God has known all along that you have sin. God knows this; but you yourself do not know this. Therefore God has given you the law to transgress so that you will know about yourself. God knows that you are no good, but you think that you are fine. Therefore, God has given the law. After you transgress against it once, twice, and a number of times, you will say that you have sin. Salvation will not come to you until then. Only when you admit that you do not have a way, that it is impossible for you to go on conducting yourself in such a way, will you be willing to receive the Lord Jesus as your Savior. Only then will you be willing to receive God's grace.

We have already seen that in order to receive grace one needs to humble himself. We are sinners, and we have committed sins. What causes us to humble ourselves? It is the law. Human beings are proud. All human beings think that they are strong and consider themselves to be good. But God gave us the law, and once we look at the law, we have to humble ourselves and confess that we are really not good at all. This is what Paul was talking about when he said that before he had read from the law that we should not covet, he did not know what it was to covet. However, once he saw the law, he realized that there was coveting within him (Rom. 7:7-8). This does not mean that before Paul saw the law there was no coveting in him. There was coveting within him long before. He had always coveted, but he did not realize that it was coveting. It was not until the law told him so that he realized it. Therefore, the law does not cause us to do anything that we have not done before; the law merely exposes what is in us already. That is why I say that God gave man the law not to keep it, but to break it. Nor does the law afford man an opportunity to transgress; rather, the law shows man that he will transgress. The law allows man to see what God has already seen.

Romans 7 explains this matter very clearly. Let us look at this chapter, beginning with verses 7 and 8, "What then shall we say? Is the law sin? Absolutely not! But I did not know sin except through the law; for neither did I know coveting,

except the law had said, 'You shall not covet.' But sin, seizing
the opportunity through the commandment, worked out in
me coveting of every kind; for without the law sin is dead."
Without the law, I do not feel that coveting is sin, even though
there is coveting within me. Hence, coveting within me is
dead; that is, I am not conscious of it. However, after the law
comes, I resolve not to covet anymore. But I still covet, and the
sin is made alive. Verse 9 says, "And I was alive without the
law once; but when the commandment came, sin revived and I
died."

Friends, remember that God gave you the law for one
reason only: to show you that you have always been full of sin.
Because you did not see your own sin, you acted proudly. The
law came to try you out. You may say that you do not covet.
However if you just try not to covet, what will be the eventual
result? The more you try, the weaker you become and the
more covetous you will be. You purpose not to covet, but the
moment you purpose this way, you find yourself coveting
everything. You covet today, and you will covet tomorrow; you
covet everywhere you turn. Now sin is alive, the law is alive,
and you are dead. Originally sin was dead and you were fine,
but now that the law has come you cannot avoid coveting. The
more you try not to covet, the more covetous you become.
The problem is that man's being is fleshly, and because man
is fleshly, his will is weak, his conduct is rebellious, and his
desires are filthy.

Verse 10 says, "And the commandment, which was unto
life, this very commandment was found to me to be unto
death." If man can truly keep the law, he will live. But I
cannot keep it; hence, I die.

Verse 11 says, "For sin, seizing the opportunity through
the commandment, deceived me and through it killed me." If
the law had not told me that I should not do this or that, sin
would go easy on me and would not be that active in me. But
ever since the law came and told me that I should not covet,
sin through the commandment has tempted me and put this
matter of coveting in my mind. The law tells me that I should
not covet, and I purpose not to covet; but instead of not coveting, I covet even more.

For a period of time I felt that I had been lying. I did not lie deliberately, but I would sometimes unintentionally say too much about something or too little about something else. When I realized this, I resolved that from then on with me yes would be yes and no would be no. Regardless of whom I spoke to, I resolved to speak accurately. Before I resolved this, I really did not lie that much, but after I made the decision, it became so easy for me to lie. I was actually getting worse. The following Sunday I sent a note saying that I would not give a message that day. When I was asked for a reason, I said, "I have found out that my speaking is full of lies. This is quite serious. I am afraid that even my message will be all lies." When I did not pay attention to lying, lying seemed dead. Of course, that does not mean that I did not lie. However, it was not until I started paying attention to lying, not until I was enlightened by the law to deal with my lies, that I felt that all my words were lies. It seems that lies were standing right next to me. Therefore, I have found that originally the lies were dead, but now the lies have been made alive. Everywhere I turn, the lies are there. Sin has killed me through the law and I become helpless.

Verse 12 continues, "So then the law is holy, and the commandment holy and righteous and good." We should never consider the law evil. The law is always holy, righteous, and good. "Did then that which is good become death to me? Absolutely not! But sin did" (v. 13a). At the beginning, sin was dead and I was not conscious of it; but when the law came to check me out, I became dead. "Did then that which is good become death to me? Absolutely not! But sin did, that it might be shown to be sin by working out death in me through that which is good, that sin through the commandment might become exceedingly sinful" (v. 13). Initially, we did not sense that sin is that sinful. But when the law came and we tried to keep it, we realized where our sins are and how sinful and thoroughly evil they are.

You can see the function of God's law here. The law is like a thermometer. A thermometer will not give you a fever. but if you have a fever, the thermometer will surely make it manifest. The law will not cause you to sin, but if you have sins,

God's law will immediately show you that you are a sinner. Originally, you did not know that you are a sinner, but now you do.

The law came to judge man's sin. The law was established because man has sin. You never see God keeping the law because there is simply no possibility for God to transgress the law. Hence, no law is put upon Him. God never told the Lord Jesus to love the Lord His God with all His heart, with all His soul, with all His strength, and with all His will, and to love His neighbor as Himself. The Lord Jesus simply did not need it. He spontaneously loves the Lord His God with all His heart, with all His soul, with all His strength, and with all His will; He spontaneously loves His neighbor as Himself, even beyond Himself. Therefore, the law is useless to Him. And God did not tell Adam not to covet and not to steal. Why would Adam need to covet? Why would Adam need to steal? God had already given everything on the earth to him. The Ten Commandments were not given to Adam because Adam had no need of them. Rather, the law was specifically given to the Israelites because it showed fleshly man his inward condition and his sin within. If no Chinese had ever stolen, there would be no need for a clause in Chinese law concerning stealing. Because man steals, there is a clause in the law which says that one should not steal. Hence, the law exists because of sin. When man sinned, the law came in.

Now let us come back to Galatians 3 and continue with verse 19: "Why then the law? It was added because of the transgressions." Now we are clear. God purposed before the times of the ages to give grace to man. Later He gave Abraham a promise. In eternity it was merely His purpose. With Abraham, it was something spoken: He would deal with man in grace. Why then did God give man the law four hundred and thirty years after that? It was added because of the transgressions. In order for man's sins to become transgressions, the law was given to man. In this way, man realized that he had sin and would wait "until the seed should come to whom the promise was made" (v. 19). It was not until the whole world saw that they were sinners and that they were really hopeless that they were willing to receive the Lord Jesus Christ whom God had promised. Even if God had given man His salvation earlier, man would not have taken it. Man does not want God's grace, but because man has transgressions and is hopeless, he will possibly receive God's grace.

Verse 19 ends in this way: "It being ordained through angels in the hand of a mediator." The "it" here refers to the law mentioned above. The law was not only added because of transgressions, but was also ordained by a mediator. There are these two features to the law: it was added because of transgressions, and it was ordained through angels in the hand of a mediator. Why was the law ordained through the hand of a mediator? Verse 20 explains: "But a mediator is not a mediator for one." Have you ever been an intermediary or a go-between? An intermediary acts on behalf of two parties. Why does the law have a mediator? It is because with the law there is the side of God and the side of man. Man has to do certain things for God before God will do certain things for man. When parties A and B draft a contract, the contract states what A must do and what B will do in return and vice versa. A mediator will then serve as a witness between the two parties. The law states what God's responsibility to man is and what man's responsibility to God is. If either side fails, the whole matter falls through.

Hallelujah! What follows in verse 20 is wonderful: "But God is one." But God is one! The law implies two sides. If either side has problems, the whole matter falls through. In giving the law, God said that we should do this and that we should do that. If we fail to do them, the whole matter will fall through. But in making the promise, "God is one," regardless of how we are. In promise and in grace, there is no mention of our side, only of God's side. As long as there is no problem on God's side, there will be no problem at all. The question today is whether God can save Abraham and whether He can preserve him. The question is not how we are. In the promise, there is nothing that involves us, nothing that depends on how we are.

The principle of the law can be compared to buying books from our gospel bookroom. If I spend $1.60, I can purchase one copy of *The Spiritual Man.* If I give the brothers there the money, they will give me the book. If they have the book but I do not have the money, the transaction will not be made. Nor will the transaction be made if I have the money but they do not have the book. If one side has a problem, the deal falls through. Therefore, the law is of two sides. If one side fails, the whole matter falls through. But what about the promise? The promise is like our magazine *The Christian;* one does not have to pay for it because it is free. The law is: if you do something for me, I will do something for you in return. If you do certain things, you will get something back; if you cannot do them, you will not get anything. Hence, the law is of two sides. By making a promise, God gives us the grace regardless of whether we do well or not. It has nothing to do with us; how we are is not a problem at all. Thank God that promise is of one side only. All that is needed is one side.

Verse 21 says, "Is then the law against the promises of God? Absolutely not!" Those with little knowledge may say that the law contradicts grace. It is right to say that law and promise are two completely different things, but there is no contradiction at all; the law is merely the servant of the promise. It is something used by God and something inserted by God. Law and promise may appear contradictory in nature, but in God's hand they are not contradictory at all. The law was used by God to fulfill His purpose. Without the law, God's promise would not have been fulfilled. Please remember that God uses the law to fulfill this goal. Hence, law and promise do not contradict each other at all.

Paul concludes in this way: "For if a law had been given which was able to give life, righteousness would have indeed been of law" (v. 21). If a man could obtain righteousness by the law, he could have life through the law. However man cannot do this. Therefore, "the Scripture has shut up all under sin" (v. 22a). What did God use to shut us all up? He used the law. Whoever is shut up by the law has to admit that he is a sinner. God shuts up all under sin "in order that the promise out of faith in Jesus Christ might be given to those who believe" (v. 22b). Hallelujah! The law of God is something God uses to save us. It is not something God uses to condemn us. The law is absolutely something used by God. Tonight every one of us here has been shut up. Every one of us is a sinner. God has used the law to show us that we are sinners so that He may save us.

# CHAPTER FIVE

# GOD'S RIGHTEOUSNESS

In the previous meetings we have seen that man has sinned and that God's salvation is based on the fact that man has sinned. If man had not sinned, there would be no need for salvation. Since man has sinned, God has given the law to show man that he has sinned. God's law came to the world to cause man's transgressions to abound. Originally, man had only sin; he did not have transgressions. But when the law came, man had not only sin, but transgressions as well. After man transgresses, he realizes that he is a sinner. Thank the Lord that though we have sin and though we have transgressed, God, who is love, purposed to give us grace and mercy. He purposed to do something for us to solve the problems that we cannot solve ourselves.

In this meeting, however, we must see something else. Although God loves us and shows mercy on us and although He fully intends to grant us grace, there is one thing that makes it very difficult for God to do this. God cannot bestow grace upon us immediately; He cannot give us eternal life directly. There is a dilemma which God must solve before He can grant grace to us. The problem, which the Bible mentions frequently, is God's own righteousness.

The phrase *God's righteousness* has confused many theologians for centuries. If we read the Bible without prejudice and preconceived notions, God will show us what His righteousness is. We can see this matter clearly without much difficulty. Tonight we hope to see, by the grace of God, what God's righteousness is. In other words, we hope to see the difficulty God encounters when He saves us.

## HIS SALVATION MATCHING HIS RIGHTEOUSNESS

If God is to save us, He must save us to a condition that matches, or measures up to Himself. If God is to give us salvation, He cannot give it in a manner that conflicts with His nature, His method, and His way. We are sinners full of transgressions and, therefore, have no thought of righteousness at all. If we wanted to be saved, we would probably use any means possible, whether straight or crooked, good or bad. We would try to be saved by any of a thousand and one ways. As long as we can be saved in some way, it is good enough for us. We do not care if the procedure is proper or if the method is right. As long as we are saved, we are satisfied. We could not care less from where the salvation comes, and whether or not it is right. In this sense, we are like thieves. All that a thief cares about is getting the money. He does not care where the money comes from. As long as he gets the money, he is satisfied. He has no concept of right and wrong; he has no concept of righteousness and unrighteousness. But we must realize that salvation is not just a matter of us getting saved, but of *God* saving us. Although we would be satisfied no matter how we are saved, God cannot say that all there is to salvation is getting us saved, without caring about whether the way we are saved is right or wrong. God undoubtedly desires to give us grace and to save us. Without doubt, He wants to give us His life. God is full of love, and He is more than willing for us to be saved. But if God is to save us, He has to save us in an excelling way. Therefore, God's saving us is a big problem. God desires to save men. But what method can He use so that man can be saved in a most righteous way? What method is most reasonable? What method will match His own dignity? It is easy to be saved, but it is difficult to be saved righteously. This is why the Bible speaks so much about God's righteousness. It tells us again and again that God saves man in a way that matches His own righteousness.

What is God's righteousness? God's righteousness is God's way of doing things. Love is God's nature, holiness is God's disposition, and glory is God's own being. Righteousness, however, is God's procedure, His way, and His method. Since God is righteous, He cannot love man merely according to His own love. He cannot grant man grace merely according to what He wants. He cannot save man merely according to His heart's desire. It is true that God saves man because He loves man. But He must do so in a way that is in agreement with His own righteousness, His own procedure, His own moral standard, His own way, His own method, His own dignity, and His own majesty.

We know that it is easy for God to save man. But it is not easy for God to save man in a righteous way. Just imagine how easy it would be for God to save us if the matter of righteousness were not a problem. There would be no difficulty at all. If God had not loved us, nothing could be done for us and everything would be hopeless. But God has loved us and has had mercy on us. Furthermore, He intends to give us grace. If the issue of righteousness had not come in, God could say, "Have you sinned? All right, just do not commit the mistake again." God could then overlook our sins. He could let us go and send us away. If God forgives carelessly not judging the sinner's sin and dealing with his sins according to the law, where is His righteousness? Here is where the difficulty lies.

Some time ago, a brother got caught up in a complicated matter and was put in jail by the government. I knew that though he was not completely without fault, the mistake was really with other people. Because of this, I was willing to help him out. I went to Nanking and talked to a few of the people who were involved in the matter. I told them about the situation and asked if they could help out a little. There were nine of us there, and all of us were busy people. We held nine meetings together over a period of eleven days, trying to come up with a way to help this man. Eventually, all these people admitted that they had the way and the authority to release the man, but that they could not release him without incriminating themselves. Hence, we had to find a way to release the man that, at the same time, would be legal.

Undoubtedly, God is full of love for us. God wants to save us. But He must do so legally. If He does not save us legally, He cannot save us at all. God's love is limited by His righteousness. God cannot act contrary to Himself and irresponsibly declare that our sins are written off, that everything is fine, and that we can get off free. If God were to forgive us irresponsibly, what law, what righteousness, and what truth would be left in the universe? All of these would be through.

God wants to save us, and we need to be saved. The question is whether or not there will be unrighteousness in our being saved. There are many today who accept bribes from others and are partial because of private relationships. They often help others out, and others often receive benefits from them; but we all agree that these people are not proper. They are not righteous but corrupt. They may have much love, but what they do is not righteous. God cannot save us at the expense of involving Himself in unrighteousness. God must save us while preserving His righteousness. It is important for God to save us, but He must do so according to His righteousness. God could save us immediately with His love. But He must also save us very righteously.

How can this be done? It is not an easy matter for God to save us without violating His righteousness. How can God justify sinners without getting into unrighteousness? How can God save sinners without involving Himself in unrighteousness? How can God forgive sins in a righteous way? God is willing to save us, but He wants us to be able to say, at the time we receive His life and are saved, that He has justified us in a most righteous way.

### GOD'S SALVATION FOR THE DEMONSTRATION OF GOD'S RIGHTEOUSNESS

There is one book in the Bible, the book of Romans, that tells us how God deals specifically with this one problem. Let us read Romans 3:25-26, beginning with the second part of verse 25: "For the demonstrating of His righteousness, in that in His forbearance God passed over the sins that had previously occurred, with a view to the demonstrating of His righteousness in the present time, so that He might be righteous and the One who justifies him who is of the faith of Jesus." Here I must add a word. Some versions make a mistake in translating verse 25. They translate: "To declare His righteousness *for* the remission of sins that are past, through the forbearance of God." But the word "for" should not be used in this verse. Instead it should read: "For the demonstrating of His righteousness, in that in His forbearance God passed over the sins that had previously occurred." Further, in verse 26 the word "and" should be understood as linking two things that occur at the same time. Hence, this clause should be understood in this way: "that He might be righteous and the One who justifies him who is of the faith of Jesus." While God justifies those who believe in Jesus, He is shown to be righteous, and man is to acknowledge Him as being righteous.

Verse 25 deals with the problems in the past, and verse 26 deals with the problems in the present. The problems in the past relate to the people of the Old Testament times. The problems in the present relate to the people of the New Testament times. Verse 25 deals with an Old Testament issue. Verse 26 deals with a New Testament issue. Those in the Old Testament times transgressed the law for four thousand years. They were full of sins and transgressions. But God did not send them into perdition or destruction immediately. During those four thousand years, day by day God forbore and passed over the sins previously committed. We do not see the lake of fire immediately after the garden of Eden. Although God told man that in the day that he ate of the fruit of the tree of the knowledge of good and evil he would surely die (Gen. 2:17), when Adam did eat of the fruit, he did not go immediately into the lake of fire. Why not? Because God passed over the sins of the Old Testament times; He exercised His forbearance over them. God exercised forbearance and passed over the sins committed by man in the past. But a question arises immediately. Was God righteous in exercising forbearance and passing over man's sins in the Old Testament? What was God's purpose in doing this? Actually, in passing over man's sins and in exercising forbearance, God was declaring His righteousness.

God does not want us to think that after we are saved our salvation is an illegal one. God would not have man harbor such criticisms. God wants to show us that there is nothing illegal or unrighteous in His ways. Concerning the sins of the Old Testament times, He says that His forbearance and His passing over were for the demonstrating of His righteousness. Concerning the sins of the present time, He says that what is done is also for the demonstrating of His righteousness. He desires that in justifying those who believe in Jesus He would be known as the righteous One.

God's salvation is not some "backdoor merchandise." God wants our salvation to be one that comes from the "front door." Our salvation has to be right and proper. He will not allow anyone to say that our salvation is improper. He does not offer a fraudulent salvation. A fraudulent salvation is rejected by God. God's intention is to save us, but He will do so in a way that is related to His nature, His moral standard, His dignity, His law, and His righteousness. God cannot save us lawlessly.

Here we have a problem. If God were willing to use whatever means possible to save us and if He were to ignore the matter of righteousness altogether, He could say to anyone, "Go; you are free." There are men who are foolishly good. If God were to say this, He would be a foolishly good God. God would never be like this. If God did not love you, it would be easy—He would just let you die and perish when you sin. But He cannot allow this to happen because He loves you. The problem is that the sin of man and the love of God are together. When the righteousness of God is added to these two, salvation becomes the most difficult thing on earth. If man had not sinned, everything would be fine; and if God had not loved, there would be no problem either. If someone commits a crime and must die, it has nothing to do with me if I do not love him. Today many are taken from prisons to be executed. The matter concerns me little if I do not love them. It is difficult only if I love them and if I want to rescue them. If they have not sinned, the matter would be easy to deal with. And if I do not love them, the matter is also easy to handle. Further, if they have sinned and I love them but have no righteousness, the matter can still be taken care of easily; I can handle the matter irresponsibly through bribery. But if I am a righteous person, I cannot resort to such fraudulent and improper methods. I would not let them go illegally. If I am to rescue them, I have to rescue them righteously. To carry out such a salvation becomes the most difficult task on the whole earth. These three matters—love, sin, and righteousness—cannot easily coexist. Love is a fact;

sin is also a fact; and righteousness is a necessity. Because these three are together, God must come up with a way to save us and to satisfy His heart of love, while at the same time preserving His righteousness. Accomplishing such a work would be a masterpiece indeed. Hallelujah! The salvation which God has prepared for us in His Son Jesus is such a masterpiece. He is able to save us from our sins and demonstrate His love, and He is able to do so in a most righteous way. This He does through the work of redemption by the Lord Jesus.

## THE COMING OF CHRIST BEING
## GOD'S REQUIREMENT IN RIGHTEOUSNESS

The coming of the Lord Jesus Christ to the earth was God's requirement in righteousness; it was not God's requirement in grace. This is a very serious word. If there had been love without righteousness, the Lord Jesus would not have needed to come to the earth, and the cross would have been unnecessary. Because of the problem of righteousness the Lord Jesus had to come. Without righteousness, God could save us any way He wants to. He could overlook our sins, or He could forgive them lightly. He could take a permissive attitude toward our sins, or He could be completely unconcerned about them. If God said, "Since all have sinned, I will let you go this time; just do not sin again," there would be no need for a Jesus of Nazareth in the first place. Apart from the requirement of righteousness, there was no need for Jesus of Nazareth to come. The coming of Jesus of Nazareth was a requirement of righteousness.

When sin entered the world, God's government was damaged. His prescribed order in the universe was broken; His glory was trodden under; His holiness was profaned; His authority was rejected; and His truth was misunderstood. When sin entered the world, Satan laughed and the angels testified that man had failed and had fallen. If God were to judge sin mercilessly, He would be without love. But if He were to let man's sins go without judging them, He would be without righteousness. Because God loves the world and, at the same time, He is righteous, He had to send the Lord Jesus

to us. Because He is righteous, He had to judge sin. Because
He is love, He had to bear man's sins for him. I must emphasize these two statements: God must judge because He is
righteous. And God bears man's judgment and punishment
because He is love. Without judgment, we see no righteousness; with judgment, we see no love. However, what He did
was to bear the judgment on our behalf. In this way, He manifests both His love and His righteousness in Jesus Christ.

## THE CROSS MANIFESTING
## GOD'S RIGHTEOUSNESS AND LOVE

Hence, the cross is where God's righteousness is manifested. The cross shows us how much God hates sin. He is
determined to judge sin. He was willing to pay such a great
price as to have His Son nailed on the cross. God was not willing to give up His righteousness. If God were willing to give
up His righteousness, the cross would have been unnecessary.
Because God was not willing to give up His righteousness, He
preferred to have His Son die rather than give up His righteousness.

The cross is also the place where God's love is manifested.
The burden for our sins should be on us. If we do not bear it, it
is unrighteous. But to bear such a burden is too much for us.
For this reason, He came and bore it for us. That God was
willing to bear the burden shows His love. That God actually
did bear the burden shows His righteousness. For God to have
us bear the punishment is righteousness without love. For
God to have us not bear the punishment is love without righteousness. Because He takes away the punishment and bears
it for us, there is both righteousness and love. Hallelujah! The
cross meets the requirement of righteousness and the
requirement of love. Our salvation today is not "backdoor
merchandise"; we have not received it fraudulently or improperly. We have not been saved illegally. We have been saved in a
clear and definite way through judgment.

For us forgiveness is free, but for God there is no such
thing as free forgiveness. For Him, forgiveness comes only
after the redemption from sins. For example, if you break
the law and the court requires you to pay a thousand dollar

fine, you must pay the fine before your case will be dismissed. In the same way, we are saved only after being judged on the cross. Our salvation comes after we suffer the judgment for sin in Christ. It is a salvation that comes only through judgment. Hallelujah! We are judged; then afterwards we are saved. God's love is here, and God's righteousness is also here.

Let me give an illustration. Suppose that there is a brother who is a millionaire, and suppose that I am one of his debtors. Let us say that I owe him a big sum of money, an amount as large as the ten thousand talents mentioned in the book of Matthew (18:24). When I borrowed the money from him, I signed a promissory note. On the note the amount that I owe him and the date and month that the amount must be repaid in full was listed, together with the terms and conditions of penalty. Suppose that now I go to him and say, "I spent all the money that I borrowed from you, and it is impossible for me to earn this money back and repay you at such a time as this, when the economy is slumping. I even have a problem taking care of my food and living. Please have mercy on me and let me go. Let me have the promissory note back." If I implore him this way, can he return the note to me? The promissory note clearly records the amount that I borrowed from him and the period of time in which I must repay him. This is a contract not only for me to keep, but one that he has to abide by as well. As the debtor, I have the responsibility to repay him the money within the set time. As the creditor, he also has a responsibility to fulfill, which is to return the promissory note to me only upon receipt of the money. If he returns the note to me before receiving the money, even though he does this out of his love and concern for me, he is not being righteous. Because we human beings are simply unrighteous and are used to unrighteous acts, it seldom occurs to us that free forgiveness is a form of unrighteousness. But God cannot do something unrighteous. If God forgave us freely, He would be unrighteous. Furthermore, going back to the illustration, let us suppose that this brother returns the note to me without receiving the money. This will affect me in a negative way. The next time I have money I

will be indiscreet in using it. I have found that I can use others' money easily and loosely. Hence, this brother's free
forgiveness is unrighteousness with him and a bad influence
on me.

Now suppose that this brother is righteous, but does not
want me to repay. What can he do? Let me tell you what I
once did in a similar situation. Someone once came to my
home to borrow money. He was a nominal Christian, so I told
him that according to the Bible Christians should not borrow
money. But he begged me to loan him the money all the same.
Originally I considered simply giving him the money. But I
knew that he was irresponsible with others' money because
some brothers had come to me beforehand and told me that
this person borrowed often from the brothers, and warned me
not to loan him anything. So on second thought I decided that
I would not simply give the money to him, but would loan it
instead. When I handed him the amount he asked for, I asked
him when he would return it to me. I pressed him for a payment date, even though I knew that I would never be paid
back. Borrowing was his habit; it was his life. But I could not
tell him that I did not expect to be paid back, for that would
have invited more borrowing. Therefore, I made him set a
payment date. When the date arrived, I purposely wrote a
letter to him, reminding him that the due date had come.
After he received my letter, he came to see me. But before he
was able to say very much, I interrupted him and told him to
go home and see his wife, for she had something to tell him.
So off to his home he went. Actually, prior to his coming to see
me, I had taken the exact amount of money he owed to his
home and had given it to his wife. I told her that when her
husband came home she should tell him that I had sent him
this sum of money for the payment of his debt. When the husband reached home, the wife told him what I had said. Then
he opened the package and found the exact amount of his
debt. He understood what to do next. He came back to my
home and returned the money to me. In this act, you can see
love and you can see righteousness. If this man had been
forced to pay, there would have been no love. But if I had
allowed him not to pay, I would have been unrighteous, for

I had said specifically that the money was given as a loan. Not only would I have been unrighteous in myself, but I also would have exerted a bad influence on him. The next time he would have been more irresponsible. Thus, I did what I did.

We owe God "ten thousand talents of silver," but we have no way to repay. Now God is doing the same thing for us. Because He loves us, He cannot ask us to pay Him back. But because He is righteous, He will not tell us that we have no need to repay at all. For us to pay Him back is impossible. Yet for God to release us from our obligation is unrighteous. Thank and praise Him that He has come to give us the "money," that we can pay back what we owe Him. The collector is God, and the payer is also God. Without collecting, there is no righteousness; but if we are made to pay, there is no love. Now God Himself is the collector; hence, righteousness is maintained. And God Himself is also the payer; hence, love is maintained. Hallelujah! The collector is the payer. This is the biblical meaning of redemption from sins.

Therefore, Jesus the Nazarene came and bore our sins in His body onto the cross. God Himself came to bear our sins. Our sins were judged by God in the person of Jesus Christ. The blood of the Lord Jesus shed on the cross is proof of this judgment. We come to God by this blood. Through the Lord Jesus we tell God that we have been judged. Now we are turning over to Him what the Lord Jesus has paid for us. It is true that we have sinned. But we are not irresponsible; there has been the judgment. It is true that we had a debt. But we are not avoiding it; the debt has already been paid. We have the blood, which signifies the accomplished salvation of the Lord Jesus, as the receipt proving that God has paid our debt back to Himself. This is why the blood in the Old Testament was sprinkled seven times within the veil. This is why it had to be brought to the propitiation cover on the ark. God has to forgive every sinner who comes to Him through the blood of the Lord Jesus. There is no way for Him not to forgive us.

Let us return to the previous illustration. Suppose I borrowed ten thousand talents of silver from a brother and I have no money to pay him back. One day he comes to my home and says, "You owe me ten thousand talents of silver.

Now you must pay me back. I am not an irresponsible or loose person. Whatever I do, I do seriously. You have to pay me back. Now here are ten thousand talents of silver. Bring this to my house tomorrow and pay back your debt. Then you can take back your promissory note." I would expect that when I go to his house with the money the next day I will be able to redeem the promissory note. But suppose that after I hand him the money, he says that because the money was given to me by him the day before, he will not return the promissory note to me. Can he do such a thing? When I hand him the money, does he have the right not to hand me back the promissory note? No. He had the right not to give me the money the day before. If he did not give me the money the day before, at most I can say that he does not love me. I cannot say a word more. But if he has given me the money and I pay him back, he is unrighteous if he still keeps my note; it is not simply a matter of him not loving me. If he is righteous, he has to hand me the note when I hand him the money.

## GOD BEING BOUND TO FORGIVE US
## BECAUSE OF RIGHTEOUSNESS

Therefore, before the Lord Jesus came to the earth and was crucified on the cross, it would have been fine for God to refuse to save us. God could have left us unsaved. Had God not given us His Son, all that we could have said was that God did not love us. We could not say anything more. But because God has indeed given us His Son and put our sins upon Him that we might be redeemed from our sins, God can do nothing else but forgive our sins when we come to Him through the blood of the Lord Jesus and through His work. Hallelujah! God has to forgive our sins! Do you realize that God is bound to forgive our sins? If you come to God through Jesus Christ, God is bound to forgive your sins. It was love that brought His Son to the cross, but it was righteousness that caused God to forgive our sins.

John 3:16 says, "For God so loved the world that He gave His only begotten Son." Out of love God gave us His only begotten Son. But 1 John 1:9 says, "If we confess our sins, He is faithful and righteous to forgive us our sins and cleanse us from all unrighteousness." The work of the cross was accomplished for us through the love of God. But today when we come to God through the accomplished work of Jesus Christ, God has to forgive us based on His faithfulness and righteousness.

Hence, if the Lord Jesus had not come, God would be free not to save us. But now that the Lord Jesus has died, even if God were unhappy about saving us, strictly speaking He still has to do it. If He received the money could He refuse to return the note? God cannot be unrighteous, because if He is unrighteous, He Himself becomes a sinner. Therefore, God is bound to forgive all those who come to Him through the blood of the Lord Jesus. Hallelujah! God cannot refuse to forgive them. I want to shout that this is the gospel. Since God has given us His Son, He is bound. Do you think that we can pay God back now? Today through the Lord Jesus, not only can we pay God back, but we have more than we need to pay Him back. We have an overflow. For where sin abounds, there grace much more abounds. Sin is abundant. But the grace in God's Son is more abundant, even superabundant. For this reason, it is through the Lord Jesus alone that one can be saved.

Everyone has to admit that there is nothing unrighteous with God when we come to Him by the Lord Jesus and when He gives us life and forgives our sins. Our heart can never say that God, in forgiving our sins, saved us lawlessly when He passed over our sins, exercised forbearance toward us, and justified us who believe in Jesus. We can never say that God has dealt irresponsibly with our sins. On the contrary, we must say that God has saved us in the most righteous way. Our salvation is a proper and upright salvation. Our sins have been judged; hence, we are saved. No one can say that God has saved us by using unrighteous procedures. Rather, we must say that God has saved us by the most righteous procedures.

## GOD'S RIGHTEOUSNESS
### MANIFESTED APART FROM THE LAW

Now let us come back to Romans 3. Verses 19 to 26 are quite a difficult passage in the Bible. But after what we have

seen concerning God's righteousness and the righteousness
that the Lord Jesus has accomplished, Romans 3:19-26 is
wonderful. Verse 19 says, "Now we know that whatever
things the law says, it speaks to those who are under the law,
that every mouth may be stopped and all the world may fall
under the judgment of God." Why did God give man the law?
It was given so that man would have nothing to say before
God, so that every mouth may be stopped. God wants to show
man that everyone is a sinner and that everyone has sinned.
There is not one who has done good. Verse 20 says, "Because
out of the works of the law no flesh shall be justified before
Him; for through the law is the clear knowledge of sin." The
ultimate purpose of the law of God was to show man that he
is a sinner. The purpose of the law was not for man to be
saved through it. The tone of the law is completely condemna-
tory. The law says that man should be condemned, that he
should die, and that he should perish.

If the matter stopped here, there would be no gospel and
everything would be over. But the matter does not stop here.
Man cannot live by the law, but God has other ways. If
you cannot pay back the money, God has other ways to pay
it back for you. The first two words in verse 21 are marvelous;
they mark a big turn in this matter. "But now." Thank the
Lord that there is a turn! "But now, apart from the law, the
righteousness of God has been manifested." God's righteousness was originally manifested in the law. But if that were
the case now, we would be doomed. What does it mean to
say that God's righteousness was manifested in the law? It
means that whatever you owed God you had to pay back.
If you sinned, you had to perish. If you transgressed, you
had to go into perdition. Thus, the law would manifest God's
righteousness. To punish sinners would be the most righteous
thing for God to do. But thank the Lord, God's righteousness
is no longer manifested in the law. If His righteousness were
manifested within the law, God would have to judge sinners.
But the righteousness of God is manifested apart from
the law, in which case, judgment falls on God Himself. The
end of verse 21 says, "Witness being borne to it by the Law
and the Prophets." Even the prophets in the Old Testament,

including David and all the other prophets, testified to the same thing.

How is God's righteousness manifested? Verse 22 says, "Even the righteousness of God through the faith of Jesus Christ to all those who believe, for there is no distinction." Since all have sinned and fall short of the glory of God (v. 23), how can we obtain God's grace? Verses 24 and 25 say that we are "justified freely...through the redemption which is in Christ Jesus; whom God set forth as a propitiation place." God has sent Jesus to redeem us from our sins and has set Him forth as a propitiation place. I believe we all know what the propitiation place is. The propitiation place is the covering of the ark in the Old Testament tabernacle; it was the place where God bestowed grace upon man. Every place on earth is defiled by sin. But this place, and only this place, is without sin. Now Jesus has become the propitiation place. How has He become such a place? By His blood being the surety. God has set forth Jesus as the propitiation place, and now through the blood of Jesus I can come by faith to God. God cannot do anything else but bestow grace upon me. Only after God has done this can we say that His forbearance and His passing over of sins in the Old Testament was righteous; and only after God has done this can we say that His justifying those who believe in Jesus in the New Testament is also righteous. We are saved today not because God glossed over our sins but because God has dealt with our sins. Before God we are not forgiven debtors, but paid up debtors who are forgiven.

This is something most precious in the Bible. This is the only way that Christians can have boldness before God. Have you ever realized that inasmuch as love is precious, it is never that reliable? You cannot bring a person to court just because he has not loved you for a few days. There is no such thing as love in a law court. But if unrighteousness occurs or if sin arises, the law will speak. God likes to give us a handle, something for us to hold on to. Through such a handle, our faith can be strengthened and the promises of God can be fulfilled in us. This handle is the Lord Jesus Christ. God knows that we may doubt, so He works faith into us through His Son. We can say to Him, "God, since You have given me Your Son and have allowed Him to die, You must forgive my sins."

Sometimes we hear people praying, "O God, I want to be saved. Please save me! I have sinned, but I am determined to be saved. Please be merciful to me and have the Lord Jesus die for me." When such ones pray, they may cry bitterly. They act as if God's heart is very hard and believe that before God would forgive them or turn His heart toward them they have to cry much. Those who pray this way do not know what the gospel is. If the Son of God had not come to the earth, their crying and imploring before God might work. But the Son of God has come, and the problem of sin has been solved. The redemptive work on the cross has been accomplished. When people come to God, there is no need for poor begging anymore. Since God has given us His Son, He can forgive sins through His Son. He is faithful to do so; He is not being a liar by doing so. And He is righteous to do so; there is nothing unrighteous in it. When righteousness is involved, faithfulness is also involved.

Most people today are ignorant first of God's righteousness and then of the fact that the Lord Jesus has accomplished God's righteousness. People do not know that God's righteousness is manifested apart from the law. They still try to work up righteousness before God. They are like the man who owes ten thousand talents of silver. There is absolutely no way to repay the debt. But the man still tries to save six cents by getting off at an earlier stop, hoping to save to repay his debt. He is still calculating, hoping to save a little here or there, to do this or that, to generate a little money for the repayment of the debt. He still wants to say to his creditor that though he owes ten thousand talents, he does have a few pennies with him. He does not realize that the full sum has already been sent to his home.

Man has no idea what God has done in His Son. Because of this, the apostle Paul tells us what attitude man should have. Concerning God's righteousness, we need to look at two passages in the Bible. The first passage is in Romans 10. Verses 3 and 4 say, "For because they were ignorant of God's righteousness and sought to establish their own righteousness, they were not subject to the righteousness of God. For Christ is the end of the law unto righteousness to everyone who believes." I love these two verses. When we read these verses in relation to the gospel, our hearts must be warmed up. These verses say that the Jews did not know that God's righteousness had been established; they were still seeking to establish their own righteousness. They tried their best to be good, to exchange their work for their salvation, and to exchange their righteousness for life and all that God has given to them. But Paul said that all those seeking to establish their own righteousness are not subject to the righteousness of God. Not to be subject to the righteousness of God is not to be subject to the work that God has accomplished in His Son Jesus. God's righteousness is accomplished in His Son Jesus. The cross of Jesus is both a manifestation of God's love and an accomplishment of God's righteousness. On the cross of Jesus, God's righteousness was accomplished. If any man wants to establish his own righteousness today, he is denying the sufficiency of the Lord's work on the cross. Never think that we can add something to the work that the Lord Jesus has finished. Never think that we can help it or patch it up a little. All those who seek to establish their own righteousness are not subject to God's righteousness at all. If someone sends a sum of money to my home to pay back a loan he has made to me and I still try to save a few pennies to repay him, I am in reality despising what he has given me. All those who seek to establish their own righteousness are blaspheming God.

Why is "Christ...the end of the law"? Christ as "the end of the law" means that Christ includes everything that the law has. In other words, God has not just given you ten thousand talents of silver; all the money in the world has been given you. How can you save a few more pennies? The end of the law is Christ. How are you going to find any more righteousness? If a man is very big, and he occupies the whole chair, can you squeeze yourself into the same chair? The end of the law is Christ. How are you going to establish your own righteousness? Thank and praise God that what He has given us is the best! I would say a strong word in a most reverent way: God has "exhausted" His omnipotence in His Son Jesus. The end of the law is Christ. All those who believe in Him must receive righteousness. Those believing in Jesus are bound to receive. There is no possibility for them not to receive. I like this thought. It is impossible for us not to be saved. God has given us His Son, who does not only possess the little that you need, but even everything. God can never forsake those who have believed into His Son. God has no way to reject us. All those who come to God through the Son must receive righteousness. There will be no hassle; the guarantee is sure.

The other passage of Scripture is 2 Corinthians 5:21. We have been saved, but we still live as humans. It is true that we are now saved and that our sins are forgiven, but what do we do while living on this earth? We are all Christians today, and are all the children of the Lord. Regarding His children, God declares something most amazing here: "Him who did not know sin He made sin on our behalf." God has made the Lord Jesus sin. Originally the Lord Jesus was without sin at all; He had nothing to do with sin. Now God has judged Him as though judging sin itself. God judged Him this way "that we might become the righteousness of God in Him." Today in the Lord Jesus Christ, you and I are the showpiece of God's righteousness. When people see us, they see God's righteousness. We, the sinners, through the Lord Jesus becoming sin for us and through His bearing of our sins to forgive us, have now become the righteousness of God in the Lord Jesus Christ. We are the living righteousness of God walking on earth. In Christ we are the representatives of God's righteousness.

If you do not know what God's righteousness is, all you need to do is find a saved person and take a good look at him. You will then know what God's righteousness is. If you want to know what God's righteousness is, just find a Christian and you will know that God has not dealt with our sins irresponsibly. He has made sin Him who knew no sin. Because the Lord Jesus has died, the work of redemption is accomplished. For us to be in the Lord Jesus today is an expression of the righteousness of God. When a person sees someone who believes in the Lord Jesus, he sees God's righteousness. If someone wants to know what God's righteousness is, I can stand up and tell him, "Just look at me. God loves me so much. He loves us to the uttermost. He is not loose concerning sin at all. This is why He caused the Lord Jesus to die on the cross. Look at me, a saved sinner today. I am the showpiece of God's righteousness in Christ."

Today we declare two great messages to the world. Both of them are what the world desperately needs. The first is that God loves man. This is a most wonderful fact. But that is not all. The other great message is that God in His righteousness has forgiven man's sins. Now man can come to God with all boldness and full faith, reminding Him that He has forgiven his sins.

At the end I would like to ask you a question. Why is the parable of the prodigal son in Luke 15? It seems that there is something lacking in this parable of the prodigal. After the prodigal squandered his estate and came home, the father should indeed love him, but he should have said at least a few words of reprimand to the son, perhaps something like this: "You have taken all your estate and have spent everything; even your stomach is empty now." But the father did not say a word like this. No wonder the older son had to say something. Even we have to say something. Is it not unrighteousness when there is sin and it is not dealt with? If Luke 15 had only the parable of the prodigal, we would have to conclude that God is not righteous, that God has not judged sin, but has glossed over it. In the parable of the prodigal son there is not so much as one word of rebuke. But thank and praise the Lord that there are three parables in Luke 15. The first is the parable of the shepherd saving the sheep. The second is the parable of the woman seeking the lost coin. The third is the parable of the father receiving the prodigal son. Immediately in the first parable we have the good shepherd forsaking his life for the sheep. The Lord Jesus has already come and died. The sin of the prodigal was already judged in the first parable. Because of what happened in the first parable, there is the second parable, in which a woman lights a lamp to seek for the lost coin. Since the Lord Jesus has accomplished salvation, the Holy Spirit can come to enlighten with His light. After this the Father does not see the problem of sin anymore. The problem of sin has been cleared up in the parable of the shepherd giving his life for the sheep. In addition, the inward feeling has been enlightened in the parable of the woman lighting the lamp. The wrongs have been realized already. By the time the Father comes, all He needs to do is to welcome the prodigal. The Lord Jesus has forgiven our sins. The Holy Spirit has enlightened us and has caused us to be convicted concerning sin, righteousness, and judgment. Hence, by the time the Father comes, the matter of sin need not be mentioned anymore; He only has to do the work of welcoming us. In the previous two parables, God's righteousness as well as His love were already manifested.

Suppose a person has not yet come to God, but he sees that he is a sinner and realizes that the Lord Jesus has judged his sins. The Good Shepherd has borne his sins away and the Holy Spirit has enlightened him concerning his sins. When such a one returns home, he has to realize that the matter of sin is forever gone; it has been dealt with on the cross. Remember that the Father's house is not the place to talk about sin. It is not the place to talk about our squandering. The cross is the place to talk about sin; it is the place to talk about our squandering. If you are at home, God can most righteously choose not to talk about your sins. We can eat and drink to our heart's delight. We can live, wear the costly garments, rest, and make merry to our heart's delight. God has said that once we were lost, but now we have been found, that once we were dead, but now we have come to life. There is no problem here any longer. Hallelujah! God's grace is sufficient for us. In this way, we realize that God's grace is a faithful and righteous grace.

## THE RIGHTEOUSNESS OF SALVATION

One thing we have to know is that before the Lord Jesus died, it was unrighteous for God to forgive our sins, but after the Lord Jesus died, it would be equally unrighteous for God not to forgive our sins. Without the Lord Jesus' death, God's forgiveness would be unrighteous on His part; He could never do this. With the Lord Jesus' death, He would be held equally unrighteous if God would not forgive. Please remember, a redemption without blood is unrighteous. On the other hand, when one has the blood and is denied salvation, this is also unrighteous.

Once I went with a brother to Kiukiang. While we were on the boat traveling and sharing the Word with others, I began to speak to a person about our faith. At the same time our brother spoke to another person, who was Moslem. During the conversation, our brother asked the man if he had any sin. The man tried to tell him how good Mohammedanism is and how great Mohammed was. But our brother said, "I am not asking you about these things. My question is this: Do *you* have any sin?" He confessed that he did. Our brother then asked him, "What then are you going to do about it? Is there any way that you can be forgiven?" The man answered that if he wanted to be forgiven, he had to feel remorseful at heart and do good, and do this and that and many other things. After the man had listed all the things that should be done, our brother said, "This is precisely the point of controversy. You have said that when one sins, remorse can bring in forgiveness. But I say that when one sins, there must be punishment. Without punishment, there can be no forgiveness. You think that a sense of remorse will earn someone forgiveness. But I say that forgiveness only comes through judgment. If I have sinned in this city and I escape to a far away country, I can be remorseful over there, and I can perform many charities. I can be a nice man there. But none of these will revoke my sin. Your God is a God who forgives without judgment. But my God is a God who forgives only after judgment." The Moslem then asked, "How can you be forgiven then?" "This is why," said our brother, "You need to believe in Jesus. Only by believing in Jesus will you be forgiven. Your sins have been judged in the Lord Jesus, and when you believe in Him, you will be forgiven." Here is the righteousness of God. Today men consider whether or not God is love. They do not realize that God is not only love, but He is also righteous. It is not that God only wants to forgive man's sins. He has to forgive them in a way that will not conflict with His nature and His righteousness. This is what men fail to see.

## THE APPLICATIONS
## OF GOD'S RIGHTEOUSNESS

We should now ask, how is God's righteousness applied to us? God's righteousness is applied to us in two ways. God's righteousness can first be applied in its giving us peace in our heart. Feelings are unreliable; therefore, we may not trust God's feelings. Love is likewise unreliable. If someone's love changes, no one can penalize him or her for it. But we can lay hold of righteousness and make claims based on righteousness. If God only loves us, He may spare us from the judgment of sins or may let us off easily, if that is something that He can do. But what if one day God is not happy with us anymore and does not want to go easy on us anymore? If God does not love us anymore and if He becomes angry and unhappy with us, we would suffer. Under such circumstances, we could not have any assurance about God, and our hearts would never be at peace. But now that God has given us His righteousness, we are at peace, for we know that our sins have been judged in the person of Christ. Hence, we can have a bold conscience and definite assurance when we come to God, and our heart can have peace. Peace cannot be obtained through love; peace can only be obtained through righteousness. Although in reality God's love is reliable, from man's point of view it is not as reliable as God's righteousness. When a person first begins to trust in God, he should learn to trust more in His righteousness than in His love. Later, as he progresses, he should learn to trust more in God's love than in His righteousness. Such a trust belongs to an advanced stage of the Christian life. This is the life of people like Madame Guyon. But at the beginning, we should take righteousness as the basis of our faith. Without righteousness, faith has no basis. Thank God that our sins have been forgiven. Thank Him that He will never judge us anymore. As the hymn says,

> God would not have His claim on two,
> First on His Son, my Surety true,
> And then upon me laid.

Our hearts are at rest, for our sins have been judged.

God's righteousness has another application: It causes us to realize the loathsome nature of sin. In order to preserve His righteousness, God was willing even to crucify His Son on the cross. God would rather sacrifice His Son than sacrifice His righteousness, His truth, and His law. God would not do one thing that is contrary to His nature. Therefore, we can see how loathsome sin is. If God cannot be careless about sin and would rather judge His Son in order to deal with sin, we also cannot be careless toward sin. In God's view, His Son can be sacrificed, but sin cannot be left undealt with. Every believer in the Lord Jesus must see then that no sin can be glossed over. God's attitude toward sin is very strict.

Now all our sins are forgiven. The Lord Jesus has died, we are forgiven, and everything is taken care of. Here I would like to give you one more illustration. One day I was at Hsiao-feng Park reading my Bible. Suddenly, the sky blackened and thunder began to roll. It looked as if it was going to rain immediately. I closed my Bible quickly and ran to a little house behind the park. But after a while the rain had not yet come, so I walked home hurriedly. On the way home the sky was still quite dark; thunder was rolling, and the clouds were very thick. Yet the rain did not come—not one drop fell on me the entire way home. On another occasion some time later, I went to the same park to read again. This time also the sky blackened like the previous time. Thunder started to roll again, and the clouds were overcast and thick. I counted on my experience from the last time, so I was quite at ease and moved slowly. But unfortunately this time the rain came, and I got wet. I had no choice but to run to that little house again. By the time I reached the house, the rain was pouring down. I did not know how heavy the rain would be. But, eventually, the sky cleared, the clouds dispersed, the thunder ceased, and I walked home again. This time, like the previous time, there was not a drop of rain while I was on my way home. But let

me ask you a question: On which occasion did my heart have
more peace? On both occasions no rain fell on me as I walked
home. But which time did I have more peace? Was it the first
time, or was it the second time? Although the first time there
was no rain on the way home, I did not know when the rain
would come; as a result, my heart was held in suspense. On
the second occasion there was also no rain on the way home,
but my heart was at peace because the rain had already
passed and the sky was clear. Many people hope that God's
grace would gloss over their sins. They are like I was on my
first trip home. Although there is no rain, darkness still
hangs overhead; thunder still rolls and the clouds still cover.
Their hearts are still held in suspense. They do not know
what will happen to them. But praise and thank the Lord, the
salvation we have received is one that has already "passed
through the rain." It is a salvation that has "passed through
thunder." Our "rain" has already been poured out on Calvary,
and our "thunder" has already rolled on Calvary. Now everything is over. We rejoice not only because our sins have been
forgiven but because they have been forgiven after being
dealt with. They were not glossed over. God has dealt with the
problem of our sins. His Son's resurrection has become
the evidence of this work.

Today is the day of grace. But we must remember that
grace reigns through righteousness (Rom. 5:21). Grace cannot
come directly; it must come through righteousness. God's
grace does not come to us directly. It comes to us through Calvary. Today some say that if God loves us, He can forgive us
without judgment. That would be grace reigning without
righteousness. But grace is reigning through righteousness.
Grace needs the righteousness of Calvary before it can reign.
Today our receiving of grace is based solely upon God's righteousness. Our sins are forgiven after they are dealt with.
When we see the cross, it is right to say that this is God's
righteousness. It is also right to say that this is God's grace.
The cross signifies God's righteousness, and it also signifies
God's grace. To God, the cross is righteousness; to us, it is
grace. When we behold the cross today, our heart is fully at
rest because we know that the grace that we have received

was obtained through God's righteous way. We know that our salvation is clear, complete, proper, and upright. Our salvation does not come through smuggling and fraud. Rather, it comes through judgment on sin. Thank and praise the Lord! The cross has solved the problem of sin, and the resurrection has confirmed that the solution is indeed true.

# CHAPTER SIX

# THE WORK OF CHRIST—REDEMPTION

By the grace of God, we have seen in the past few evenings what God's salvation is. Tonight is the sixth evening. I hope to give a quick review of what we have covered in the previous five meetings. Then we will continue. We have seen sin, the law, God's love, His grace, and His righteousness. We have seen how man became a sinner and how the law came in to expose man's sins. We have also seen that though man is proved to be a sinner, God still loves him. Not only has God loved us, but He has also shown us mercy and grace. We have also seen how God's grace has been manifested, what the nature of this grace is, how it came about, and that it can never be mixed with human effort. Last night we saw that, in spite of God's love and His desire to give us grace, there was one hindrance to grace's coming to us. If one thing had been left unsettled, God's grace could not have come to us. Though grace is now here to reign, it reigns only through righteousness (Rom. 5:21). Grace cannot reign by itself. Hence, the Lord showed us how righteousness was manifested. His righteousness has dealt with our sins. At the same time, it enables us to receive grace from God. We have covered these during the last five evenings. Now, we will go on with the gospel of God and His salvation.

The salvation accomplished by God through the Lord Jesus has manifested God's grace. At the same time, it satisfies God's righteous requirements. At this time we will cover the work of the Lord Jesus. This is an excellent and sweet subject. It deals with the way the Lord Jesus accomplished God's salvation. We have to see how the Lord Jesus satisfied God's demand and how He has manifested God's grace. At the same time, we have to see how the Lord Jesus satisfies the heart of the Christian so that we would be satisfied with His work also. A song which we sing says, "God's heart is satisfied with the work of the Lord Jesus, and our hearts are also at rest with His work." God is satisfied, and we are satisfied. If time permits, I hope that we can cover both of these aspects.

## THE LORD JESUS BEING BOTH GOD AND MAN
## FOR THE ACCOMPLISHMENT OF REDEMPTION

The first thing we have to see is that the Lord Jesus is God. We may say that only God can bear man's sin. Never consider the Lord Jesus as a third person coming to die a substitutionary death. Do not think that God is one party, we are another party, and the Lord Jesus is a third party. The Bible never considers the Lord Jesus as a third party. On the contrary, it considers Him as the first party. You may have been told that the gospel is like a debtor, a lender, and the lender's son. The debtor has no money to pay back his debt. The lender, being very severe, insists on the payment. But the lender's son steps forth to pay the debt on behalf of the debtor, and the debtor becomes free.

This is the gospel that man preaches today. But this is not the real gospel. If this were the case, at least two points would not be fair and would be contrary to the Bible. First, this kind of understanding makes God the mean One and the Lord Jesus the gracious One. In such an illustration, we do not see God loving the world. Rather, we see only His righteous demand and the demand of the law. We see a severe God, One who is without grace and One whose words to man are always harsh. We see that the Lord Jesus loves us and gives grace to us. This is a wrong gospel. However, although this is a wrong gospel, God still uses it. Actually, I was saved through this kind of illustration. But although I was saved, during the first three years I could never praise God. I always felt that the Lord Jesus was good, that I should thank and praise Him, that without Him everything was hopeless, and that it was fortunate that He came. But I felt that God was very harsh, severe, and mean. He was not at all lovable. It seemed that everything good was with the Lord Jesus and everything bad was with God, that God was terrible and the Lord Jesus was lovable.

But this is not the Bible. The Bible says that God so loved the world that He gave His Son to us (John 3:16). God sent His Son to us because He loved us. This is why we were brought back to God after the Lord Jesus accomplished His work on the cross. If God had not loved us and had not sent us the Lord Jesus, the most that the Lord Jesus could have done would have been to bring people back to Himself; He could not have brought people back to God. Thank the Lord that the One who loved us is God. Thank Him that He Himself sent His Son to us. It was the Father who was moved with compassion. It was the Father who loved us. It was the Father who planned out salvation. It was the Father who had a will in eternity past. First, the Father purposed everything, and then the Son came. Hence, it is wrong for man to think that there are three parties. There are only two parties, God and man. The Lord Jesus is God's gift to man. However, this gift is something living and with a will, rather than lifeless and without a will. Thank God that salvation is something between God and man. The Lord Jesus is a gift. Today the One we have to face is God. We come to God through the Lord Jesus. This is the first thing we have to realize.

Second, if there were three parties, the Lord Jesus would not have been qualified to die for us. It is true that when the Lord Jesus died for us, God's righteousness was met and man's sins were forgiven. But is this righteous to the Lord Jesus? Suppose there are two brothers. One brother has committed a capital crime and has been sentenced to death. The other brother is very willing to die for him and is therefore executed on his behalf. He is innocent, and also a third party. He dies instead of the other. The Bible does not show us that the Lord Jesus died for us this way. It does not show us that God had a demand, that His law had to be satisfied, and that in order for man to meet the law's demand, the Lord Jesus came to fulfill God's law. There is no such thing. What position did the Lord Jesus take when He came to accomplish redemption? We have to consider this matter carefully and accurately from the Bible.

I would like you to be aware of one thing. The world thinks that there is only one way to deal with the problem of sin.

Preachers who preach wrong teachings say that there are three ways to deal with sin. But for God, there are only two ways to deal with sin. Some explanation is needed here. Before one reads the Word of God, he may think that any of three ways can solve the problem: man can solve it, God can solve it, or a third party can also solve it by substitution. The unsaved ones who do not know God consider that there is only one solution, which is for man to solve it by himself. But God's righteousness shows us that there are only two ways to solve the problem. One is by God Himself and the other is by man himself. What do I mean by this? Let us first consider what man thinks. He thinks that he is a sinner and should therefore bear the judgment of sin and the wrath of God. He thinks that he should perish and go into perdition. The only way is for him to solve the problem by going to hell. He will take responsibility for what he has done. If one sins, he goes to hell and bears his own judgment of sin. This is one way to solve the problem. When one owes money, he sells all that he has. He may even have to sell his wife, children, house, and land, if that is what it takes to solve the problem. This is righteous. Then there is the other wrong concept. For those who have heard the gospel, they consider that the Lord Jesus is a third party coming to take our place and solve the problem of our sin. Man has sinned and has incurred the judgment of sin. Now all the judgment is laid on the Lord Jesus; He bears all the judgment. Such a teaching seems right. But you will see shortly that this is not accurate.

For the sake of those with unclear concepts, I will say a word first. In the Bible, there are two important doctrines, which are the bearing of sins and the ransom for sins. Please do not think that I do not believe in substitution. But the substitution that some talk about is not the substitution in the Bible, because their kind of substitution involves unrighteousness. If the sinless Jesus is to be a substitute for sinful men, it is, of course, a bargain for us. But is it righteous to treat the Lord Jesus this way? He did not sin. Why should He be killed? This is not the kind of substitution that the Bible speaks of. If the Lord Jesus is to die on behalf of all the sinners in the world, then those who believe in Jesus as well as those who do not believe in Him will likewise be saved. The Lord has died for them both, whether or not they have believed. One cannot turn the wheel backward and reverse the Lord's death just because some do not believe. One can turn back the wheel on other things. But this is not something reversible. Why does the Bible say that those who do not believe have been judged and shall perish? (John 3:16, 18). The reason is that the Son of God only died a substitutional death for us who believe. He is not a substitute for those who do not believe.

What then is the way to solve the problem of sin according to the Bible? There are only two righteous ways to solve the problem. One is to deal with the one who has sinned, and the other is to deal with the one who has been sinned against. There are only two parties in the world that are qualified to deal with this problem. There are only two persons in the world who have the right to deal with the problem of sin. One is the one who has sinned against another. The other is the one who has been sinned against. When a person sues another in court, no third party has the right to speak anything. In a court proceeding, only the one who has sinned against someone and the one who has been sinned against have the right to speak. Concerning the sinner's salvation, if the sinner does not take care of it himself, then God has to take care of it for him. The sinner is the sinning party, and God is the party being sinned against. Either party can deal with the problem of sin in a most righteous way. On the sinner's side, it is righteous for him to suffer judgment and punishment, perish, and go into perdition. But there is another way which is equally righteous. The party that has been sinned against can assume the punishment. This may be quite inconceivable to us, but it is a fact. It is the party being sinned against that bears the sins. It is not a third party that bears our sins. A third party has no authority or right to step in. If a third party comes in, it is unrighteousness. Only when the party that is being sinned against is willing to suffer the loss can the problem be solved. Since God has love and also has righteousness, He would not allow a sinner to bear his sins, for that would mean that God was righteous without love. The only alternative is for the party being sinned against to step in. Only by God bearing our sins will righteousness be maintained.

Do you know what forgiveness means? In the world, we have forgiveness. Between individuals, there is forgiveness. Between a government and its people, there is also forgiveness. Even between nations, there is forgiveness. With God and man, there is also forgiveness. Forgiveness is something universally recognized as a fact. No one can say that forgiveness is something unrighteous. It is something one does cheerfully to another. But the question is: who has the right to forgive? If a brother has stolen ten dollars from me, and I forgive him, it means that I have taken up the consequence of his sin. I have taken up the loss of these ten dollars. As another example, let us say that you have hit me in the face. The blow was so severe that I bled. If I say that I forgive you, it means that you have committed the sin of hitting, and I have suffered the consequence of hitting. The sin was committed by you, but I suffered the consequence of it. This is forgiveness. To forgive means that one party sins, and another suffers the consequence of that sin. Forgiveness is the taking up of the responsibility of the sinning party by the party sinned against. A third party has no right to come in to forgive. He cannot come in to recompense. If a third party comes in to forgive and recompense, it is unrighteousness. If the Lord Jesus comes in as a third party to substitute for the sinner, it may be fine for the sinner, and God may also have no problem with it, but there is a problem with the Lord Jesus. He has no sin. Why did He have to suffer judgment? Only the sinning one can bear the consequence of sin; he has the right to bear his own responsibility and suffer judgment for his own sin. And there is only one who can take up his sins—the one whom he has sinned against. Only the one sinned against can take up the sin of the sinning one. This is righteousness. This is the principle of forgiveness. Both God's law and man's law recognize that this is righteous. Man has the right to suffer loss. Inasmuch as man has a free will, God also has a free will. A person with a free will does have the right to choose to suffer loss.

What then is Christ's redemption? The redemptive work of Christ is God Himself coming to bear man's sin against Him. This word is more lovely to the ear than all the music in the world. What is the redemptive work of Christ? It is God bearing that with which man has sinned against Him. In other words, if Jesus of Nazareth was not God, He would not be qualified to bear our sins righteously. Jesus of Nazareth was God. He is the very God whom we sinned against. Our God has come down to earth personally and borne our sins. Today, it is God rather than man who has borne our sins. This is why it was a righteous bearing. We cannot bear it ourselves. If we were to bear it, we would be finished. Thank God that He Himself has come to the world to bear our sins. This is the work of the Lord Jesus on the cross.

Why then did God have to become a man? It is good enough for God to love the world. Why did He have to give His only begotten Son? One has to realize that man has sinned against God. If God requires man to bear his sin, how can he do it? The wages of sin is death. When sin motivates and acts within, it ends in death. Death is the rightful penalty of sin (Rom. 5:12). When man sins against God, he has to bear the consequence of sin, which is death. Hence, God is the other party. If He is to come and take up our responsibility and bear the consequence of our sin, He has to die. But 1 Timothy 6:16 tells us that God is immortal; He cannot die. Although God is willing to come into the world and bear our sins, and although He is willing to die and go into perdition, it is impossible for Him to do this. Death has simply no effect on God. There is no possibility for God to die. Hence, for God to bear the judgment of man's sin against Him, He has to take on the body of a man. This is why Hebrews 10:5 tells us that when Christ came into the world, He said, "A body You have prepared for Me." God has prepared a body for Christ so that Christ could offer Himself up as a burnt offering and sin offering. The Lord says, "In burnt offerings and sacrifices for sin You did not delight" (v. 6). Now He is offering up His own body to deal with man's sin. Hence, the Lord Jesus became a man and came into the world to be crucified on the cross.

The Lord Jesus is not a third party; He is the first party. Because He is God, He is qualified to be crucified on the cross. Because He is man, He can die on the cross on our behalf. We must distinguish between these two statements clearly. He is qualified to be crucified because He is God, and He is able to be crucified because He is man. He is the opposite party; He has stepped over to man's side to suffer punishment. God has become a man. He has come among man, joined Himself to man, taken up man's burden, and borne all his sins. If redemption is to be righteous, Jesus of Nazareth must be God. If Jesus of Nazareth is not God, redemption is not righteous. Every time I look at the cross, I say within myself, "This is God." If He is not God, His death becomes unrighteous and it cannot save us, for He is but a third party. But thank and praise the Lord, He is the party opposite us. That is why I made the statement that only two parties are able to deal with our sins. One is we ourselves, in which case we have to die ourselves. The other party is the God whom we have sinned against, in which case He dies for us. Other than these two parties, no third party has the right or authority to deal with our sins.

## THE MAN JESUS HAVING
## THE RIGHTEOUSNESS ACCORDING TO THE LAW
## AND BEING QUALIFIED TO REDEEM MAN

Jesus of Nazareth has come into the world. While He was on the earth, His works demonstrated that God loves us. But at the same time, He fulfilled the law. He was truly submissive to God. He was a holy man and a submissive man. In Him we see a perfect man. Jesus of Nazareth was full of righteousness. He was a righteous man. Throughout history there was only one man who could be saved by the law. This was Jesus of Nazareth. He did not need to keep the law, yet He kept the law. The Bible says that only those who keep the law can inherit the righteousness that is of the law. With righteousness, there is life. The law says that he who keeps it will live. To keep it is to abide by the law. All who have the righteousness of the law have life. The only purpose for God to say this to the whole world is to condemn man and prove to him that he is a sinner. God gave us the law to prove to us that we are sinners. Thank and praise the Lord. There is only One who has life by the law. This One is Jesus of Nazareth.

Let us for the moment set aside the fact that He is God and consider Him as a man, a very ordinary man. He kept the law and lived. He lived on earth for over thirty-three years. Not only did He not sin, He did not even know sin. He was tempted in all things. But He was not tempted by sin. Note this: the Lord Jesus was not tempted by sin. When many read the book of Hebrews, they receive a wrong understanding based on a wrong translation. The Greek text shows us clearly that although the Lord Jesus was tempted in all things, He was never tempted by sin. He was in the flesh and therefore had weaknesses. But He knew no sin. He was never tempted by sin. If you consult an accurate translation, you will see this clearly.

Are the Lord Jesus' righteous acts of any benefit to us? Indeed they are. The righteous acts of the Lord Jesus prove that He is God. Because of these righteous acts, the Lord Jesus did not have to die for Himself. The righteous acts of the Lord qualify Him to die on the cross on behalf of our sins. If the Lord Jesus had any sin, His death would have been for Himself; He would not have been able to die for us. Since the Lord did not have any sin at all, He was qualified to be offered up as a sacrifice for our sins. Christian theology says that God has made the righteousness of the Lord Jesus ours. God has transferred the Lord's righteousness to us in the same way that banks transfer money from one account to another. The Lord kept the law for us. We have disobeyed the law. But the obedience of the Lord Jesus has earned us God's satisfaction. But let me ask emphatically: Has the Bible ever mentioned the "righteousness of the Lord Jesus"? Who can find a place in the New Testament that speaks of "the righteousness of the Lord Jesus"? If you read the entire New Testament, including the Greek text, you will discover that the New Testament never mentions the words *the righteousness of Christ*. One place seems to say this, but it does not refer to Christ's own personal righteousness. Men do not like to read God's Word today. They like to study theology.

Theology, however, is created by man. It does not come from God's Word. Theology tells us that God has imputed Christ's righteousness to us. The Bible does not have this concept. On the contrary, the Bible is opposed to this concept. The righteousness of Jesus of Nazareth is His own righteousness. It is indeed righteousness, but it is the righteousness of Jesus of Nazareth. This righteousness qualifies Him to die for us and be our Savior, but God has no intention to transfer the righteousness of Jesus to us.

John 12:24 is a precious verse in the Bible. It says that unless the grain of wheat falls into the ground and dies, it abides alone. A man like the Lord Jesus was just one grain before God. Only after He has died are there many grains. Salvation begins with the cross. Although we must have Bethlehem before we can have Golgotha, we are saved through Golgotha, not Bethlehem. The Son of God is absolutely righteous. He was the one righteous grain. But His righteousness cannot save us. It cannot be imputed to us. God does mention the righteousness of Christ in the Bible. But He never says that Christ's righteousness is to be ours. The Bible says that Christ is our righteousness. It never says that Christ's righteousness is our righteousness. I would like to bring this out, for this will exalt the cross of the Lord Jesus Christ. The Bible says that Christ is our righteousness. Christ Himself is our righteousness. We go to God in Christ. Christ is our righteousness.

Once I asked a Western sister what she wears when she goes before God. She said that she puts on the righteousness of Christ to go to God. She took the righteousness of Christ as her garment to go to God. I asked her where this is found in the Bible. It is not the righteousness of Christ that has become our righteousness. Christ has never transferred His righteousness to us. Rather, it is Christ Himself who has become our righteousness. We are saved by the righteousness of God, not by the righteousness of Christ.

We have seen what God's righteousness is. God's righteousness brings us forgiveness and saves us from judgment. It is not the righteousness of Christ that does this. The righteousness of Christ is only the qualification for Him to be our

Savior. Christ has never transferred His righteousness to us. If the righteousness of the Lord Jesus were transferable to us, He could have done this while He was living on earth. He did not have to go to the cross, and we could have been saved then. If that is the case, His life would have become a ransoming life. But there is no such doctrine as a ransoming life. There is only the doctrine of a ransoming death. Only the death of the Lord Jesus will save us. His life is our example. We cannot be saved by His life. His righteousness condemns us. The more righteous He is, the more we are in trouble. There is absolutely no way for His righteousness to be imputed to us. If God were to put us side by side with the righteousness of the Lord, we could only go to hell. But thank God that He has died and become our righteousness. This is why we are saved. Salvation comes from the cross. It does not come from the manger. Salvation comes from Golgotha; it does not come from Bethlehem. If the righteousness of the Lord Jesus could save us, He would not have had to die. Therefore, when we read the Bible, we should not be affected by theology. We will be much clearer if we are taught by the Bible rather than by theology. Man's word can help, but it can also damage. We would rather put man's word aside.

Let us go on step by step. We first saw that it must be God who comes to bear our sins. Then we saw that Jesus of Nazareth came to bear our sins. But His righteousness on earth was more of a condemnation to us. When were we saved through the Lord Jesus? Let us consider a type in the Bible. Between the Holy Place and the Holy of Holies in the tabernacle, there was a veil. God was within the veil in the Holy of Holies. Outside the veil was the world. The Bible tells us that this veil signifies the flesh of the Lord Jesus (Heb. 10:20). In other words, the Holy of Holies can only be seen by the Lord Jesus as a man on earth and those who live a life like the life of the Lord Jesus. Not all can see God. Only the Lord Jesus can see God. No one in the entire world can see the Holy of Holies. It has been veiled. Man was able to see the Holy of Holies when God removed the veil from heaven and combined the Holy of Holies, the Holy Place, and the outer court into one. This was accomplished at the time the Son of

God was crucified on the cross. At that time, the way to the Holy of Holies was opened. This is why Hebrews 10:19-20 says that we have boldness to enter the Holy of Holies by the blood of Jesus through the veil. This torn veil is the flesh of the Lord Jesus. Now we have boldness and the full assurance of faith to come to God. The righteousness of the Lord Jesus on earth has no direct relationship with us. Thank the Lord that He did not stay on earth forever. If He were to remain on earth forever, He would still be the one grain. Thank God that He has died and produced us, the many grains. Thank the Lord for the cross.

### THE TWO ASPECTS OF THE LORD'S CROSS

Here is a question. The Lord died on the cross, but what is the significance of His death? Who sent Him to the cross? Everyone who reads the Gospels knows that the Jews sent Him to the Gentiles, and the Gentiles crucified Him on the cross. If I remember correctly, Pilate was a Spaniard. How can we say that the Lord Jesus died to bear our sins? He was clearly crucified by man. In Acts 2:23 Peter told the Jews that they had nailed Jesus to the cross through the hand of lawless men. Here it says that it was the Jews who nailed the Lord Jesus to the cross. But what did the Lord Jesus do on the cross? Before He went to the cross, He was praying in the garden of Gethsemane. Was His prayer, accompanied with sweat like drops of blood, caused by man's persecution and opposition? Was it because Judas was bringing men to arrest Him? Or was it because He had to go to the cross to redeem us from sin? Was it not because God made the sinless One to become sin for us and laid the sins of the whole world upon Him, so that He would bear our sins upon the tree? There He prayed, "Father, if You are willing, remove this cup from Me" (Luke 22:42).

If the cross was something out of man's hand, if it was just the tool for some evil men to kill Him, and if there was only the human aspect to the Lord Jesus, then I would not like to listen to this prayer of the Lord. I would not like to hear Jesus of Nazareth kneeling there praying to the Father to remove the cup from Him if possible. For the past two thousand years, many martyrs and disciples of the Lord had a much stronger voice than He did when they were about to die. Many martyrs, when locked inside cells and dungeons, prayed that the Father would glorify them, that they would rather die for the Son, and that they would rather testify to the Lord's Word with their blood. If it had not been God who had commenced to place the burden of sins on the Lord at Gethsemane, and if it had not been God who had laid the burden of bearing our sins on the Lord Jesus, we would have to say that the Lord Jesus did not even have as much courage as those who believed in Him. Hence, the problem is that the cross has the aspect of man and the aspect of God. Man crucified the Lord Jesus on the cross. But the Lord said that no man takes His life away; He gave it up by Himself (John 10:17-18). Man could crucify the Lord a thousand times or ten thousand times, but unless He Himself gave His life away, nothing could have been done to Him. Man considers that He was crucified by man. We consider Him to be crucified by God to redeem sins on our behalf.

We have to find out from the Bible what God did on the cross. First, let us read Isaiah 53:5-10: "But He was pierced because of our transgressions; / He was crushed because of our iniquities; / The chastening for our peace was upon Him, / And by His stripes we have been healed. / We all like sheep have gone astray; / Each of us has turned to his own way, / And Jehovah has caused the iniquity of us all / To fall on Him. / He was oppressed, and it was He who was afflicted, / Yet He did not open His mouth; / Like a lamb that is led to the slaughter / And like a sheep that is dumb before its shearers, / So He did not open His mouth. / By oppression and by judgment He was taken away; / And as for His generation, who among them had the thought / That He was cut off out of the land of the living / For the transgression of my people to whom the stroke was due? / And they assigned His grave with the wicked, / But with a rich man in His death, / Although He had done no violence, / Nor was there any deceit in His mouth. / But Jehovah was pleased to crush Him, to afflict Him with grief. / If You make His soul a trespass offering, / He will see a seed, He will extend His days, / And the pleasure of

Jehovah will prosper in His hand." The apostles quote Isaiah 53 many times in the New Testament. The One spoken of in this passage of the Scriptures is the Lord Jesus. What did the prophet say when he wrote this portion of the Scripture? The last sentence in verse 4 says, "We ourselves esteemed Him stricken, / Smitten of God and afflicted." At the beginning, the prophet thought that He was smitten and stricken by God, that He was punished for His own sins and smitten by God for His transgressions. But in verse 5, there is a turn. God showed him a revelation by means of the word *but*. We think that He was merely suffering from punishment and smiting. *But* He was not suffering from punishment and smiting. "But He was pierced because of our transgressions; / He was crushed because of our iniquities; / The chastening for our peace was upon Him, / And by His stripes we have been healed. / We all like sheep have gone astray; / Each of us has turned to his own way" (vv. 5-6). The next sentence is very precious, "And Jehovah has caused the iniquity of us all / To fall on Him" (v. 6). This is what the Lord has done. We can see that there is the aspect of man to the cross and there is the aspect of God. Although it was the hands of man that nailed the Lord Jesus up, manifesting man's hatred for God, it was also God who had laid all of our sins upon Him and crucified Him. The cross was God's doing; it was something that Jehovah accomplished.

What happened at the cross? "He was oppressed, and it was He who was afflicted, / Yet He did not open His mouth; / Like a lamb that is led to the slaughter / And like a sheep that is dumb before its shearers, / So He did not open His mouth. / By oppression and by judgment He was taken away; / And as for His generation, who among them had the thought / That He was cut off out of the land of the living / For the transgression of my people to whom the stroke was due?" (vv. 7-8). To be cut off out of the land of the living is to die. Those who stood by the cross at the time the Lord was crucified marveled and wondered why this man was being crucified. They did not know the reason why such a thing happened. The prophet said that "He did not open His mouth," and that He is brought "like a lamb that is led to the slaughter / And like a sheep that is dumb before its shearers." Who knew that He was cut off out of the land of the living for the sin of the people? Who knew that it was God working on Him to accomplish the work of redemption? The cross was the way that the Lord accomplished redemption through His death. Verse 9 says, "And they assigned His grave with the wicked, / But with a rich man in His death, / Although He had done no violence, / Nor was there any deceit in His mouth." Verse 10 is very precious: "But Jehovah was pleased to crush Him, to afflict Him with grief. / If You make His soul a trespass offering." The cross is a work that God did. It was God Himself who bore our sins on the cross. He solved our problem of sin. Never give any credit to Judas for delivering the Lord Jesus to the Jews. Never think that without Judas the Lord would not have been able to be the Savior. Even if there had been a thousand or ten thousand Judases, it would still be useless. It was the Lord Jesus Himself who bore our sins.

When the Lord Jesus was praying in the garden of Gethsemane, He may have seemed like the weakest of all men, without any courage. He prayed for the Father to take the cup away from Him (Luke 22:42). But when He came out from the garden and met many evil men, He said, "I am," and "they drew back and fell to the ground" (John 18:6). Please remember that He did not fall while being confronted with man's evil. On the contrary, He caused them to fall. While He was at Gethsemane, considering the suffering involved in bearing man's sins, how the sinless One would be made sin, and how He was to take upon Himself the judgment of sin, He prayed for the cup to be removed from Him if possible. Had it not been for the question of redemption, the Lord Jesus would not have even matched a martyr. How brave were the many Christian martyrs when they marched to the lions' den. But the Lord Jesus pleaded to have the cup removed from Him if possible. Physically speaking, the Lord Jesus was vastly different from all the martyrs. But for redemption, for solving the problem of sin, for God to come to man and bear man's sin, even He had to ask for the removing of the cup if possible. The Bible says that it was Jehovah that made Him an offering for sin. It was Jehovah who laid on Him the iniquity of us all. It was something Jehovah did. The cross was the work of God; it was not the work of man. The cross is God Himself coming to earth to bear man's sins. The cross is not the crucifixion of the Son of God by man.

Do you remember what the Bible says about the sixth to ninth hours? The sun's light failed (Luke 23:44-45). The Jews could mock Him, and the Gentiles could chastise and shame Him, but the sun was beyond the Jews' control. The Gentiles did not have the authority to manipulate the sun. Man could clamor and trumpet, but the earthquake was not something that Pilate could summon. Why was the sky darkened? These phenomena happened because God Himself had come to bear our sins. This was not something done by man. If it had been done by man, would God have added to His Son's pain when He was hanging on the cross? Would God not have sent twelve companies of angels to come and rescue Him? Such would indeed have happened had it not been for the redemption for sins. We thank and praise God that His Son came to redeem us from sins. This was why He said, "My God, My God, why have You forsaken Me?" (Matt. 27:46). No believer throughout the past two thousand years has ever said these terrible words when they died. For two thousand years, whether the believers died in peace or in woe, they were more bold than He was. Why was the Son of God rejected there by God? If it had merely been man's hand and man's crucifixion, that would have been the time He needed God's presence even more. When man plotted to persecute and kill Him, God should have manifested His presence more. That was the most crucial moment. God should have been with Him. Why did God leave Him instead? It was solely because the Son of God had become sin and had borne the judgment. That was the reason He cried, "My God, My God, why have You forsaken Me?" God had forsaken Him. We who have believed in the work of redemption know that the work of the cross was for Him to be judged by sin. The cross of the Lord shows us how evil sin is and how much of a price God has paid for the work of redemption.

Besides Isaiah 53, another clear testimony of the Scripture

can be found. In Romans 3:25, God set forth Christ "as a propitiation place." This also shows clearly that the work was done by God. Deuteronomy 21:23 tells us that he who is hanged on a tree is accursed of God. When the Lord was hanging on the cross, He was not accursed of man. Rather, He was accursed of God. That is why He can deliver us from the curse. First John 4:10 says that God loved us and sent His Son as a propitiation concerning our sins. It was God who sent His Son to be a propitiation. It was not man who crucified Him. Second Corinthians 5:21 also says, "Him who did not know sin He made sin on our behalf." This was something that God did. The cross is the work of God. It was God who sent the Lord Jesus to pass through the cross. Acts 2:23 mentions both the aspect of God and the aspect of man. "This man, delivered up by the determined counsel and foreknowledge of God, you, through the hand of lawless men, nailed to a cross and killed." The Lord Jesus was killed by the Jews through the hand of lawless men. However, such a death was according to the determined counsel of God. This shows us that everything was done by God. We have sin, and sin can only be taken care of by God Himself. For this reason, God came to the world to be a man. While He was a man, He was indeed righteous. But this righteousness was not imputed to us. It was the death of the Lord Jesus that delivered us from the curse of the law (Gal. 3:13). He did not deliver us from sin while He was living, but when He died. On the cross, it was God who crucified Him, rather than man. Man's hand is useless. It was God who took the opportunity to make manifest man's sin.

## REDEMPTION AND SUBSTITUTION

Now we have to ask one question. Since the Lord Jesus died on the cross and since God made Him the propitiation place, how can we be saved? What is the difference between redemption and substitution? Are they similar in any way? We have to realize that the work of the Lord Jesus is a work of redemption. But the result of this redemptive work is substitution. Redemption is the cause, and substitution is the result. The scope of redemption is very large. But the scope of substitution is not quite as large. It is quite interesting that the Bible never says that the Lord Jesus died on behalf of the sins of all. It only says that the Lord Jesus died on behalf of all (2 Cor. 5:14). His redemptive work was to satisfy the righteous requirements of God. When the Lord accomplished redemption on the cross, this work of redemption had absolutely nothing to do with man. I want to impress you strongly with this word. Redemption is absolutely not related to us. The work of redemption is between God and sin. What is the work of redemption? It is God Himself coming to the world to solve the problem of sin. Once the problem of sin is solved, the work of redemption is done.

The blood of the Passover lamb was sprinkled on the side posts and upper posts of the doors (Exo. 12:7). God said that when He saw the blood, He would pass over the house (v. 13). The blood was for God to see. It was not for the firstborn to see. The firstborn did not need to see the blood; they stayed in the houses. The blood was to meet God's righteous requirements; it was not to meet the requirements of the firstborn. With the firstborn, there was no such thing as redemption. If we read the Old Testament, we will discover that the blood for the atonement (i.e., redemption) of sin was brought into the Holy of Holies. It was sprinkled on the veil seven times (Lev. 16:14-15). On the day of Atonement, the high priest had to take the blood and sprinkle it on the mercy seat of the ark. The blood was offered to God. It is true that the blood had to be smeared on the thumb, the ear, and the toe of a leper. But that was done with respect to consecration. It was a matter of consecration to God. Man had no such requirement. Redemption has to do with God; it is God coming in to solve what man cannot solve by himself. This is why the Bible says, "And He Himself is the propitiation for our sins, and not for ours only but also for those of the whole world" (1 John 2:2). Redemption includes the whole world. In such a redemption, everyone, even those that have not been saved, are included.

God has come and dealt with our sins. The Lord Jesus has satisfied God's righteous requirements so that we can receive the substitution of the Lord Jesus. His redemption is an abstract preparation. By believing in Him, this redemption becomes a substitution to us. Before God, it was not a substitution, but a redemption. It is important to know this. If we are not clear about this matter, we will be confused about many other doctrines. Redemption is before God, and substitution is for us. Redemption is to satisfy God's requirements, and substitution is for us to receive the benefit. What He accomplished was redemption; what we have received is substitution. I do not mean that there is no such teaching as substitution in the Bible. There is indeed such a teaching. But all the teachings in the Bible concerning substitution are written for Christians. They are not written for unbelievers. To the Gentiles we say that Jesus has died for them and accomplished redemption. To the Christians we say that the Lord Jesus has substituted them in bearing their sins.

In the passage that we have read from Isaiah 53, notice that it says, "But He was pierced because of our transgressions; / He was crushed because of our iniquities; / The chastening for our peace was upon Him, / And by His stripes we have been healed" (v. 5). Please observe that it says "our" instead of "your." He bore the suffering for our sins. Hence, our sins are forgiven. It is for us and not for the whole world. When Peter quoted Isaiah 53, he said, "Who Himself bore up our sins in His body on the tree" (1 Pet. 2:24). It was always "our" and not "your." Hence, we have to be careful when we preach the gospel. It is better that we adhere more to the Bible. The Bible never says to sinners that Jesus died for their sins. The Bible says that Jesus died for them (Rom. 5:8). There is such a thing as Jesus dying for them. But there is no such thing as Jesus dying for their sins. For Jesus to die for them is a fact. But the problem of sin is not solved yet. It is true that all the problems of sin are solved before God already. But if one has not participated in this work, his sins are not yet solved, and he has no part in the substitution of Jesus. When one receives the Lord Jesus, his problem of sin is taken care of. This is substitution. Without this, there is no substitution. In other words, redemption has been accomplished, but salvation has not yet been accomplished. If I were to ask you when you were redeemed, you should reply that it transpired two thousand years ago. But if I were to ask you when you were saved, you should say that it happened in a certain year on a certain day and month. Redemption is something that happened long ago. Salvation is something present. Redemption was accomplished by Christ. Salvation is realized in us. We were redeemed two thousand years ago. But we may have been saved for only a few years. I do not know how to say it more clearly. This is very clear to me. God's work of redemption is a matter regarding Himself; it is to satisfy Himself and has nothing to do with us. It is something absolutely before God. God Himself was the One who did the work. When we come and see what God has accomplished, and believe and accept it, we will receive this substitution.

Let us use another illustration. There is a crossing that joins the east and west bank of the Whampoa river. It is free of charge. The name of the place is called The Free Crossing. Suppose I were a robber who had robbed and stolen many times there. However, now I am different. What should I do if I want to have a thorough dealing concerning my past theft and robbery? Even if I want to repay, where should I go? Those from whom I stole are now nowhere to be found. What should I do? For the sake of righteousness and in order to repay, I may start a free service to ferry people across the river. Anyone can come for the ride, and no money is charged. I may do this to repay the money that I stole from people in this area. I offer this kind of free service as a solution to the problem of my unrighteousness. This free service is to me a solution to unrighteousness. But to others, it is a substitution; I am paying the fare on others' behalf. This is the way that the Lord Jesus deals with the problem of punishment. God sent the Lord Jesus to accomplish redemption in order that the problem of sin, as well as His own holiness and righteousness, might be taken care of. When one believes, he will enter into this work, and the Lord Jesus will take away his sins.

Hence, the New Testament says, "Christ also has suffered once for sins, the Righteous on behalf of the unrighteous" (1 Pet. 3:18). He "Himself bore up our sins in His body on the tree" (1 Pet. 2:24). All of these were done for us. On the night the Lord was betrayed, He took the cup and blessed it, and gave it to the disciples, saying, "This is My blood of the covenant, which is being poured out for many for the forgiveness of sins," (Matt. 26:28). It was for *many,* not for *all.* In the future, we will see innumerable ones, with palm branches in their hands, who are washed by the blood (Rev. 7:9, 14). Thank the Lord. He accomplished redemption for His own sake, so that we can be substituted. We can say nothing but to thank and praise Him.

CHAPTER SEVEN

# THE WORK OF CHRIST—RESURRECTION BECAUSE OF OUR JUSTIFICATION

We have already mentioned that the Lord Jesus died for us and for our sins (Rom. 5:8; 1 Cor. 15:3). We have also seen how the Lord accomplished God's righteousness and, at the same time, manifested God's grace. Now we have to ask a question. How do we know that the redemptive work of the Lord Jesus Christ has been accomplished? How do we know that such a work was accepted by God? Although we say that the Lord Jesus has fulfilled God's righteous requirements, what does God have to say about this? How can God show us that His Son has indeed accomplished the work of redemption and indeed met His requirements? It is true that the Lord Jesus died for us and for our sins and that His work was accomplished. On the cross before He died He clearly said, "It is finished!" (John 19:30). It is true that He finished the work of redemption He set out to do on earth. He was able to say that it was finished. Every one of us who has looked forward to His salvation can also say that it is finished. But how do we know that the Lord's work of redemption is acceptable to God when it is presented before Him? How do we know that the redemptive work of the Lord Jesus was approved by God? It is all right for us to say that the Lord's work has passed the test. But what does God have to say? We can say that Jesus died on the cross and accomplished the work of redemption. But how do we know that our God is fully satisfied with such a work? We know that the Lord's work of redemption is most reasonable to us. But how do we know that the same is true to God? We say that the work of redemption is fully righteous, but would God say that it is righteous also? When we look at the cross, we say that all things are settled. But when God looks at the cross, is everything settled in His eyes? We have to realize that there is no way to know whether or not God is satisfied based on the cross of the Lord Jesus alone; there is no way to find out whether or not God considers it final. If there were only the cross, if we only had the Lord's death, if the cross alone were to remain with us until today, and if the Lord's tomb had never been emptied, we would not know what the work of the Lord's death has accomplished for us. Regarding the redemptive work of the Lord, there is not only the aspect of the cross but the aspect of resurrection as well.

### THE LORD'S RESURRECTION IS THE PROOF OF GOD'S ACCEPTANCE OF HIS REDEMPTION

Tonight we are not going to speak about everything related to the resurrection of the Lord Jesus, just as we did not share about everything related to His death the last time. Earlier we spoke only about the objective aspect of His death. Tonight we will also consider only the objective aspect of the Lord's resurrection. Objectively, the Lord died a substitutionary death for us; He died on behalf of all (1 Pet. 3:18; 2 Cor. 5:14). At the same time, He died for our sins (1 Cor. 15:3). This is what the Lord's death accomplished. What then is the purpose of His resurrection? God raised up the Lord Jesus from the dead as a proof that the work of redemption has been accomplished. God has justified and approved it. Now He is satisfied.

Many of us have had experience working in business. Suppose you have a secretary who has proposed a plan to you. After you look at the plan you may write "OK" on it. This means that the work is approved; it is all right. Now it can be carried out. The Lord has died for us and the work has been accomplished. The resurrection of the Lord is God's signing of an "OK" on the work and death of the Lord Jesus. This means that this death is now approved. Man's problem of sin is now solved. Since the Lord has resurrected, the problem of our sins is fully solved. If the Lord had not resurrected, though the redemption would have been accomplished, our hearts would be held in suspense. There would still be a certain uneasiness within us, for though we would know that redemption had been accomplished, we would not know whether it had been accepted. We realize that we are fully redeemed from our sins when we see that the Lord Jesus has resurrected. Resurrection is the proof. It shows us that the cross was right and the redemption was approved. Resurrection is the proof that the work of the cross has been accepted and received by God.

Let us consider an illustration. Suppose I owe a certain person a sum of money. I may owe him so much that there is no way for me to repay my debt. This, of course, is not a very good illustration. But we will use it here for the sake of clarifying one aspect of the truth. It should not be applied to all aspects of the truth. Let us say that I go to a brother and say to him, "You know that person to whom I owe the money very well. You two are good friends. Please plead for me a little. I have no way to pay back what I owe, even if I pawn everything at a pawn shop. I have a problem even in taking care of my own living today. Please do me this favor by all means." My creditor does not live here in Shanghai; he lives in Soochow. At my request, the brother makes a special trip to Soochow and tells the man, "Mr. Nee is really poor. He cannot even take care of his own living. This little sum of money is nothing to you. Why don't you let it go and write off his debt?" Suppose my creditor is very generous. He says, "Since you come to plead for Mr. Nee's debt, I will forget about it. He does not have to return it to me anymore. Take this promissory note back to him." Then he goes on and says to this brother, "We have not met each other for years. Since we are good friends and since you are here in Soochow, you should take a trip to Tiger Hill and the Winter Mountain Shrine. Why don't you stay here for a few days." He invites him to stay in Soochow and lavishly hosts him. Suppose this brother left on May 10 and settled the business on that day. However, by May 20 he is still not back in Shanghai. While he is feasting in Soochow, I am worrying in Shanghai. I do not know whether or not this brother has finished the business. Perhaps he has not come back because of some difficulty. He did not come back on the night train on May 10. Perhaps the business has not yet been settled. He did not come back on May 11. Neither did he come back on May 19 or 20. As long as he has not come back to Shanghai, my heart cannot have peace because I do not know if the business has been settled. The business was settled on May 10, but I have not yet received news on May 20. As long as he has not come back, my business is not finished. I still consider myself a debtor, and my heart is still ill at ease. When will the business be transacted? Only when he returns to Shanghai will I know that the matter is cleared up. Friends, this illustrates the resurrection of the Lord Jesus. When He died for us, He solved the problem of sin. As soon as He died, the fact of sin was taken care of. But if He had not resurrected from the dead, and if He had not come back, then our hearts would have been held in suspense; we would not know what had happened. The Lord Jesus went through death for us. He went through the punishment of the law and the wrath of God for us (Gal. 3:13). But if the Lord Jesus had not come back, we would not know if the work was finished. We would not know if God had accepted the work of the Lord. For this reason, the Lord Jesus must come back. He must resurrect. Then we will know that the work is settled. Praise the Lord. The work is settled. If the work had not been settled, the Lord would not have come out and resurrected. His resurrection proves that our sins have fully been cleared up.

Romans 4:25 says, "Who was delivered for our offenses and was raised for our justification." Why was the Lord Jesus delivered? It was because of our offenses. If we had had no offenses, the Lord would never have had to be delivered. It was because of the offenses that the Lord was delivered to man. In the same way, His resurrection was because of our justification. In Greek the two clauses have the same structure. Jesus was delivered because of our offenses and was resurrected because of our justification. Some Bible translators have misinterpreted Paul's meaning. They thought that resurrection is for the purpose that man may be justified. They thought that it is first the resurrection of the Lord, then our justification. But Paul was saying and the Holy Spirit was saying that He was resurrected because we have been justified. To put it simply, it is because we have been justified that the Lord was resurrected. Some versions say that resurrection comes first, then justification. But the Holy Spirit says that justification comes first, then resurrection. First there is the matter of our offenses. Then there is the death of the Lord. In the same way, first there is our justification, then there is His resurrection. He was delivered because of our offenses, and He was resurrected because of our justification. This means that the resurrection of the Lord Jesus is our proof of justification. Because we have been justified, God raised up the Lord Jesus. Since the Lord has satisfied God's righteous requirement, God resurrected Him.

My friends, tonight I have to announce to you some very good news. Although some have believed in the Lord, they are still in fear and trembling. They feel like they are walking on the edge of a precipitous cliff or on thin ice. They think that they have committed their souls, their lives, and their eternal future to the Lord's cross. They do not know whether this trust in the Lord will be safe or not. If they find out at a later date that this trust does not result in salvation, then they are in trouble. I may believe in the cross of Jesus for the redemption of my sins today. But if it fails me on that day, then I am in trouble. Today I may say that it is not a matter of doing good or of keeping the law and that all I have to do is rely on the cross of Jesus. But what happens if God says in that day that this is not all right? What shall I do? How do I know today that the cross of the Lord is sufficient? My friends, you should not look at the cross; you should not worry about whether the cross is sensible or not and whether it is right or wrong. All you need to look at is the Lord's resurrection. If the work of the Lord's cross was not proper or right, God would not have resurrected Him. Hence, He resurrected because we were justified. Because we are justified when we trust in the blood of Jesus, the Lord Jesus was resurrected.

### RESURRECTION BECAUSE OF
### OUR JUSTIFICATION

It is wonderful that Romans 3 tells us that we are justified freely through the blood of the Lord Jesus and that Romans 4 follows by telling us that because we are justified, the Lord Jesus was resurrected (v. 25). His death is the basis of our justification, while His resurrection is the proof of our justification. Since He died, we are justified; since we are justified, He resurrected. We are justified before God because of His death, and He was resurrected because of our justification. His resurrection is God's proof to us that His blood is able to justify us. Suppose someone were to ask if His blood is effective or not. There is no way to see the blood. We cannot see the blood at all because the blood was put on the side posts and the upper post of the door (Exo. 12:7). It was brought into the Holy of Holies and put in the place of atonement for sin (Lev. 16:14-15). It was only for God to see. We only know about the redemption of the Lord Jesus. We do not know how the blood of the Lord Jesus has satisfied God's demand. No matter how much we know, we will never be clear about this matter. In the whole universe, only One knows the full value of the Lord's blood, and this One is God. God knows in full the value of the Lord Jesus' blood. We only know it in part. We will never know it by our mind, our prayer, or our wisdom. We do not know why the blood of the Lord Jesus washes away all our sins. We can only say that He has died for us and for our sins. We still do not know the value of the Lord's work on the cross. However, God knows this value. How does God show that the work of His Son is of great value? How does God show that the propitiation sacrifice of His Son has indeed propitiated us? He shows it by giving us the resurrection as a proof. Resurrection proves that He is satisfied with the cross. In resurrection, God is saying that He has approved the cross and that the cross has passed the test. Now God is presenting resurrection as an evidence. We are justified. Therefore, the Lord Jesus resurrected. Because God saw that the work of the Lord had fulfilled all the righteous requirements of God, everyone who comes to God is now justified. Since God is satisfied, the Lord Jesus resurrected.

The illustration that we have given may not be very good. Let me give you a more accurate illustration. Let us not say that I owe money. Let us say instead that I have sinned. In this case a brother is not going to plead for me. Instead he will bear my punishment, if there is such a thing in law as bearing others' punishment. I have sinned and should be put in jail for three months or confined to manual labor for two or three months. But I have brain disease, heart disease, a lung problem, a kidney disorder, and all kinds of other sicknesses. However, this brother is very healthy and is willing to be my substitute. When will I know that my case is over? I should be the one to go to jail. But he has gone in my place. Although I have not spent one day in jail and although I am staying peacefully at home and can conduct my business as usual, as long as he is in jail, my heart is still not at ease. I am worried that one day the judge may say that he cannot be my substitute and that I have to come myself. It is not until the day that he is released and walking on the street that I know that my case is over. If my case was not yet over, he would not have been released. The Lord Jesus has died for us. But we do not know what God has to say about this. I know that the Lord has come to redeem us from sin. But how do I know that God will acknowledge this way of redemption as proper? I do not know if the Lord's redemption is adequate or proper. I do not know if the redemptive work of the Lord has been fully settled. But since the Lord came out from death, I realize that everything has been taken care of.

Last year when we were buying a piece of land, a few times I took the money to the bank myself. Some of the money was in notes. The other money was in coins. I wrapped them up in a big bundle and wrote on a bank slip the amount of cash included. Then I handed in the package. I thought that if any of the notes or coins were counterfeit, I would have to rewrite the slip. While I was standing by the counter, I kept worrying. How do I know that the amount was correct? How do I know that all the notes were genuine? How do I know that all the coins were genuine coins? The teller would at times take a note and examine it under the light. After he had counted all the money, he put his signature on the slip and passed it to another senior officer, who also signed the slip. The slip was then passed to another man sitting opposite to him who signed the slip again. Finally, the slip was handed to me. By then I knew that the transaction was completed, and I took the slip home. I did not have to worry anymore about whether the notes were genuine or whether the coins were real. As long as the three signatures were genuine, everything was all right. If after I returned home, I still worried that one of the notes might be counterfeit and could not eat or sleep because of this, there had to be something wrong with my mind. The question was no longer whether the notes had the right color, the right print, or the right paper texture. As long as the bank took the money and put its signature on the slip, the money was genuine, and all the problems were over. In the same way, as long as we see the Lord resurrected, everything is all right. The resurrection of the Lord tells us that we are justified. What does it mean for us to be justified? It means that God has acknowledged the redemption of Jesus His Son. After this, He justified us and then resurrected His Son. Resurrection testifies that His death is proper. Hence, if you still do not have peace and still do not know God's view concerning your salvation and whether you can be saved before God through the Lord Jesus, all you need to ask is whether the Lord has resurrected. His death takes care of redemption. His resurrection takes care of justification. Without justification, He could not have resurrected. This is why I have often said that resurrection is the receipt that God issued for the sacrifice that the Lord Jesus offered. Resurrection is God's receipt to us. It acknowledges the payment as adequate.

If you have faith in a certain person and you know that he has good credit, you would not necessarily need a note of receipt from him if you loan him a hundred, a thousand, or even ten thousand dollars. You know that he would not cheat you. But if it is a person that you do not know, one whom you have never been acquainted with and whose credit you know nothing about, you would definitely want a note of receipt from him. You do not know what he would do with your money. Thank the Lord. He knows that we are of little faith. He knows that we would doubt Him and that we would not believe in Him immediately. Although He has given us His Son and caused His Son to suffer judgment and accomplish redemption, and has even declared that whosoever receives His Son would be justified, He knew that man would still not believe in Him. Therefore, He has resurrected His Son from the dead to be a proof of our justification. His Son is the proof of our justification before Him.

My friends, you have a receipt in your pocket now. Suppose I am now saved, but after a few years God were to say, "Now you have to go to hell. You have to go into eternal perdition." Of course, this is something that will never happen. I would ask, "Why?" Suppose He says, "Because you have sinned. You are not good." I would say, "Has not the Lord Jesus accomplished redemption?" Suppose He would say, "The redemption of Jesus is not enough. You must go to hell." I would then say, "Why is the Lord's redemption not enough?" God might say, "Don't you think that I know everything. When I say that it is not enough, it means it is not enough." What should I say then? I say that I have indeed done wrong, but I am trusting in the Lord's redemption. But God says that though the Lord's redemption has been accomplished, it is not completed. I would then say to Him, "If the work of the redemption of the Lord Jesus was not thorough enough, You should not have resurrected Him. If You resurrected Him, You were telling us through this resurrection that everything was all right. How can You say that it is not enough now?" If I were to say this to God, even He would have to acknowledge that I am right. Hallelujah! The purpose of His resurrection is to show us that His works are proper.

If there is no resurrection among us, then how do we know what happened on the cross? How do we know what the Lord negotiated with God on the cross? We heard these words on the cross, "My God, My God, why have You forsaken Me?" (Matt. 27:46). Another word that we heard was, "It is finished!" (John 19:30). One word tells us that God forsook Him. Another tells us that it was finished. If the Lord Jesus had died only, then the whole world could only have hope in Him; it could not have assurance in Him. Man could hope to receive eternal life in Him. He could hope to be justified and forgiven in Him. But he could never have the assurance to say that he is saved or has received eternal life, or that his sins have been forgiven, or that God has justified him. The reason I have the assurance that my sins are forgiven and that I am saved through faith is that I have seen the resurrection of the Lord

Jesus. His resurrection shows us that the cross has satisfied
God's heart.

## THE BIBLE CAUSES US
## TO BELIEVE IN RESURRECTION

I am one who preaches the cross. Among us, many
co-workers also preach the cross. Today we are all those who
believe in the cross. We all believe that His death has saved
us. He did not die for Himself. Rather, He died to redeem us.
But let me ask you a question. Can you find one place in the
entire Bible that says that we should believe that the Lord
Jesus has died for us? Where in the entire New Testament
does it say that we should believe in the Lord's death for us?
There is no such place. This is most peculiar. There is not a
single verse in the entire New Testament that tells us that we
should believe in the Lord's death for us. Do not misunderstand and think that I despise the work of the cross. I am very
much for the work of the cross. But one must pay attention to
the word of the Bible. There is not a single place in the New
Testament that says that we should believe in the Lord Jesus'
dying for us. There are countless places in the Bible that tell
us that Jesus died for us and for our sins. But there is not one
place that tells us to take His death as the object of our faith.
The Gospel of John tells us that we have to believe (3:15-16,
18, 36). But it does not speak about believing in the cross. It
only speaks of believing in the Lord.

There is another thing that is equally peculiar. The New
Testament tells us to believe that God has raised Jesus from
the dead. The Bible does not say that the cross or the death of
the Lord Jesus is the object of our faith. Rather, it says that
resurrection is the object of our faith. I believe we all know
the verse in Romans 10:9, "That if you confess with your
mouth Jesus as Lord and believe in your heart that God has
raised Him from the dead, you will be saved." Why does the
Bible not ask us to believe in the cross of the Lord, but asks us
to believe in His resurrection? Why does the Bible never ask
us to believe in the cross of the Lord Jesus, but ask us to
believe that God has raised Him from the dead? Brothers, we
must consider this a little. This is very crucial. If it were up to

our reading of the Bible, we would think that the cross is the most important thing, and that there should be at least one word that says that we should believe in the Lord's death on the cross. But there is not a single word about this. Why is this the case? One brother may answer that if Christ has not resurrected, our faith is in vain. It is true that twice in 1 Corinthians 15 it says that if Christ has not been raised, then our faith is vain (vv. 14, 17). But this word does not help us to solve the problem. On the contrary, it makes our problem all the more difficult. If there is no resurrection, our faith is in vain. Hence, resurrection is something that we should believe in. We know that redemption is a matter between God and the Lord Jesus. It is not God's demand on man. Redemption is not something that the Lord has done to satisfy man's heart. It is the Lord Jesus' satisfaction of God's demand of holiness, righteousness, and glory. The Lord's death and the redemptive work that He accomplished are transactions that went on between God and the Lord Jesus. It is not something that is sounded out as the object of our faith. The basis of our faith is God's raising of Jesus from among the dead.

Hence, today our faith is not in the blood of the Lord Jesus' redeeming us from sin. We can never fully understand this matter. Even a man as spiritual as Andrew Murray, who knew God so well, said that he did not know how much value there is to the blood of the Lord Jesus. Even he said that when he went before God, he could only pray, "God, I do not know how much worth is the blood of Your Son before You. But I ask that all the worth of Your Son's blood be realized in me." The Lord's blood is of such worth that if I would only say so much, I will not be able to receive all that He has done, and His work would be limited by my speaking.

We do not know the worth of the blood. But we do know the worth of resurrection. The blood of the Lord satisfied God's demand, and we do not know how great that demand is. But we do know how great the satisfaction is. I do not know how much I owed. Perhaps it was ten talents or perhaps ten million talents. But I know that the death of the Lord is sufficient to save me. How do I know this? It is because He has resurrected. I am not trusting in the money I put into the bank to be enough or not enough. This is not what I am trusting in. I do not even have to trust that all the money that I have put in was genuine. What I am trusting in is that God would not give me a counterfeit receipt. Even if the redemption of the Lord were wrong, whatever mistakes there could be, God would never issue a wrong receipt. Hence, though I do not know how much the blood has met God's demand, I do know that it has satisfied God's demand. If the Lord had not satisfied God, God would not have resurrected Him. Therefore, you can believe in a most ignorant way. You do not have to ask whether the blood of the Lord is sufficient, or whether the Lord's work of redemption is approved. You only have to ask if God has resurrected the Lord. Since the Lord Jesus has resurrected, all you have to do is believe. We believe in resurrection. This is why the Bible only requires us to believe in resurrection; it does not require us to believe in the cross. The work of the cross is only conveyed to us to let us know what the Lord has done before God. What we preach and believe is the resurrection of the Lord Jesus. It includes His death and His life. Once I see the receipt, immediately I know that the amount is adequate and that every bank note is genuine.

Tonight I can sleep well because the Lord Jesus has resurrected. If the Lord had not resurrected, even though He has died and redeemed us, we still could not sleep in peace. How do I know that His blood is sufficient? How do I know that the problem of sin is solved? Hallelujah! There is the resurrection. Because we are justified, He has resurrected. Hence, we believe in His resurrection. I do not know how many are sitting here who are still worried about their salvation, who are still doubting and are not sure. When you ask yourself whether you have trusted in Jesus, you may say yes. When you ask yourself whether you believe that Jesus has died for you, you may also say yes. But in you there is still a question. You may think that to believe in Jesus is not sufficient to be forgiven of your sins, that you may still have to do some good works. You may still think this and that. But you only need to know one thing. Why did God resurrect the Lord Jesus? Why did God issue a receipt? The fact that God is willing to issue you the receipt proves that the amount that you have put in was right. When God raised His Son from the dead, it proved that the redemption that His Son accomplished was a righteous one. God cannot do anything unrighteous. Resurrection proves that the work of the Lord Jesus is effective before God. This is why the New Testament emphasizes so much our believing that God has raised His Son from the dead.

The two verses that we mentioned earlier in 1 Corinthians 15 are very precious. Verse 14 says, "And if Christ has not been raised, then our proclamation is vain; your faith is vain also." Verse 17 then says, "And if Christ has not been raised, your faith is futile." If Christ has not resurrected, one will not know what has become of the things that he has believed in. Another wonderful thing is seen in 1 Corinthians 15:3 which says, "Christ died for our sins according to the Scriptures." But in verse 17 it says, "If Christ has not been raised...you are still in your sins." Do not these two verses contradict each other? Verse 3 says that He has died for our sins. That means He has solved the problem of our sins. Why does verse 17 say that if Christ has not been raised, we are still in our sins? This verse is quite peculiar. Perhaps you would have changed that to, "If Christ has not died for you, you are still in your sins." If we changed the words *been raised* to *died,* we would readily be able to understand it. Since Christ has died for us, we are no longer in sin. But verse 3 says that Christ has died for our sins already. Now verse 17 says that without Christ's resurrection, we are still in our sins. What does this mean?

My friends, the matter is actually very clear. On the one hand, Christ has died for our sins. But when do we know that we are no longer in sin, and when do we know that we have been freed from sin? It is when the Lord Jesus was resurrected. It is when the Lord was resurrected that we realized that we were redeemed from our sins. We have to distinguish between these two. The redemption and deliverance from sin before God is due to the Lord's death; it is not due to His resurrection. But for us, it is the Lord's resurrection, rather than His death, that we realize. For my creditor, the time a debt is settled is when he sees the money. But for me, it is settled when I see the receipt. My creditor only looks at the money, and I only look at the receipt. God's eyes only see the death of the Lord Jesus, and our eyes only see His resurrection. God does not need the resurrection of the Lord as His proof. He knows very well that the Lord's death is adequate for redemption. The problem is that we do not know. A receipt is not written for the one who receives money. It is written for one who pays the money. No receipt is prepared for the creditor. All receipts are made out for the debtors. They are written to give the debtors peace of mind. Hence, before God the Lord's death is sufficient for our sins. As long as He dies, God is satisfied. Resurrection tells us that He is satisfied, that the death of the Lord has redeemed us from sins. But if the Lord has not resurrected, even though we have been redeemed from our sins, we still would not know it. With the death of the Lord, the problem of sin is forever dealt with before God. Without resurrection, we would not have the confidence that our sins are indeed dealt with. The fact of forgiveness lies in His death. The assurance of forgiveness lies in His resurrection. The Lord's death redeems us from sins, and the Lord's resurrection allows us to know that we have been redeemed from our sins.

## THE LORD'S DEATH BEING FOR GOD
## AND HIS RESURRECTION BEING FOR US

Hence, there are these two sides in the Bible. Without the death of the Lord Jesus for us, we would not have been redeemed from our sins. The Bible says that Jesus has died for our sins. But we see that we are still in sins. Although God has finished His side of the work, matters are still unsettled on our side. That is why the Lord Jesus must resurrect before we know that our sins have been forgiven. Death is for God, and resurrection is for us. Death is God's demand, and resurrection is the sinners' demand. Death is the solution of sin before God, and resurrection is the removal of doubt in man's heart. With death, the record of sin is done away with. With resurrection, we realize the proof of forgiveness and a not guilty verdict. Thank the Lord that there is resurrection. What happens when one comes to God and wonders if he is saved or not? Such a one may indeed have believed in the Lord Jesus Christ. But he may still wonder if he is really saved. Now before God, the receipt has been issued already. If such a one still wants to doubt, it is because he chooses to doubt. If the Lord Jesus has resurrected, then our problems are solved.

Please make a point to remember these three passages— Romans 4:25, 10:9, and 1 Corinthians 15:17. These three places show us what resurrection has accomplished for us objectively. Up until now, we have seen quite a few things. We have covered sin, the law, grace, God's righteousness, the work accomplished by the death of the Lord Jesus, and the work accomplished by His resurrection.

A brother has asked the question: What does 1 John 2:2 mean? I would answer in this way. The words "the sins of" in the phrase "the sins of the whole world" in some versions are not in the original text. The Chinese Union Version reads, "And He is the propitiation for our sins: and not for ours only, but also for the sins of the whole world." If such is indeed the case, then the whole world would have been saved already, for the Lord Jesus has become a propitiation for the sins of the whole world. But in Greek it should read, "And He Himself is the propitiation for our sins: and not for ours only, but also for the whole world."

For a reader of the New Testament to understand the Lord's redemption and His substitution, he first has to know the distinction between ourselves and our sins, that is, between the sinner and the sins of the sinner. Second, he has to know the difference between all and many. Third, he must know the difference between sin and sins. There are differences between the three pairs of things: ourselves and our sins, the all and the many, and sin and sins.

The Bible says many times that the Lord Jesus died for all. But not once does it say that the Lord Jesus died for the sins of all. Second Corinthians 5:14 says that, "One died for all, therefore all died." Paul could not say that since One died for the sins of all, therefore all died. The Lord Jesus died for all. But He did not die for the sins of all. If the Lord Jesus had died for the sins of all, then whether or not one believes, he can be saved, for all the problems of sins are solved. But the Lord Jesus died for all. If we go to Him, we will receive Him as our substitute and receive His redemption.

The Bible does say that the Lord Jesus died for sins. But in such cases, it says that He died for the sins of many, and not for the sins of all. The night before last, a brother tested me with a verse. He asked why the book of Hebrews says that the Lord Jesus was offered up for our sins. Hebrews 9:28 says, "So Christ also, having been offered once to bear the sins of many, will appear a second time to those who eagerly await Him, apart from sin, unto salvation." You can see that when it talks about Christ's bearing of sins, it says "to bear the sins of many," and not "to bear the sins of all." Following this, it gives an explanation, "to those who eagerly await Him." This means all those who are purchased by the blood. It is the innumerable multitude in Revelation 7:9-17. It is the many. That is why it can say that He was offered up for their sins. But it cannot say that He was offered up for the sins of all. The wording of the Bible is never loose. If Christ bore the sins of all, if He bore all the sins of everyone in the world, then we would not have to preach the gospel anymore. But this is not the case. What we have is the many.

Hence, Matthew 26:28 records that when the Lord Jesus took the cup, He said, "For this is My blood of the covenant, which is being poured out for many for the forgiveness of sins." Again we have "many," and not "all." If it were "all," then everyone's sins are forgiven. The Bible only says that the Lord Jesus died for all. This word merely shows us that the Lord's death is an open one and that everyone can receive the benefit of His death. If there is anyone here who is not saved tonight, I would say that Christ has died for you. But as for me, the Lord Jesus died for my sins. As long as you ask for it, the effectiveness of the Lord's death will be upon you, and you will have a share in it. But you must come to Him before the effectiveness of the Lord's death can be yours and can work on you. The Lord Jesus died for all, and He died for the sins of many. There is a distinction between the two. We have to take note of this.

Let us read two more passages. Romans 5:18-19 says, "So

then as it was through one offense unto condemnation to all men, so also it was through one righteous act unto justification of life to all men. For just as through the disobedience of one man the many were constituted sinners, so also through the obedience of the One the many will be constituted righteous." If we want to understand these two verses, we must give them some thought and pay attention to them. Readers of the Bible agree that these two verses are some of the most difficult verses in the New Testament. We have to pay attention to the wording of them. First, in verse 18, it says, "all men," but in verse 19, it says, "the many." Second, in verse 18 there is the Greek word *eis,* which is equivalent to the English word *to* or *toward.* One version translated this as "by the offence of one judgment came upon all men to condemnation; even so by the righteousness of one the free gift came upon all men unto justification of life." This is not a very accurate translation. The verse can be translated here as "through one offense *unto* condemnation to all men, so also it was through one righteous act *unto* justification of life to all men." Now we have to pay a little closer attention to this matter. Verse 18 speaks about one offense, and verse 19 speaks about one man. The one offense denotes the sin of Adam (Rom. 5:14). The one-time sin of Adam was unto the condemnation of all men. This means that the one offense was for the condemnation of all men. Have you seen that just once was enough? It is like saying that once a person makes a fortune, he is prepared to buy many things. The one offense was for the condemnation of all men. In the same way, the one righteous act of Christ was for the justification unto life to all men. It is not correct to translate the verse as the previously mentioned version does, for it would mean that through the one righteous act of Christ, all would have been justified and received life. What is the meaning of *eis,* translated "unto" in this verse? It means a preparation. It is like the government's printing of many bank notes in the central bank. It is a preparation to be used later for exchange. Even if everyone comes to exchange the notes, the government is prepared. Verse 18 says all men. This means that everyone can receive life. There is no problem here at all. But verse 19 is different. Here it says, "For

just as through the disobedience of one man the many were
constituted sinners, so also through the obedience of the One
the many will be constituted righteous." Here we have the
many. Through the disobedience of one man, who is Adam,
the many were constituted sinners. Here it does not say that
all men were constituted sinners. Why is this so? Let me give
you an honest testimony. It may seem as if I am joking. But
six years ago, when I first read about the difference between
the many and the all, I was a little concerned for the apostle
Paul. While I was looking up the original text, I thought if
Paul were to use words the way our translators did, it would
be a disaster. I was almost praying there, "Don't let such a
word be *all* but be *many*." Eventually I found out that it is
indeed *many*. What does it mean if we say that through the
disobedience of one all men were condemned? This would
mean that everyone who is in Adam is a sinner. There would
not be one righteous one. This would not be too serious. But
the next sentence would be more serious: Through one righteous act all men are justified. This would mean that the
gospel need not be preached anymore, for everyone is saved
and is justified. There is no mention here of the matter of
believing or not and receiving or not. Through the obedience
of the One all are saved. Even the unbelieving ones are saved.
But this is, of course, not the case. What it says here is,
"Through the obedience of the One the many will be constituted righteous." Therefore, what the work of the Lord Jesus
has gained is for the many. One must differentiate between
*all* and *the many*.

At the same time, we must also differentiate between ourselves and our sins. Romans 5:8 says, "While we were yet
sinners, Christ died for us." But 1 Corinthians 15:3 says that
"Christ died for our sins according to the Scriptures." To be
"for us" is a preparation. But to be "for our sins" is a kind of
realization. Even if a person is not yet saved, he can still
preach the gospel. But he can only say that God sent His Son
to die for us. This is absolutely right. But only those who have
been saved can say that God sent His Son to die for our sins.
This is because our relationship with the Lord Jesus is in the
matter of sins. Hence, we can say that the Lord Jesus died for

our sins. First Peter 2:24 says, "Who Himself bore up our sins in His body on the tree." There is a distinction here. To a sinner, we can only say that the Lord Jesus died for him. We cannot say that the Lord Jesus died for his sins.

It will help you to understand if I illustrate this by a simple example. Suppose I have borrowed some money, but have no way to repay. A brother knows that my account number in the Shanghai Bank is No. 51. Suppose he deposits a sum of money into account No. 51. Then he writes a letter to me telling me that he has deposited a sum of money in the bank for me and that I can now repay my debt. He has paid the money and has sacrificed himself to prepare the money for me. But let me ask, Has my debt been cleared yet? I can pay back the debt. The money is in the bank. But the debt is not paid yet. It is only when I go personally to the bank and withdraw the money and pay back the debt that I can say that this brother has paid the debt for me. In the same way, the Lord Jesus has died for us. This death was prepared for us. But it is only when we receive the Lord Jesus that we can say that He died for our sins. Hence, brother, when you quote 1 John 2:2, you must be careful about the wording. Jesus Christ has become a propitiation for our sins, and not for us only, but also for the whole world. You can see how accurate the Holy Spirit is in choosing the words through His apostle. The Lord Jesus died for our sins. But the death of the Lord Jesus was not only for us, but for the whole world, so that the whole world may receive this death. One has to be careful here. Do not add the words *the sins of* to "the whole world." It is unfortunate that many have not seen this. We cannot add anything to the word of God, nor can we subtract anything from it (Rev. 22:18-19).

Finally, there is still one thing that we have to take note of. It is the difference between sin and sins. We cannot say that the Lord Jesus died for the sins of the whole world, for *sins* means all the wrongdoings and all the punishment that we need to bear. If the Lord Jesus died for the sins of the whole world, then all the wrongdoings of all the world were removed. Whether a man believes or not, he is saved. But the Bible is very careful in the use of words. It only says the sin of the world. It does not say the sins of the world. John 1:29 says, "Behold, the Lamb of God, who takes away the sin of the world!" The word "sin" is singular. The problem of sin is brought into the world through one man and brought out of the world through one man. What is mentioned here is the "abstract" dealing of the problem of sin by the Son of God. Objectively speaking, sin entered the world in an "abstract" way through Adam. Today the Lord Jesus is taking away and dealing with the problem of sin in an "abstract" way. This does not mean that He has borne the guilt of each individual sin. If He has borne the guilt of each individual wrongdoing, then the whole world would have been saved already. Thank and praise the Lord that the Word of God does not have any loophole. It never makes a mistake.

# CHAPTER EIGHT

# THE WORK OF THE HOLY SPIRIT— ENLIGHTENING AND FELLOWSHIP

In the past few evenings we have seen how God manifested His grace and accomplished His righteousness. We have also seen how God through His Son Jesus died for us and for our sins, thus accomplishing the work of redemption (Rom. 5:8; 1 Cor. 15:3). His work of redemption justifies us before God through faith in His blood (Rom. 3:24-25). His resurrection from the dead becomes the assurance of our faith. Through this resurrection we know that God has accepted the sacrifice of the Lord Jesus. The work of the Lord Jesus has satisfied God's requirements. His resurrection is a proof to us of this fact. All who believe in the blood of His Son and who come to Him through His redemption are now justified.

Tonight I will not cover the other aspect of the Lord's work, which is His ascension. Since many brothers and sisters already know about this, I will just mention it in brief. The ascension of the Lord Jesus is His appearing before God on our behalf, that we might be accepted in Christ. What is ascension? In the Bible ascension means only one thing objectively, which is for one to be accepted before God. Today the Lord Jesus has appeared before God (Heb. 9:24). We also appear before God in Him. In this way God accepts us in the same way that He has accepted Christ.

## THE WORK OF THE HOLY SPIRIT— ENLIGHTENING TO SEEK OUT SINNERS

Tonight we must mention another matter. The gospel is inadequate if it mentions only the work of the Father and the Son without mentioning the work of the Holy Spirit. There must be the mention of the Holy Spirit also. The work of the gospel is of three aspects. Luke 15 shows us three parables. On the one hand, we see the loving Father waiting to receive the sinners. On the other hand, we see the good Shepherd coming to the world to seek for the lost sheep. One sees the Father waiting at home for the repentant and saved sinner, and one also sees the Son coming to the world to save sinners. But after the Lord's work was completed and before the sinner reaches home, there was another parable, which is the woman patiently and carefully seeking the lost coin with a lighted lamp.

First, one sees the Lord Jesus coming to earth to seek for the sinners. Second, one sees the woman lighting the lamp to enlighten, sweep, and seek for the lost coin. Hence, the Holy Spirit is working together with the Father and the Son to seek out the sinner for the accomplishing of the gospel work. The Son came to die for the sinner; the Father receives the sinner home; and the Holy Spirit works to enlighten man's heart and to show man his real position.

If a person does not have the light of the Holy Spirit, it is possible that he can be like Judas, who saw his sin, was suffering and had no peace within, but would not see his own position before God. Without the light, he would not see his position of perdition. Man's feeling concerning sin goes only so far as to realize that he has done wrong. He does not realize that he is a lost one before God. We are willing to admit that we are sinful. But without the enlightening of the Holy Spirit, we will not admit that as a result of sin, we became lost persons before God. In the eyes of God, we are lost persons.

There is the possibility of a fleshly counterfeit even in the matter of sin-consciousness. The flesh can replace the work of the Holy Spirit. Many tears in revival meetings are but results of man's flesh. They are not produced through the work of the Holy Spirit in man. It is one thing for man to know that he has sinned. It is another thing for man to know that his relationship with God is wrong. The Holy Spirit patiently and carefully enlightens man and shows him that he is lost. What the Holy Spirit does is to show man that his position is wrong. Hence, the first feeling of everyone who has experienced the work of the Holy Spirit of God is not something related to sin, but the feeling that he is away from home. His relationship with God is cut off. He has developed a problem with God. He is a lost man.

Our problem before God does not lie merely in how much we have wasted ourselves in eating, drinking, fornication, or gambling. It is a problem of being away in a distant country. When the Holy Spirit enlightens man, the first thing He does is show man that he is in a distant country. When one reads the last parable in Luke 15, he has to take note of what the prodigal said to the father. He did not say that he had squandered all his father's estate with harlots. The first thing he realized when he came to himself was that in his father's house there was an abundance of bread. Why then was he living with the hogs in a distant country and not able even to satisfy his hunger with the carob pods which were for the hogs? When the Holy Spirit enlightens a person, he will realize that he has a problem with God, that he has left his Father's house, and that he is away from his Father. My friends, when a person in the world has come to the end of himself in his sinful condition, he may, like Judas, become aware of his sins. But without the light of the Holy Spirit, he will not feel that he has left the Father's house and is in a distant country. I am not saying that sins are not serious. Sins are sins. But the Bible shows us that man's chief sin lies in the fact that he is lost. He is standing on an improper ground. He may not be in an improper condition. Of course, all those who are in an improper condition must stand on improper ground. When the Holy Spirit enlightens us, first He shows us that we are on an improper ground. Then He shows us our improper condition. This is the enlightening of the Holy Spirit.

Hence, although there is the love of the Father and the work of the Lord, there is still the need for the Holy Spirit to prepare man's heart. He still has to work in man's heart so that man will receive all that the Lord Jesus has done. One can say that the Lord Jesus is our objective Savior from God and that the Holy Spirit is our subjective Savior from God. The Lord Jesus is the Savior who accomplished redemption for us outwardly, and the Holy Spirit is the Savior who accomplishes salvation for us inwardly. All of us sitting here have been enlightened by the Holy Spirit. We all know that we are the lost sheep, that we have all turned to our own ways (Isa. 53:6). We all like sheep were lost. Our problem was not sickness or lameness, but taking a wrong path. The path that one takes is very important. In John 16:8-9, the Lord Jesus told us that when the Holy Spirit comes, "He will convict the world concerning sin and concerning righteousness and concerning judgment." What does it mean to be convicted concerning sin? We are convicted concerning sin "because they do not believe into Me." We have developed a problem with Him, and we have come into conflict with Him. We are convicted of sin because we have not seen His blood and His authority, because we have not met His demands, and because we now have a problem with Him. The greatest sin of man is the refusal to believe in the Lord Jesus. The Holy Spirit comes to show us that we have developed a problem with the Lord Jesus and with God. Our position is wrong.

But let me ask a question. Is it possible that a person in a distant country can be a good son? Is it possible that he can be frugal and thrifty? Is it possible that he can be a diligent worker? Is it possible that he can be discreet in making friends? We know that this is impossible. If a person has wandered to a distant country and is wrong in his relationship with his father, he must be wrong in all other relationships. That is why the prodigal began to live dissolutely. When the Holy Spirit enlightens a person, not only will He show him that he is in a lost position, but He will also show him that his past conduct has been wrong. The Holy Spirit does not overlook past sins. He pays attention to all sins. However, He turns one's attention to all the sins only after He has shown such a one his perishing position. The Holy Spirit first shows you how dangerous a position you are in, then He shows you how many sins you have. The light of the Holy Spirit enlightens and exposes all the areas in which you have transgressed against others. It exposes all unrighteousness and all the hidden sins in our words and thoughts.

God's chastisement is for His healing. The Holy Spirit's rebuking is for His comforting. God is not pleased to chastise and punish His children without reason. The only reason God punishes is that man would obtain peace. The reason the Holy Spirit shines on man and shows man his shortcomings and his waywardness is that man would accept all the work of the Lord Jesus Christ on the cross. Without the enlightening of the Holy Spirit, we are not able to see even one of our sins.

## GOD POURING OUT THE HOLY SPIRIT
## UPON MAN FOR HIS SALVATION

What should we do now that the Holy Spirit has enlightened and we have seen our position? There is one thing we continually neglect in our preaching of the gospel, which the Bible pays attention to all the time. We have to realize that the work of the Lord Jesus for the sinners is indeed precious and crucial. But likewise the work of the Holy Spirit for the sinners is equally precious and crucial. The Bible shows us that not only does the Holy Spirit come to enlighten us and to show us our sins, our lost position, and our unrighteousness before God and men, but this Spirit is also sent from God and is poured forth upon all flesh for the purpose that man everywhere could be saved through His work (Acts 2:17-18, 21).

Some who know a little more than others concerning the truth of the Bible think that it is easy to receive forgiveness and to accept the Lord Jesus as Savior. All he has to do is to kneel down and pray and accept Him from his heart. Perhaps he does not even have to kneel down; he only has to accept in his heart. But many people do not have this knowledge. They may be weak or from inaccessible lands and may not have had the chance to listen to the truth. They may think that it is a very difficult thing to be saved. They may think that they have to pray for a long time, and they have no assurance whether God would listen to their prayers. If I were to ask you today if you are saved, you can answer quickly that you are saved. But such a statement would sound strange to one from an inaccessible land. They would wonder how you could be saved. To them it is a most difficult thing to be saved. They would say that they have prayed for many years and are still not sure if they are saved. They hope to be saved, and they try

their best to be saved. But they still do not know if they are
saved. It seems as if they are not yet saved. To them, salvation
is something very difficult to achieve. But my friends, just as
the work of the Lord Jesus is complete, the work of the Holy
Spirit in causing us to appropriate the Lord's work is also complete. The Bible shows us clearly that God sent the Holy Spirit
for the purpose that we, the sinners, would receive the Holy
Spirit's work and be saved. The Son of God came for the sake of
the whole world. In the same way, the coming of the Holy
Spirit is also for all flesh. As long as we are a man in the flesh,
we can obtain the Lord's work for us.

## WHOEVER CALLS UPON
## THE NAME OF THE LORD SHALL BE SAVED

Let us read Romans 10:13: "Whoever calls upon the name
of the Lord shall be saved." The subject of Romans 10 is on
God causing the Lord Jesus to die and resurrect for us. In the
few verses prior to this verse, God asks if there is anyone who
can bring Christ down from heaven to die for us and if there
is anyone who can bring Christ up from the abyss to resurrect
for us (vv. 6-7). There is no such person. Such a work can only
be done by God alone. It is God Himself who has caused
Christ to die for us. It is also God Himself who caused Him to
resurrect for us. Hence, everyone who calls on the name of the
Lord today is saved.

I do not know if you realize that it is a most wonderful
thing to be saved just by calling on the name of the Lord.
In the original language, the word *call* means that we only
need to say His name. Today in order to contact a brother, all
I have to do is to go to his door and knock twice with the door
handle. This is to call upon him. I do not have to beg him to
listen. I do not have to implore him. I only need to go to him
and inform him with a word. This is the meaning of calling.
The Chinese version translates this word as *implore*. This is
incorrect. Although one cannot say that the Greek word carries no sense of imploring, it does mean more of an invoking.
Since God has caused the Lord Jesus to die and resurrect for
us, all who desire to be saved need only to go to God and tell
Him. They will then be saved. As long as you would go to the

Lord Jesus and call His name once, you will be saved. All you need to do is to open your mouth once. You do not need to do anything else because He has already completed all the work. All the work has been completed. That is why we say that we are justified by faith, and not by works (Gal. 2:16). If you think that even to call once is a work, then God says just believe a little in your heart and it will be enough. Verse 8 says, "The word is near you, in your mouth and in your heart." Since the Lord has done the work of death and resurrection, we have nothing to do. As long as we open our mouth once, everything is done. Whoever calls on the name of the Lord shall be saved.

You may ask why it transpires so quickly. It is true that the work of Christ has been accomplished. But why will I be saved just by calling? How can the Lord's work in death, resurrection, and ascension be applied to me so quickly? Acts 2 is an added explanation to this. Verse 17 says, "And it shall be in the last days, says God, that I will pour out of My Spirit upon all flesh." We have to remember that in the last days God will pour out of His Spirit upon all flesh. What is the result of this? Verse 21 says, "And it shall be that everyone who calls on the name of the Lord shall be saved." Verse 17 is linked to verse 21. God says that He will pour out of His Spirit upon all flesh. Then He says that whoever calls on the name of the Lord shall be saved. Everyone who calls on the name of the Lord will be saved because God has poured out His Spirit upon all flesh. The Holy Spirit is working now on all flesh. If there is anyone today whose sins have not been forgiven and who still does not know how to be saved and receive eternal life, who does not know that the Lord Jesus is his Savior, he must remember that God has poured out the Holy Spirit. The Holy Spirit is upon you already; He is waiting for you. Once you call, you will be saved.

God says that He would pour out of His Spirit upon all flesh. Why is there Pentecost? God gave us Pentecost because He wanted to pour out the Holy Spirit upon all flesh. Now one only needs to open his mouth and say, "O Lord!" and the Holy Spirit will come into him. The Holy Spirit is like the light. As long as there is a crack, light will come in. You may not realize how well light goes through cracks. If you do not believe this, just go next door. If you drill a hole in the wall, as soon as the drill is taken out, the light enters. You do not have to look for it because it comes in immediately. As long as there is a crack, the light will come in. Today God has poured out the Holy Spirit upon all flesh. As long as you are alive, the Holy Spirit is upon you. Whenever you say, "O Lord!" the Holy Spirit begins working. This is the meaning of calling on the name of the Lord. The ancient Chinese say that one must appeal to heaven, to earth, and to his parents. Now we only need to appeal to the Lord once. When one mentions prayer, he always thinks of supplication more than invocation. Actually, all we need to do is invoke Him. Once we open our mouth, the Holy Spirit comes in. When the Holy Spirit comes in, the accomplished work of the Lord Jesus is brought to us.

## THE WORK OF THE HOLY SPIRIT— FELLOWSHIP

The work of the Holy Spirit is fellowship. The characteristic of God is His love. The characteristic of the Lord Jesus is His grace, and the characteristic of the Holy Spirit is His fellowship. Second Corinthians 13:14 says, "The grace of the Lord Jesus Christ and the love of God and the fellowship of the Holy Spirit be with you all." God is love, and His characteristic is love. The Lord Jesus is grace, and His characteristic is grace. Lastly, the characteristic of the Holy Spirit is fellowship. The Holy Spirit has nothing in Himself. He brings the love of God and the grace of the Lord Jesus into you by the way of fellowship. This is the work of the Holy Spirit. The Holy Spirit has not accomplished a work of love. He has not accomplished a work of grace. The Holy Spirit conveys to you what God and the Lord Jesus have accomplished. Hence, the work of the Holy Spirit is fellowship. The Holy Spirit after the Lord's ascension is just filled with the work of the Lord Jesus. He is like the light. As long as there is a crack, He will come in. When He comes in, He will bring the grace of the Lord Jesus and the love of God into you. This salvation is surely complete.

Some time ago, a very famous servant of the Lord in England died. Of course, his death was under God's sovereignty. None of us can say anything about that. But humanly speaking, we can say something about his death. He was very weak and had been sick for years. The doctors had prescribed a kind of medicine for him. Whenever he inhaled that medicine, he became strong again. He put this medicine by his chest of drawers. Many times, when he suffered much and felt like dying, he would breathe in the medicine and become well. Although the medicine did not smell good, it was very effective. The night that he died he felt uncomfortable again. He tried to reach for the medicine but was too weak to open the drawer. The next morning others found him in his bed with his hand stretching for the medicine. He died there with half of his body outside his bed. It was not a matter of the lack of the best and most effective medicine. He had lived by that medicine for eight or nine years already. Every time he was about to die, he inhaled the medicine and became well again. Why did he die this time? It was not because there was no medicine, and it was not because he did not want the medicine. It was because the medicine did not get into his hand. In the same way, we are those who are about to perish. The Lord Jesus has accomplished the work. God's medicine has been prepared. As long as we take it, we will be healed. But who will give this medicine to us? There is the doctor to prescribe the medicine. There must also be someone to apply the medicine. The work of the Holy Spirit is to convey the work of the Lord Jesus to us. The love of God is in the grace of the Lord Jesus, and the grace of the Lord Jesus is in the fellowship of the Holy Spirit. Hence, all those who have received the fellowship of the Holy Spirit receive the grace of the Lord Jesus, and all those who have received the grace of the Lord Jesus have a taste of the love of God.

When the Holy Spirit comes, He gives you the light and shows you your failures and degradation. He shows you that you are lost. God has worked to such an extent that once you open your mouth and say a word and once your heart has a place for the Lord and would invoke Him, you will be saved. You do not have to go to a great cathedral to be saved. You do

not have to pray to be saved. You do not have to step forward
to the altar to be saved. The Holy Spirit is poured out upon all
flesh already. Wherever you are, the Holy Spirit is there. Hallelujah! This is a fact! Today the Holy Spirit has already been
poured out upon all flesh. You do not need to look for Him. He
is looking for you. You can call on the street or in a house. You
can receive God's salvation in the sweetest place or the most
unpleasant place. You can have it in the most crowded place
or the most quiet place. The Holy Spirit has been poured out
upon all flesh. No matter where you are, as long as you call
on the name of the Savior, you will be saved.

Romans 10 talks about the fact, and Acts 2 talks about the
reason. Romans 10 only tells us that whoever calls upon the
name of the Lord shall be saved. It does not tell us the reason.
Acts 2 tells us that the Holy Spirit is upon all men. Hence, as
long as one opens his mouth, he shall be saved. The Holy
Spirit has already entered in. When man calls on His name,
he shall be saved.

## THE HOLY SPIRIT AND THE WORD OF GOD

There is another thing that the Holy Spirit does and this
concerns the Word of God. Many people do not see the relationship between the Holy Spirit and the Word of God. Hence,
they do not treasure the words of the Bible that much. How
can man receive the work of the Lord's cross? Many are bewil-
dered about this. Many sinners even pray, "Lord Jesus, be
merciful to me and die for me." They do not know what
redemption is at all. Here we see the preciousness of God's
Word. After God has accomplished His work through His Son,
He declares it to us and shows us through the words of the
Bible. In other words, God has placed the grace that the Lord
accomplished for us in His own Word and has sent this Word
to us.

If we subtracted the work of the Lord Jesus from the Word
of God, what would we have? If we took away the work of the
Lord Jesus from the Word of God, God's Word would become
zero; nothing would be left. The reason that God's Word is
God's Word is that in it there is the fact of the Lord's work.
What is a word? A word is a recorded fact. Without facts,

words become lies. With the facts, the words become real. If the Lord's work for us is not real, the Word of God is not trustworthy. But if the work of the Lord Jesus is a fact, if God has accomplished His righteousness through the Lord Jesus, and if God has accepted us in the Lord Jesus, God's Word must be trustworthy. Hence, we have to remember that the work of the Lord Jesus is contained in the Word of God. Here we see the relationship between the Holy Spirit and the Word of God.

The Holy Spirit is the doorkeeper of God's Word. I like my English name, Watchman. It means one that guards and keeps watch. God has put the accomplished work of the Lord in the Holy Spirit. Today the Holy Spirit is carefully watching. He is like a doorkeeper. As soon as a person receives the Lord, immediately He opens up the matters in God's Word to him.

A few days ago a brother sent me a box of candy. The box was very big and had flowers printed on it. It was wrapped in peach-colored paper with a letter attached, saying that the candy was a gift for me. I can say that what I received was a paper box. I did not receive the candy itself. I did not even taste the candy. What was in my hand was a paper box. But what I had actually received was the candy because the candy was in the box. What I took home was the box. But at the same time, I took the candy that came with the box. What we receive today is the Word of God. But what we receive into us is the work of the Lord Jesus. When we receive the Word of God, we get the work of the Lord, for the Lord's work is in God's Word. When one believes today, he is not believing that the Lord has done something for him. He is believing in the Word of God. But when one believes in the Word of God, the Lord's work is automatically applied to him. Hence, if you say that you are not very smart and that you cannot understand the work of the Lord, I will say to you that God does not require you to believe in the work of the Lord. He only requires you to believe in God's Word. When you believe in God's Word, you will obtain His work in the Word. Apparently, what I took home was the paper box. How do I know that it contained candy? When I went home, I removed the colored paper and opened the box and took out the candy. Thank the Lord. This is how the Holy Spirit works. We receive God's Word by faith, and the Holy Spirit opens up the work of the Lord that is contained in God's Word. Therefore, we must realize that the work of the Holy Spirit is fellowship. The Holy Spirit conveys the work of the Lord contained in God's Word to us. Without the Holy Spirit's conveying, God's Word remains only the Word. But when the Holy Spirit comes, the Word is opened up. Hence, God has prepared the Lord Jesus. He has also prepared the Holy Spirit for this work of fellowship.

## THE HOLY SPIRIT CONVEYING THE LORD'S WORK AND THE LORD HIMSELF TO US

Now we must see how the Holy Spirit conveys the work of the Lord to us. The Lord's work includes all that He has done on the cross, in His resurrection, in His ascension, in His second coming, and in everything that He bestows upon us. We cannot go into detail concerning all these items. There is too much to say about them. To speak of them, we would have to mention the work of the Holy Spirit in the entire New Testament. Tonight we can only mention it in brief. The coming of the Holy Spirit is not merely for conveying the Lord's work to us. It is also for conveying the Lord Himself to us. The purpose of the fellowship of the Holy Spirit is to convey the Lord Jesus and His work to us. If a man has not received the work of the Lord, the Holy Spirit conveys this work to him. If a man has not received the Lord Jesus, the Holy Spirit conveys the Lord Himself to man. At the time we were saved, the work of the Holy Spirit was to convey the work of the Lord to us. Later His work is to convey the Lord Himself to us. The ministry of the Holy Spirit is to manifest the Lord Jesus.

A week ago, two sisters came to me asking me how to translate the English phrase *to minister with Christ* into Chinese. This is a difficult phrase to translate. It means to serve others with Christ, like serving someone with a cup of tea or a bowl of rice. The work of the Holy Spirit is to serve the Lord Jesus to us. When we received the Lord, the Holy

Spirit transferred the Lord's work to us. Hence, all the work that the Lord has accomplished, such as the gift of repentance, forgiveness, cleansing, justification, sanctification, and joy, are accomplished by the Holy Spirit in us. Matters such as regeneration or the receiving of eternal life are accomplished in us through the Holy Spirit. The work of the Holy Spirit is to convey the life of the Lord Jesus to us. It is similar to a wire conveying electricity from the power plant at Willow Tree Creek to us. Through the Holy Spirit, we receive a new life, a new heart, and a new spirit (cf. Ezek. 36:26). When we receive a new spirit and a new heart, the Lord Jesus is able to abide in us through the Holy Spirit. Hence, regeneration is the Holy Spirit preparing a new temple for the Lord.

Since we are of the flesh, the Lord Jesus cannot dwell in us. We are like the world under judgment at the time of Noah. After the water subsided, Noah released a dove from the ark (Gen. 8:8-9). But the dove found no place of rest; it could not abide anywhere. In the same way, we are full of sin. The Lord Jesus can find no place to abide in us. That being the case, God gave to us the Holy Spirit. The Lord accomplished everything objectively. Now the Holy Spirit gave us a new spirit subjectively, so that the Son of God can abide in our spirit. The Holy Spirit came first to prepare a dwelling for the Lord Jesus. Then the Lord came to live in us.

On the one hand, the Holy Spirit gave us a new life within. On the other hand, day by day He conveys God's truth and purpose into us. This is why the Lord says that when the Spirit of reality comes, He will guide us into all reality (John 16:13). Furthermore, there is another item of the work of the Holy Spirit, which is to communicate to us the gifts, such as prophecy, tongues, healings, miracles, revelations, words of wisdom and words of knowledge, faith, and all kinds of other gifts.

## THE HOLY SPIRIT PRESERVING
## THE ETERNAL FRESHNESS OF THE LORD'S WORK

I do not want to enumerate in detail all the items of the Holy Spirit's work of fellowship. I will only stress one thing: all of the work of the Lord Jesus is conveyed to us today through the Holy Spirit. Even the Lord Jesus Himself is conveyed to us through the work of the Holy Spirit. This is God's salvation. Many people do not understand the Holy Spirit's work of fellowship. They ask me how the Lord's work that was accomplished nineteen hundred years ago could be applied to us today. Actually, if there were not the work of the Holy Spirit, their question would be fully justified. How can a work accomplished nineteen hundred years ago be applied to us today? What the Lord accomplished nineteen hundred years ago was not left to "dry in the wind and the sun." God has preserved and nurtured this work in the Holy Spirit. That is why this work remains so fresh. Today we can receive the work of the Lord Jesus. This work can be the same as it was before.

Once I went to a shop and the shopkeeper gave me a can of imported vegetable soup. The can looked old and ugly outside. It was covered with dust. The shopkeeper recommended it very much and was willing to sell it to me at a discount. I bought it and took it home. When I examined the date afterwards, I found out that the date was older than my age. Later, when I opened it and cooked it, I found out that the soup was still quite palatable. If the Lord Jesus' work were not preserved in the Holy Spirit, the question of time and space would come in. How could the Savior who died on Calvary nineteen hundred years ago come into me? But with the Holy Spirit, there is no question of time and space. God has preserved the work of the Lord in the Holy Spirit. Now the work of the Lord is living. This is why the Holy Spirit is able to convey the work of the Lord into us.

I have a brother who studies biochemistry. He conducts experiments all the time. In order to cultivate a certain bacteria, he has to use a certain kind of chemical. As long as he maintains a certain temperature, the bacteria will live. If the temperature becomes too high or too low, or if other elements are added into the culture, the bacteria will die. The best environment to preserve the work of the Lord is the Holy Spirit. Once the work of the Lord leaves the Holy Spirit, it will not be able to live and will die. The same is true with the Christian life. A Christian life can never be separated from the Holy Spirit. If the truths understood by the Lord's children are separated from the Holy Spirit, they will gradually dry out and die. Hence, all spiritual matters have to be in the Holy Spirit. Apart from the Holy Spirit, everything will die. Nothing will survive. We have to see that the Holy Spirit is the source of life. In Him is life. Apart from Him, everything is dead.

Through the Holy Spirit, God conveys everything of Himself and the work of the Lord into us. God has prepared everything related to our salvation. Furthermore, the Holy Spirit has come and is ready to convey everything that God has prepared. If there is anyone who is not saved yet, he cannot say that God has not loved him, or that the Lord Jesus has not accomplished redemption for him. He cannot say that the word is too far from him and is unreachable.

My friends, do you have a mouth? Some people may argue that they are dumb and that they do not have a mouth. But they have a heart. They can be without a mouth. But they cannot be without a heart. Romans 10:8-9 says, "The word is near you, in your mouth and in your heart...that if you confess with your mouth Jesus as Lord and believe in your heart that God has raised Him from the dead, you will be saved." Why is this? Because God has said that whoever calls on the name of the Lord shall be saved. Perhaps you wonder how it can be so simple and how it is that one can be saved just by calling. This is because the Holy Spirit has come. He will save you as soon as you call. How does one call? If he has a mouth, he can use his mouth. If he does not have a mouth, he can call with his heart. This word is not far from us. It is in our mouth and even in our heart. This word is the word of justification by faith that we have been speaking of in the past few days.

# CHAPTER NINE

# THE WAY OF SALVATION—
# FAITH VERSUS LAW AND WORK

During the past few days, we have seen that all that man has is sin. We have also seen that God accomplishes everything. He has loved us. He has given us grace. God has accomplished righteousness, has caused the Lord Jesus to die and resurrect for us. God has even sent the Holy Spirit to convict and enlighten us and to give us the strength to accept the work of God. Let me ask a very natural question. What must man do to be saved, now that God has finished all His work? God has done everything on His part. Today He has laid this finished work before man. What then is the condition for us to be saved? God has accomplished the work of redemption. How can man now receive salvation? How can redemption become salvation? How can propitiation become substitution? How can God's gift to us in His Son be communicated to us in the Holy Spirit? We are talking about the condition for salvation. What should we do on our side before what is on God's side can be communicated to us?

## THE CONDITION FOR SALVATION—FAITH

All those who read the Bible know that the condition for salvation is faith. There is no other condition except faith. Because man has fallen and is corrupted, because his thoughts are crooked, and because man's flesh is of the law, he thinks that he must do something before he can be saved. But the Bible shows us that the only condition for our salvation is faith. Besides faith there is no other condition. The New Testament tells us clearly at least one hundred and fifteen times that when man believes, he is saved, he has eternal life and is justified. When man believes, he has all these things. In addition to these one hundred and fifteen times, the Bible says that man is justified by faith, or becomes righteous through faith, another thirty-five times. In the first instance, we have the verb *to believe*. In the second instance, we have the noun *faith*. The verb *to believe* is used one hundred and fifteen times. Once a man believes, he is saved (Acts 16:31). Once a man believes, he has eternal life (John 3:36). Once a man believes, he is justified. In addition to these verses, there are thirty-five times in which the noun *faith* is used. Man is saved through faith. He receives eternal life through faith, and he is justified by faith. Hence, in the entire New Testament, at least one hundred and fifty times it says that man is saved, justified, and has eternal life through faith only. It is not a matter of who one is, what one does, or what one can do. Everything depends on believing. Everything depends on faith.

Another thing that deserves special attention is that in all these one hundred and fifty occurrences of faith and believing, no other condition is added. These verses do not say that man must believe and then do something to receive eternal life. They do not say that man must believe and do something before he can be justified. Neither do they say that man must believe and do something before he can be saved. The Lord's Word mentions faith in a clear and definite way. Nothing else is mixed in or attached to the condition of faith. Hence, the Bible shows us clearly from God's point of view that there is no other condition to salvation than to believe.

One of the most well-read and treasured books in the New Testament is the Gospel of John. If one reads it carefully, he will see that John wrote this book with no other purpose than to tell us how man can receive life and be saved and how he can be delivered from condemnation. The Gospel of John mentions eighty-six times that man receives life, is justified, and does not come into condemnation by faith alone and nothing else. Hence, the Bible shows us clearly, adequately, and simply that salvation is not based on who man is, what he has, and what he has done. The Bible shows us that when man believes, he receives (John 1:12). He receives by believing.

We have said that salvation and redemption are accomplished by God. Even the way and plan to accomplish them are laid out by God. We have also seen that grace is accomplished by God through the Lord Jesus. We have to remember that if it is grace on God's side, then it must be faith on our side. If I stretch out my hands to give a brother a cup of tea, he cannot receive it by stretching out his feet. Whatever way others use to give things to you, you have to use the same way to receive them. The way to receive must be the same as the way to give. If others call you on the telephone, then you have to answer by picking up the telephone. If others write a letter to you, you have to receive the letter. The way something is received must be the same as the way it was sent.

According to the Bible, God has given us grace through Jesus Christ (1 Cor. 1:4). For Him to do so is in the principle of grace. Since giving is in the principle of grace on God's side, then receiving is in the principle of faith on our side. Faith and grace are two inseparable principles. Grace is God giving something to us, and faith is our receiving something from God. Faith is nothing other than receiving what God has given us in spirit. This is absolutely independent from work. Only by this way can man receive God's grace. If we resort to any other means, we will not be able to receive God's grace.

Although the Bible shows us that through faith one receives God's grace, many doctrines have emerged as a result of man's misunderstanding. Man comes up with theories that are based on his own thoughts and darkened mind, involving what he should do before he can be saved. Just as man has made idols with his crooked heart and has considered them gods, he has specified conditions for salvation with his crooked heart and darkened thoughts. For this reason, I must point out the different conditions that man has set forth for salvation and consider if these ways of salvation are trustworthy or not. If man does not see God's truth and does not understand His Word, he will not realize that the condition for salvation is faith. But if a man sees God's light and understands God's truth, he will not be able to overturn the New Testament fact that salvation is through faith. The problem today is that after man realizes faith as the condition of salvation, he adds something else to faith. The point of dispute between God and man is not that of believing or not believing, but whether it is believing with repentance, believing with the works of law, believing with baptism, or believing with testifying, as a prerequisite to salvation. The Word of God tells us that once we believe, we are saved. But man today adds a word *with*. According to his darkened mind, he claims that man is saved by faith *with* something. What we will consider is not if one can be saved by faith. That matter is settled already. The question today is whether or not faith is enough. Do we need to add *with* to faith before we can be saved?

## SALVATION NOT BEING FAITH
## WITH THE WORKS OF LAW

The first question is whether man is saved through faith *with* the keeping of the law. Man's way for salvation is faith plus the keeping of the law. We have spoken concerning the question of the law already, but we will repeat it again. The Bible devotes much time to deal with this question. Preachers, therefore, must also devote much time to deal with this question. Because man pays so much attention to the law, the Bible devotes two books to deal with this problem. We have to know for what purpose God has given the law. God gave the Israelites the law, not for them to keep, but for exposing their sins. Originally, the Israelites had sins, but they had not become transgressions. From Adam to Moses, man had sins (Rom. 5:14), but he did not have any transgressions. God gave the law in order to turn man's sins into transgressions (Rom 5:13, 20a).

How were man's sins turned into transgressions? Suppose there is a person who has the disposition and temperament of walking back and forth outside the meeting hall every day. It is something that he likes to do. He has to do this every day, every week, every month, and every year. No one can explain why he does this. But in his temperament, disposition, and life, there is something that compels him to walk back and forth outside the meeting hall. Although he has such a habit, we cannot say that he has any transgression. You may not like what he does, and you may think that it is wrong, but he has no realization that this is wrong. When will he realize that it is wrong? Suppose you take two bright red ribbons and tie one to each end of the lane. When he comes the next day, he will see the two ribbons and will realize that he should not walk through them. His habit has always been to walk there because something in him compels him to walk there. Suppose he takes a look at the two ribbons and considers the bright color, the silk texture, the nice knots, and then tears them apart and walks right through. In that case, his walking is different from his previous walking. His previous walking was sin without transgression. Now it is the same walking, but he walks in transgression.

God says that the law is perfect. It is good, righteous, holy, and excellent (Rom. 7:12). But man is full of sin. He is full of sin within and without. However, from Adam to Moses, man had no transgressions although he had sin. God established the law, not in order that man would not sin, but in order to expose man's sins and make them transgressions. Today the law is here. Once a person breaks the law, he realizes that he has sinned. Hence, we can say that God gave man the law not for him to keep, but for him to see that he has sinned. When there was no law, he did not realize that he has sin. Now he knows.

The strange thing is that man takes the law, which is there to prove his sin, to try to prove that he is righteous. He turns the law around. God wants us to know through the law that we have sinned, but we want to prove through the law that we are righteous. God wants to show us through the law that we are perishing, but we want to prove through the law that we are saved. Man does not see himself. His thoughts are full of the law. He does not see that he is corrupt inside and cannot keep the law. Man's flesh cannot keep God's law. It will not submit to God's law. However, man still wants to seek out right-eousness from the law and earn life through it. God uses the law to show man that he is helpless and that he needs to receive salvation. But when man sees the ordinances, he tries to earn a little righteousness through them and be saved. Romans 3:19 says, "Now we know that whatever things the law says, it speaks to those who are under the law, that every mouth may be stopped and all the world may fall under the judgment of God." Here it says that the law was given for the purpose of stopping every mouth, so that no one can say anything, and so that everyone can be subject to the judgment of God. Following this, there is a verdict concerning us: "Because out of the works of the law no flesh shall be justified before Him; for through the law is the clear knowledge of sin" (v. 20). One can see that the original intention of the law was to expose sin; it was not to justify man. It is so clear that the purpose of God's law was to expose sin rather than to establish our own righteousness.

In the Old Testament, not only did God give man the law, He gave man the types as well. These were the ceremonial laws. They explained how to offer up sacrifices and how to pay the money for atonement. These matters typify the Lord Jesus' accomplishment of redemption and its subsequent salvation for us in the New Testament. This is what God has shown us. It is so strange that man would try to establish his own righteousness not only through the law, but also through these types. He tries to establish his righteousness through these ordinances. We even find a Pharisee praying that he fasted twice a week and that he offered to God one tenth of what he had (Luke 18:11-12). He thought that these were his righteousnesses and that through them he could be saved. Man does not see the purpose for which God established the law. He misunderstands God's purpose. Man doubts if it is that easy to be saved. He thinks that it is true that man is indeed saved through believing in the Lord Jesus. We who are Christians all the more acknowledge the need to believe. It is right to believe, but many say that we should also keep the law. What man is saying today is not whether one can be saved through the law or not. What he is saying is that those who believe in Jesus should also keep the law before they can be saved. Faith in Jesus is an undisputed doctrine in the Bible. But Christians say that one should add to that the keeping of the law. Man does not see that to believe in Jesus and to keep the law are two absolutely contradictory things. They can never be joined together. The difference between faith in Jesus and work in the law is the difference between heaven and hell. As heaven is vastly different from hell, so faith in Jesus is vastly different from the work of the law.

To whom was the law given? It was given to the Jews. Why then does the New Testament mention again and again the keeping of the law? In the New Testament, the apostles, or we should say the Holy Spirit, knew clearly that the readers of it may not necessarily all be Jews. Only a minority of those who believed in Jesus at the very beginning were Jews. One person asked me once, "You say that the Jews were the ones to receive the law. But who are the Jews?" I told him that the Jews were like guinea pigs. When a researcher of pharmaceutical products is not sure of a drug, he does not experiment with humans. Instead, he first injects it into guinea pigs. If the guinea pigs die, then the drug cannot be used. Only after the drug is proven effective will it be injected into human beings. The same is done for oral drugs. First, it is taken in by guinea pigs. If it works, then the drug is used. Otherwise it is discarded. The same is done for immunization against bacteria. If it works on guinea pigs, it will work on man. If it does not work on guinea pigs, it will not work on man. I would say in a most respectful way that the Jews are the guinea pigs. God tried out the law on the Jews. If the Jews could make it, then it could be used. If they could not make it, then it cannot be used. God did try the law on the Jews, and they did not make it. This means that the whole world cannot make it. The Jews were selected by God as objects of an experiment. The Jews are representative of the whole world. Hence, one sees that the law was officially given to the Jews. But the principle of the law is given to all men. It is given to all flesh. God gave man the law to forewarn him that man is of the flesh and is fleshly.

What is Christianity? Christianity does not tell the sons of Adam to do good. That is not Christianity. Christianity says that Adam has been crucified and removed and that the Adamic race has been annihilated through the cross of the Lord Jesus. Man in Christ receives a new life and becomes a new race. The law is useless for the new race, for there is no such thing as law in the new race. The law was given by God to the sons of Adam to expose their sins. If one wants to be saved through keeping the law, he has to realize the serious consequence of the phrase *keeping the law*. Once man keeps the law, he will have righteousness. But this righteousness would be of the flesh. In other words, it would mean that the sons of Adam, that is, the Adamic race, need not die. It would mean that man can please God with his flesh. Perhaps one would argue that he does not mean to keep the whole law, that he realizes that it is impossible to keep the whole law, that what he means is to believe in Jesus and then keep the law. But if the work of the law has a millionth fraction of ground before God, it means that Adam did not have to die. This would revoke the very nature of Christianity. Christianity is not here to establish a ground for Adam. It is not here to maintain the old creation. It is here to transfer us to the new creation. We are of the flesh, and we cannot obtain the righteousness that comes from the keeping of the law.

Since the fall of man, the cherubim and the flaming sword were guarding the tree of life in the garden of Eden (Gen. 3:24). Why were the cherubim and the flaming sword guarding the way to the tree of life? It was to prevent man from eating of the tree of life. After man became a sinner and had eaten of the fruit of the tree of knowledge of good and evil, there was no other way for him to go back to the tree of life and eat of its fruit except through the judgment of the cherubim and the slaying of the flaming sword. God shows us that man cannot eat of the fruit of the tree of knowledge of good and evil and at the same time eat of the fruit of the tree of life. Man cannot eat of both. Man cannot receive the seed of sin on the one hand and take in the Lord's salvation on the other hand.

Here lies the difference between Christianity and Judaism. Judaism says to the man in the flesh that in keeping the law he shall live. But Christianity says he cannot live, for he cannot keep the law. Christianity asserts clearly that man cannot do this. There is no possibility for him to keep the law. Hence, we can see that in the Old Testament, God gave the law for man to keep. In the New Testament, we see that man cannot keep the law at all, nor does he have to keep it. This is one of the greatest truths in the Bible. Now there is a danger of mixing faith and the law together, and annulling the principle of the Bible. Right away, Adam will have the ground, and the fleshly man will be able to live again. God's judgment is that man must die. Through Jesus Christ, God has removed man. He does not want the fleshly man to come up with anything. If man still tries to produce something from the flesh, he has overturned the principle of the New Testament. If the law is given some ground, then the flesh also will have some ground. But God says that the flesh has no ground, that all grounds have been removed.

We may wonder whether this is to annul the law. Please remember that according to the Bible, the law requires two things from us. First, the law says that he who keeps it shall live (Rom. 10:5). The law demands us to keep and to do something. Once man keeps it, he will have righteousness. If we have righteousness, we will have the reward, which is life. But there is a second aspect. The law says that the day we eat of the tree of knowledge of good and evil, we shall surely die (Gen. 2:17). On the one hand, the law requires man to keep something. On the other hand, its punishment is death for all those who do not keep the law. All who do not keep the law receive the recompense of not keeping the law. Hence, in the Old Testament, in principle, we see that the law required man to keep it and to be righteous. Those who did not keep it were condemned and punished.

In Shanghai, the traffic department has many traffic regulations. For example, to ride after dark, one has to have lights on his bicycle. If there is no light for the bicycle, then there will be a fine of sixty cents. This regulation requires two things: it requires man to install a light, and it requires those who do not do this to be punished. What then is to annul the law? To annul the law means that one does not need a light, and he does not have to be punished. What is to keep the law? To keep the law is to meet either of the two requirements. For those who have a light, they are keeping the law. For those who do not have a light, but are willing to pay sixty cents, they are also keeping the law.

The problem today is that we cannot keep the law. The law of God requires that we be righteous. If we are not righteous, then we fail. Only by being righteous can we live. But no man of the flesh is able to keep the law. None among us can have righteousness before God through keeping the law. Once man touches God's law, he will fail. Paul said in Romans 7:7 that even if God has only one law, man is not able to keep it. Paul did not transgress all the laws. He mentioned only one law, the one concerning covetousness. In the original language, covetousness is lust. Paul said, "I am helpless. The lust keeps coming back again and again. It is impossible for me not to have lust." He could not get the light of his bicycle to work, yet he had to travel in the city. For some, the problem is not that the light does not work. For them, they simply do not want to have the light. These people do not even want to light the lamp. What is annulling the law? It is when someone pleads with God saying, "O God, I cannot keep Your law today. Please let me go on account of the Lord Jesus. I have done my best. Please do not punish me." All who plead for the Lord Jesus to be lenient or for God to have mercy on them are annulling the law. On the one hand, they do not want to keep the law. On the other hand, they do not want the punishment of the law. They do not want to have a light. Yet at the same time, they want to avoid the fine of sixty cents. What about us today? Do we have our lights today? If we have the lights, then we can travel peacefully in the city. But none of us are able to have the light. Hence, the only way is to pay the sixty cents. This is what the Lord Jesus has done for us. This is the judgment that we have borne in Christ. We have to say, "Praise and thank the Lord that we are already judged in Christ!" We have been punished in Christ. God has punished us in Christ. Since the Lord Jesus has died, resurrected, and ascended, the salvation we receive now is equivalent to what we would obtain if we keep the law. The ones who have the light are free. The ones who have been punished are also free. Today if a man keeps all the laws, he will be justified and will be saved in the same way that we who have believed in Jesus are saved and justified. Of course, we are not just saved when we believe in Jesus; in saving us, the Lord Jesus grants us many other things apart from the law as well.

Paul said in Romans 3:31, "Do we then make the law of no

effect through faith? Absolutely not! Rather, we establish the law." Hence, when we are saved through faith in Jesus, we have not made the law of no effect. Since we have met the requirement of the law in us, the law has nothing to say. Never think that we should add the work of the law to our faith. For us to believe is like paying the sixty cents. For us to keep the law is like having the light. No one in the whole world would have the light and pay sixty cents at the same time. This is unreasonable. Why does one have to pay sixty cents and at the same time have the light? If he is able to have the light, then he does not have to pay the sixty cents. If there is the word of faith, then there cannot be the law. If there is the law, there cannot be the word of faith. No one can have faith and keep the law at the same time, for to do so would be to despise the Lord Jesus. It would mean that one fails to see his utter weakness and filthiness.

Please read again Galatians 2:16-17: "And knowing that a man is not justified out of works of law, but through faith in Jesus Christ, we also have believed into Christ Jesus that we might be justified out of faith in Christ and not out of the works of law, because out of the works of law no flesh will be justified. But if, while seeking to be justified in Christ, we ourselves also have been found sinners, is then Christ a minister of sin? Absolutely not!" The book of Galatians shows us that some in Galatia contended that even though man was justified through faith in the Lord Jesus, it was not enough; he still had to keep the law. They were not saying that a man should not believe. They recognized that a man was justified in Christ. But they were saying that one still needed to keep the law. Paul said a very strong word here. He said that if while seeking to be justified in Christ we have been found sinners, it meant that after we have believed in the Lord Jesus, we are still not justified, that we are still sinners, and must still keep the law before we can be saved. For example, suppose that I am sick, and I spend ten days with one doctor. Afterwards, because the sickness is still present, I have to consult another doctor. If I seek to be justified in Christ, and at the same time try to keep the law, it means that I am still a sinner and have not yet been saved. If I am no longer a sinner, then I should not need to keep the law anymore. If I am still a sinner, is Christ a minister of sin? Paul asked that if he was not justified after he had believed in the Lord Jesus, did that mean that Christ is a minister of sin? The answer is, "Absolutely not!" In the New Testament, Paul said "absolutely not" many times. In Greek, it is an idiom. It is translated in the King James Version as "God forbid." It is equivalent to the expression "heaven forbid," a very strong word. This means that even heaven would reject this. There is no reason under the sun that this should be so. Hence, one can see that a man cannot have faith in Jesus and at the same time keep the law.

In Romans 3, Paul made another clear statement. Verse 28 says, "For we account that a man is justified by faith apart from the works of the law." This is a conclusive statement. Now it is a matter of faith. It has absolutely nothing to do with the law. Thank the Lord. Jesus is enough. When the Bible pays attention to faith, it pays attention to God's grace. This shows us that everything comes by receiving. Some like to exalt men in their gospel preaching. But if we know the Bible, we will see that apart from God, man is absolutely helpless. Please remember these two sentences: man is not saved by the law, and neither is he saved by faith *with* the law. This is the first and most common mistake of man. Man has mixed faith with the law.

### SALVATION NOT BEING FAITH WITH GOOD WORKS

"The works of law" is an expression we find in the Bible (Gal. 2:16). We have covered this aspect already. A more common understanding of the condition of salvation is that salvation is by faith and also by works. Salvation by faith is a doctrine of the Bible, and man cannot argue against it (Eph. 2:8). But man says that it is also by works. Let us now consider what the Bible says about this. We are often polite and accommodating in our speaking, but the Bible is not polite in its speaking. It is very definite. Ephesians 2:8 and 9 say, "For by grace you have been saved through faith, and this not of yourselves; it is the gift of God; not of works that no one should boast." These verses tell us that salvation is absolutely by grace and through faith. The word *through* means to traverse. It is like saying that the electric light shines by electricity and through the wire. It is also like saying the water from the faucet comes by the reservoir in the water department and through the pipes. Man is saved by grace, but the channel through which salvation comes to us is faith. The channel is not works but faith. It is through faith and has nothing to do with works. It is not adding faith to works. One has to know that faith and works are basically opposed to one another. The grace of the Lord Jesus is based on the love of God. When we believe, grace and love flow into us. As a result, we are saved, have life, and are justified. None of the above are communicated to us through works.

Thank the Lord that salvation is not because of work. Why should it be so? The answer here is that no one should boast. What Ephesians 1 tells us is that God wants to have all the glory. That is why He does all the work. Suppose a certain brother is very capable and educated and has suffered much for the Lord. If another brother comes to me and says, "Brother Nee, I praise you and glorify you for the fine work that this brother has done," we would surely say that he is mentally ill. Glory can only go to the one who has done the work. There is no such thing in the world as one working and another getting the glory. Those who work deserve the wages. Whosoever works, the same should get the glory. Why has God done all the work of saving us? It is so that He would get all the glory. The reason God gave us grace is that He would get all the glory. He does not want us to work, lest we boast in ourselves. To boast is to glorify oneself. If we have done anything that deserves any glory, we will not thank and praise God before Him. Right away we will say, "No doubt, the salvation is given to me by You. It is Your work. But I have added my part to it. If I had not added my part, I would not be like I am today." Man loves to overestimate his own merits. He likes to overemphasize his own outstanding points. If God said that He would accomplish ninety-nine percent of the work of salvation and leave one percent to us, this one percent would silence the heavens. The angels would not praise anymore, and the stones would not cry out anymore. Instead of the stones becoming the sons of Abraham, the sons of Abraham would become the stones, for out of the one hundred percent, some would lay claim to one percent. They would then tell the wonder of their own work and say, "I passed through that in this way, or in that way. How did you get through? What contribution did you put in?" Everyone would be boasting about his own work, and God would have no possibility of getting the glory.

Thank and praise the Lord! Since He wants to get all the glory, He did not leave one thing for us to do. When we reach heaven, we will have to say that we are still helpless persons. We are able to get there because of "free" grace. This word "free" will stop all supplication in heaven and will fill it with thanksgiving and praise. It will be all thanksgiving and praise because everything is done by God. We have to see that this is the truth of the Bible. Man's work and God's grace cannot be mixed together. Once man works, it comes into conflict with glory. Hence, whether I am on the street, at my home, or in a Lord's table meeting, I can say from my heart, "God, I thank and praise You, because I have nothing to do with my salvation. My salvation comes one hundred percent from You. Therefore, what can I do except praise You?" God delights in praise. The Bible calls one kind of prayer loathsome, but the Bible never calls any kind of praise loathsome. Some prayers are rejected by God, but God never rejects any praise. God wants to have all the glory, for He has done all the work.

Does that mean that we can be loose and do not need to do good anymore? Ephesians 2:10 explains, "For we are His masterpiece, created in Christ Jesus for good works, which God prepared beforehand in order that we would walk in them." Verses 8 and 9 show us what God has done for us objectively. Verse 10 immediately shows us the subjective matters. God has not saved us in a foolish way. He has given us a new life, a new nature, and a new spirit within. The Lord Jesus is living in us through the Holy Spirit and has prepared us for all good works. Please remember that God has not included these good works in the previous two verses. It does not matter how many good works you do after you are saved. Salvation is still of grace. It does not matter how fast you advance spiritually, for salvation is still of the free grace of the Lord Jesus. Even if you have a work like Paul's, a result like Peter's, a love like John's, and a suffering like James's—even if you have all of these four things—you are still saved through free grace. In the future, while your work can show that you are saved, it is never your condition for salvation. My faith does not mean much. It is only a receiving of God's work.

Man is not saved by works. No one can argue against this. But man is very pitiful. Because his heart is darkened and filled with sin, because his flesh is wicked and full of the law, although he recognizes faith, he presumes that he should add works also. Man does not see that works come after he is saved by faith. Salvation has nothing to do with works. I am not saying that we do not need works. We do pay attention to work. But this is not the condition for salvation. Salvation is an altogether different problem. One must not forget that the Bible says that if we pay but a little attention to work, God's grace is annulled (Gal. 2:21). Since it is grace, it must be of faith only and not of work.

Romans 4:4 and 5 say, "Now to the one who works, his wages are not accounted according to grace, but according to what is due. But to the one who does not work, but believes on Him who justifies the ungodly, his faith is accounted as righteousness." Now we are clear. If a man can be saved by works, then salvation becomes a reward. It is no longer grace, but something that one deserves. If it is something that one deserves, then it is no longer free. The word *freely* in the Bible (3:24) means in the original language *without a cause*. In other words, there is no reason for it. The Lord Jesus said in the Gospel of John that "they hated Me without cause" (15:25). In the original language, it can mean, "They hated Me freely." The Lord never spent anything to buy that hatred, but they hated Him just the same. There was no reason attached. It was free. God's grace during those three and a half years was accomplished freely for us.

We are like the younger son in Luke 15. One day we came to God and said, "God, give me the share of the estate that falls to me." God gave us what we should have. After we took our estate, we squandered it with evil companions. Today we have come back to the Father's house. The robe, the ring, and the shoes that we wear and the fatted calf that we eat are not what we deserve. That which was rightfully ours has been spent. We do not deserve the ring. We do not deserve the robe. We do not deserve to eat the fatted calf, and we do not deserve to wear the shoes. What then is grace? When those who do not deserve to be saved are saved, that is grace. Grace is what those who should not obtain have obtained. What the younger son took away the first time was not grace. He spent that already. What he received the second time was all grace. His own portion was long spent. When he enjoys another meal at home, it is not what he deserves to get; it is the Father's grace.

Hence, if one works, the question of wages comes in, and it is no more grace. Grace is in conflict with what one deserves. How then does faith work? When it is not work or labor, but only faith in the God who justifies the sinner, that faith is reckoned as righteousness. This is the relationship between faith and grace. If it is work, then it is not grace. If it is grace, then there is only faith. To believe is to accept what God has done. It is not how much I have done. We must emphasize that, before God, we are not justified by what we have done. We are justified by faith. Today we have justification by faith. Therefore, the question of work is forever over.

Everyone who knows me well knows that I like soy sauce. It is all right if there are not many dishes at the table. As long as I have soy sauce, I can get by. At one time, one who was serving me saw that my soy sauce was almost gone. He went to the market and brought more back. Then he mixed it in with the good soy sauce. When I tasted it, I noticed that the taste was different. I asked why the soy sauce tasted different that day. I checked with the serving one whether or not he had poured the soy sauce from the same bottle. He answered yes. I wondered if my taste had changed. It did not seem that likely. I then asked if he had mixed it with something else. He had to admit that he had. Today man does the same thing to God's work and His grace. He tries to mix something else into them. Once we mix something in this way, grace is no longer grace. That is why God says that if it is of grace, then it is no more of work (Rom. 11:6). If it is of work, then it is no more of grace. Work can never be mixed with grace. Hence, we must not merely say that salvation is of faith. We must say that salvation is solely of faith.

I love Romans 3:27. This word is based on verses 25 and 26 which speak of how the Lord Jesus has become a propitiation place and how God has justified those who believe in Him. It is not unrighteous for God to do this. Hence, in verse 27 it says, "Where then is boasting? It is excluded." There is no way for us to boast. There is no possibility to boast anymore. The next sentence is very important. It says, "Through what kind of law?" This means that we have nothing to boast of anymore. By what way are we excluded from boasting? By what principle are we excluded from boasting? Verse 27 continues, "That of works? No, but through the law of faith." Paul asked how man can be excluded from boasting and how boasting can be removed. His answer is by the principle of faith. If one is in the principle of faith, then he is not in the principle of works. If it is by the principle of works, then boasting cannot be excluded. But thank the Lord. Today we have the principle of faith. Hence, we cannot boast. We can only praise.

Philippians 2:12 says, "So then, my beloved, even as you have always obeyed, not as in my presence only but now much rather in my absence, work out your own salvation with fear and trembling." Many have told us that Paul said explicitly in Philippians that we have to work out our own salvation. If we are to work out our salvation, does that not mean that we have to do something? Is it true that the Lord has done the work, but man also has to do something? This is like saying that He supplies the material, we supply the labor, and the two of us work out our salvation. A person says this because he does not understand the word of the Bible. If we are to work out our salvation, then what has the Lord Jesus done on the cross? What has He accomplished on the cross? If a thing has been accomplished, it cannot be accomplished any further. If you are a child of God, you cannot become a child of God again. On the cross, the Lord Jesus clearly said, "It is finished!" (John 19:30). The cross of the

Lord Jesus has accomplished the work of salvation. It has accomplished the work of redemption. Since the work of salvation and redemption have been accomplished, there is no possibility for us to work out this salvation. If we still want to work out our salvation, we must first overturn the work of the Lord on the cross. We must declare that the work of the Lord Jesus has not been accomplished; the Lord's work has not been finished. That is why we have to work it out.

Many times, we do not know what it means to shame others. But once you have experienced it, you will know what it is. For example, here is a sister. Someone has asked her to wash some handkerchiefs. After she has washed them, she hangs them up to dry. But another person comes along and takes the handkerchiefs away. When she asks for the reason, she is told that they were taken down to be washed. This is an open shame to the sister, for it means that the other person does not believe that the handkerchiefs are washed. It means that they think that the sister has lied. In the same way, for us to work out our salvation is not a glory to Christ but a shame to Christ. The Bible says clearly that Christ has accomplished all the work.

Then why does Philippians 2:12 say that we have to work out our salvation? The word *work out* in the original language carries the meaning of *out*. We should work *out* our salvation in fear and trembling. Did Paul's word stop here? If it had stopped here, we would not know what he meant. Verse 13 says, "For it is God who operates in you both the willing and the working for His good pleasure." Since God has operated in you, it is possible for you to now work it out. If God has not operated *in,* we have no way to work it *out.* Since God has operated *in,* you can work *out.* God has already saved you within and has given you life. Now there is no other way but to let Him come out. God does not want you to work. He wants you to *work out.* Hence, this is not a question of salvation or perdition, eternal life or eternal death. This is a question of whether or not one receives the reward after his salvation. God has already operated in you, causing you to will and to work for His good pleasure. Hence, you have to work it out. This is the proper condition of a Christian. In other words, this is your work after salvation. If a man has not yet been saved, he cannot work out his salvation. If a man does not have life, he cannot live out a life. Only after a man has been saved can he work out his salvation. Hence, one sees that there is no such thing as being saved through good works.

## THE DIFFERENCE BETWEEN
## ETERNAL LIFE AND THE KINGDOM

There is one thing we have to be clear about. To have eternal life is different from entering the kingdom of the heavens. Whoever cannot see the difference between eternal life and the kingdom of the heavens will never be clear concerning the way of salvation and the way of preservation. The Lord Jesus said that from John the Baptist until now the kingdom of the heavens is taken by violence (Matt. 11:12). The violent take it. The law and the prophecies of the prophets ended with John (11:12-13). Based on this word, some have said that we must be violent, that is, we must strive before we can be saved. If we do not strive, we will not be saved. A person says this because he cannot tell the difference between the kingdom of the heavens and eternal life. There is a difference between eternal life and the kingdom of the heavens.

The first difference between eternal life and the kingdom lies in time. Eternal life is for eternity, but the kingdom is not for eternity. When the new heaven and the new earth come, the kingdom of the heavens will be over. The kingdom of the heavens denotes God's rule. The period of God's rule is the period of the kingdom of the heavens. God's sovereignty on earth and His rule on earth will be manifested for only one thousand years. What are the heavens? The book of Daniel talks about the ruling of the heavens (7:27). Hence, the kingdom of the heavens is the sphere in which the heavens rule. When the Lord Jesus comes to rule on earth, that will be the time when the heavens rule. Today the ruling one on earth is the devil, Satan. The worldly politics and authorities today are of Satan. The Lord Jesus will not rule until the time of the kingdom of the heavens. But the period during which the authority of the heavens is realized is very short. First

Corinthians 15:24 says, "Then the end, when He delivers up the kingdom to His God and Father, once He has abolished all rule and all authority and power." The kingdom will be delivered up to God the Father. Hence, there is a time limit to the kingdom. But eternal life is forever. Everyone who reads 1 Corinthians 15 knows that at the beginning of the new heaven and the new earth, that is, at the conclusion of the millennium, the kingdom will be delivered up. Hence, there is a difference in time between eternal life and the kingdom of the heavens.

The second difference lies in the method that man enters the kingdom of the heavens and the way he obtains eternal life. The receiving of eternal life is the subject of the entire Gospel of John. The way to have eternal life is by believing. Once we believe, we obtain. We never read of another way. But to enter into the kingdom of the heavens is not a simple matter. The entire Gospel of Matthew mentions the kingdom of the heavens thirty-two times. Not once does it say that the kingdom of the heavens is received by faith. How does a man gain the kingdom of the heavens? Matthew 7:21 says, "Not every one who says to Me, Lord, Lord, will enter into the kingdom of the heavens, but he who does the will of My Father who is in the heavens." One can see that the entry into the kingdom of the heavens is a question of work rather than of faith. Matthew 5:3 also tells us, "Blessed are the poor in spirit, for theirs is the kingdom of the heavens." Here it does not say eternal life but the kingdom of the heavens. To have the kingdom of the heavens, one needs to be poor in spirit. The Lord also says, "Blessed are those who are persecuted for the sake of righteousness, for theirs is the kingdom of the heavens" (v. 10). One does not have to be persecuted to receive eternal life, but the kingdom is for those who have been persecuted for the sake of righteousness. Even if a man has eternal life, if he has not been persecuted for the sake of righteousness today and is not poor in spirit, he may still have no share in the kingdom.

There is a third difference. It lies in the attitude Christians should have concerning eternal life and the kingdom of the heavens. Concerning eternal life, God has never told us to seek after it. Rather, every time it is mentioned, He shows us that we have it already. However, concerning the kingdom, the word of the Bible says that we have to seek after it and pursue it diligently. Today, concerning the kingdom, we are in the stage of pursuit; we have not obtained it yet. We still have to put forth the effort to seek and pursue after the kingdom.

The fourth difference lies in the way God treats the kingdom and eternal life. God treats eternal life as a gift; it is given to us (Rom. 6:23). One never sees a person going to the Lord to seek for eternal life. There is not such a thing, because eternal life is free grace; it is given through the Lord Jesus to all those who believe in Him. There is no difference between a seeking one and one who is not seeking. But the kingdom is not the same. One recalls the mother of the two sons of Zebedee coming to the Lord Jesus and wishing that the Lord would cause her two sons to sit on both sides of Him in the kingdom (Matt. 20:21). But the Lord Jesus said, "To sit on My right and on My left, this is not Mine to give, but it is for those for whom it has been prepared by My Father" (v. 23). Grace is obtained once we call on Him. But the kingdom depends on whether one can be baptized in His baptism and drink the cup which He drank. Both of the disciples said that they could. But the Lord said that even though they promised that they would and could, the matter is still not up to Him to decide. The Father is the One who gives.

Furthermore, the criminal who was crucified along with the Lord said to Him, "Jesus, remember me when You come into Your kingdom" (Luke 23:42). Did the Lord Jesus hear his prayer? Indeed, He did. But He did not grant his request. The criminal asked the Lord to remember him when the Lord receives the kingdom. The Lord Jesus did not answer him that he would be with Him in the kingdom. Rather, He answered him, "Today you shall be with Me in Paradise" (v. 43). The Lord did not answer his question concerning the kingdom. But He did give him a reply concerning Paradise. As long as we call on Him, we can go to Paradise. But it is not so simple to go into the kingdom. Hence, there is a big difference here. God's attitude toward eternal life and the kingdom of the heavens is different: one is the gift of God, and the other is the reward of God.

Concerning the difference between the kingdom of the heavens and eternal life, there are other passages in the Bible which are quite interesting. Now we come to the fifth difference. Revelation 20 shows us that the martyrs receive the kingdom, although it does not say that they are the only ones who receive the kingdom (v. 4). The Bible, however, never shows us that man must be martyred to receive eternal life. If that were the case, Christianity would become a religion of death, for then man must die. But one does not see such a thing. However, the kingdom is different. The kingdom requires striving. It even takes martyrdom to obtain the kingdom. For example, poverty is a necessary condition for the kingdom of the heavens. In order to obtain the kingdom of the heavens, one has to lose his riches. The Bible shows us clearly that no person on earth who is rich according to his own ways can enter into the kingdom of the heavens. We cannot say that no rich man can be saved. We cannot say that no one can enter into eternal life who would not lose his riches. Inasmuch as it is difficult for the camel to go through the eye of the needle, in the same way it is difficult for a rich man to enter into the kingdom of the heavens (Matt. 19:24). But have you heard that inasmuch as it is impossible for the camel to go through the eye of the needle, in the same way it is impossible for a rich man to be saved and have eternal life? Thank the Lord. The poor can be saved. So can the rich. The poor can inherit eternal life. So can the rich. But to enter into the kingdom of the heavens is a problem for the rich. If we accumulate wealth on earth, we will not be able to enter into the kingdom of the heavens. Of course, this does not mean that one has to give up all of his money today. I am saying that one has to hand over all his money to the Lord. We are only the stewards. We are not the master of the house. The Bible never recognizes a Christian as the master of his money. Everyone is but a steward of money that is for the Lord. All of us are but the Lord's stewards. There is such a condition for entering the kingdom.

There is another very peculiar thing. One never sees the

questions of marriage and family come into play involving the matter of eternal life. But the Gospel of Matthew says that some will not marry for the sake of the kingdom of the heavens. Some even made themselves eunuchs for the sake of the kingdom of the heavens (Matt. 19:12). In order to enter into the kingdom of the heavens, and in order to gain a place in the kingdom, they choose to remain virgins. One does not see a married person being denied eternal life. If such were the case, Peter would have been the first one to have a problem, for he had a mother-in-law (Matt. 8:14). We see that the question of eternal life is not related to family and marriage at all, but the question of the kingdom is very much related to the family and marriage. This is why the Bible says that those who have wives should be like those who had none. Those who use the world should be as those not using it, and those who buy should be as those who do not possess (1 Cor. 7:29-31). This has much to do with our position in the kingdom of the heavens.

Finally, we have to mention another difference. In the kingdom, there are different levels of rank. Even if men are able to enter into the kingdom, there is a difference in the position that they hold there. Some will receive ten cities, and others will receive five (Luke 19:17-19). Some will merely receive reward, but others will receive great reward. Some will gain a rich entrance into the kingdom (2 Pet. 1:11). Some will enter the kingdom without a rich entrance. Hence, there is a difference in rank in the kingdom. But there is never a question of rank regarding eternal life. Eternal life is the same for everyone. One will not receive ten years more than another. There is no difference in eternal life, but there is a difference in the kingdom.

If one would consider a little, he will realize that in the Bible, the kingdom and eternal life are two absolutely different things. The condition for salvation is faith in the Lord. Other than faith, there is no other condition, for all the conditions have been met by the Son of God already. His Son's death has met all of God's requirements. But to enter the kingdom of the heavens is another matter; it requires works. Today a man is saved by God's righteousness. But we cannot enter the kingdom of the heavens unless our righteousness exceeds that of the scribes and the Pharisees (Matt. 5:20). The righteousness in one's living and conduct must surpass that of the scribes and the Pharisees before he can enter into the kingdom of the heavens. Hence, one sees that the question of eternal life is completely based on the Lord Jesus. But the question of the kingdom is based on man's works. I am not saying that the kingdom is better than eternal life. But God has a place for both.

# Chapter Ten

# THE RELATIONSHIP
# BETWEEN FAITH AND WORK IN JAMES 2

God's Word is very clear concerning the condition for salvation. God shows us that salvation is by faith and not by works. We have read enough Scriptures and seen enough clear reasons why our works cannot come into consideration. Because we believe in God's work through His Son, there must not be works of our own. Yet some who do not understand the words of the Bible have come to me, asking, "Is it not true that the book of James tells us clearly that a man is not justified by faith, but by works? Is it possible that James and Paul contradict each other? And is it possible that man is justified by both faith and works?" These ones think that James and Paul do not agree with each other. They think that the books of Romans, Galatians, and James also do not agree with each other. I have to use Paul's expression: "Absolutely not!" Let us come to the book of James and see what James himself had to say.

When we read the book of James, we must take care of one thing. We can only read what is said; we cannot add into it our own thoughts. What counts is what James said. What one adds on top of that does not count. Do not read your own thoughts into the book of James. You must see what James said and not what he did not say.

## THE SUBJECT OF JAMES BEING MERCY—
## JUSTIFICATION BEING INCIDENTAL

We will read James 2:14-26. But before we read this passage, I want to first ask a question: What is the context of these verses? Paul wrote the book of Romans with a subject in mind. He also wrote Galatians with a subject in mind. Romans says that man is justified by faith; Galatians says that man is not justified by works. Romans speaks from the positive side; Galatians speaks from the negative side. Romans declares positively how man is justified; Galatians argues negatively how to be justified and how not to be justified. Hence, the two books, Romans and Galatians, complement each another. The subject of these books is strictly justification. They deal specifically with the problem of justification. One deals with the problem from the positive side; the other deals with it from the negative side.

Many people feel that James 2 is a difficult chapter. What is the subject of James 2? The subject of Romans is justification, and the subject of Galatians is also justification. But what is the subject of James 2? The subject of this chapter covers at least mercy and help to others. What do the verses prior to this portion say? Beginning from verse 6 James says, "But you have dishonored the poor. Is it not the rich who oppress you and is it not they who drag you to the courts? Is it not they who blaspheme the honorable name by which you are called? If indeed you are fulfilling the royal law according to the Scripture, 'You shall love your neighbor as yourself,' you do well; but if you respect persons, you commit sin, being convicted by the law as transgressors. For whoever keeps the whole law yet stumbles in one point has become guilty of all. For He who said, Do not commit adultery, also said, Do not murder. Now if you do not commit adultery, but you murder, you have become a transgressor of the law. So speak and so do as those who are to be judged by the law of freedom. For the judgment is without mercy to him who has shown no mercy; mercy triumphs over judgment" (vv. 6-13). The subject of these verses is the showing of mercy. James tells us not to flatter the rich, but rather to care for the lowly and show mercy on the poor. This is what verses 1 through 13 say. Moreover, verse 1 is a continuation of chapter one. The last verse of chapter one says, "This is pure and undefiled religion before our God and Father: to visit orphans and widows in their affliction and to keep oneself unspotted from the world" (v. 27). This is James's subject. If a man says that he is a godly Christian, his godliness should be manifested in his care and giving to the orphans and widows. He should not invite someone wearing splendid clothing to sit in a good place and ask the orphans, the widows, and the poor to sit under his footstool. He should care for, show mercy, and give to the despised ones. James's subject is pure and undefiled religion. Pure and undefiled religion is manifested toward the poor, the lowly, and the despised.

After 2:14, he continues to talk about giving: "If a brother or sister is without clothing and lacks daily food, and any one of you says to them, Go in peace, be warmed and filled, yet you do not give them the necessities of the body, what is the profit?" (vv. 15-16). At the end of chapter one, the subject of James is given, that is, to care for the orphans and widows. At the end of the first section of chapter two, he says that we should show mercy to others, that we should give to the poor, and that we should not despise the poor. In the second section of chapter two, James tells us what one should do when he sees a brother or a sister without clothing and lacking daily food. All these words have to do with giving to others, showing mercy on others, not despising the poor, and helping others. Verses 14 to 26 only speak of justification in passing. Because mercy, giving, and caring for orphans and widows is the subject, justification is mentioned only in passing as a means to arrive at the goal of developing his subject. Hence, we see that James is not teaching the matter of justification in his book.

The subject of our meetings during these past two weeks has been the salvation of God. But suppose that during this period I stand up on the Lord's Day morning and give a message, not on salvation, but on overcoming, or on the kingdom, or on how to reign with the Lord Jesus in the millennium. That would be the subject of my message. While I speak, I may mention eight or nine sentences about salvation in passing. If you wish to understand the doctrine of salvation, would you not consider the other messages I gave during the rest of the two weeks? Would you ignore all that was spoken in two weeks and just take the eight or nine sentences that you hear in that one message? Romans and Galatians are specifically on justification, whereas James only mentions a few words about justification. His subject is not justification, nor is his purpose to teach justification. His purpose is to exhort others to give; the matter of justification is only mentioned in passing. A person cannot overturn Romans and Galatians with James's few words on justification. Is James then in conflict with Romans and Galatians? In a while you will see that it is not. But from the start, I want you to accurately grasp the subject of James. He was not talking about justification. He was talking about mercy, about care, and about what one should do for the orphans and widows.

### FAITH WITHOUT WORKS BEING
### OF NO PROFIT

Verse 14 says, "What is the profit, my brothers, if anyone says he has faith, but does not have works?" Notice that James does not say that this man has faith in God. Do not add into this verse what James does not say. James does not say whether this man is a believer or not. He only says that this man says that he has faith. Regardless of whether he has works or not, this man himself should not say that he has faith. If you actually have faith before God, there is no need to talk about it. Paul says that he who believes is justified. He never says that he who says that he has faith is justified. Certainly one is not justified just by saying so. I do not know what the man mentioned here is like. I do not know if he has faith or not. James does not say that he actually has faith. What we do see, however, is a boastful man. He may or may not have something within him. But whether or not he has something, he likes to make a show before others. He likes to print *faith* on his name card and show others that he has faith. Hence, James says, "My brothers, if anyone says he has faith but does not have works? Can that faith save him?" If you saw a man who is not concerned about his behavior at all, who is free to do anything, but says that he believes in Jesus, you would say the same thing as James does. You also would ask what profit it is if anyone says he has faith but does not have works. Perhaps he was fighting or arguing with someone outside a minute ago, and now he says that he has faith. If such a one had not said anything about having faith, James would not have said anything to him. The reason James says anything at all is that some do not have the works but still brag. Have you ever met such people? Such ones like to boast. They like to be exalted and glorified. Not only did James have to subdue this kind of person; we also have to subdue this kind of person.

Hence, James is not talking about having faith or not having faith. Nor is he talking about works for those who have faith. James is specifically talking about works for those who say that they have faith. He is not dealing with the works of Christians, but with the works of those who say that they are Christians. He is dealing with the works of nominal church members and nominal Christians who say that they have faith. James 2 says "if anyone." It does not say "if any Christian."

Verse 14 goes on to say, "Can that faith save him?" What is "that faith"? If faith cannot save him, then what can? James refers to "*that* faith," not simply "faith." If faith cannot save us, we do not need to preach anymore. But James refers to "*that* faith," that is, the faith that some have on their lips. Do not change around what James is saying. He is not talking about faith saving this man. He is talking about that kind of faith saving him, that is, the kind of faith that one has on his lips only. I do not know if you have ever met such people. I have met such people. They say that they are Christians, that they believe in this and that, and that their faith is this and that. Can *this* faith save them?

## FAITH WITHOUT WORKS BEING DEAD

In verses 15-16 James gives an illustration. "If a brother or sister is without clothing and lacks daily food, and any one of you says to them...." This is the man who says that he has faith. He tells the brothers and sisters in lack, "Go in peace! May the Lord bless you. May you be clothed warmly and fed bountifully." If you asked such a one why he tells others to go in peace and why he wishes others to be warm and fed, he would tell you that it is because he has faith. He would say that he believes that these ones will be clothed warmly and fed bountifully when they go home. He would say that he believes they can go home in peace. James is talking about the kind of faith that believes in empty stomachs being automatically filled and in naked bodies being automatically clothed.

"Yet you do not give them the necessities of the body, what is the profit?" The purpose of James's illustration is not to expound on justification. Rather, it is to exhort the brothers and sisters to take practical measures. Our love to the brothers and sisters should not be in word only, but in conduct as well. If you see someone lacking clothing and food, you should give him clothing and food. You have to take care of him. This is why James says this. James is against anyone's saying, "Go in peace, for I have believed for you already." James is saying that now is not the time for you to believe; now is the time for you to open up your wallet. For you now, faith is not the issue; the issue is the letting go of your money. If you hold on tenaciously to your wallet and tell others to go in peace, saying that you have faith, what good does this kind of faith do? If you encounter a poor brother or sister and would not give all that you have to help him and care for him, but would only say that you believe for him and that he can go in peace—if that is the kind of faith you exercised when you believed in the Lord Jesus, would such a faith save you? If that is the kind of faith you exercise toward the brothers and sisters and if that is the same kind of faith you have toward your justification, then I question if that kind of faith will justify you. James indicates that if that is the kind of faith you have toward the brothers and sisters, then perhaps that is the kind of faith you have toward the Lord Jesus, too. If the faith that you have toward the brothers and sisters is the same as the faith that you have toward salvation and justification, I question whether that faith can save you. If there is no basis to your believing in warm clothing and bountiful feeding, then there is no basis to your faith in salvation and justification. But if you see a brother in poverty and give him money, clothing, or food, and then believe, then there is basis for your faith.

When God saw you naked, hungry, and poor, did He say, "Be warm and filled. May you never go to hell. May you go to heaven"? If God's faith were like yours, no one would be saved on earth. But what did God do? When God saw us poor, hungry, naked, and dead in sin, He came to accomplish the work of redemption so that we could be saved. Thank the Lord. First, He set forth His work before us; then we received it. Is your faith toward the brothers and sisters a vain faith? If God were vain toward you, everything would be vanity indeed. And if you are vain toward God, your faith is also empty indeed. We know that we are justified and saved and that we have eternal life. Why is this? It is because God is not sitting in the clouds saying, "May everyone in the whole world be saved, and may everyone not go to the lake of fire." Rather, God came down personally from heaven to accomplish His righteousness and to deal with sin on the cross. Because God has done a concrete work, we can have faith today. That is why our faith is trustworthy.

Verse 17 says, "So also faith, if it does not have works, is dead in itself." James does not say that a man is not saved by believing. He does not mean that a man is not justified or does not have eternal life by believing. He means that when you hear such words from this kind of person, you know that his faith is dead. If you were to ask Paul to come here today and comment on this, even he would say that this kind of faith is dead. If one only says that he has faith, but has no outward expression of it, that faith must be dead. For no matter how great one's faith is, others still need clothing and food. They cannot cover their nakedness with the light of heaven. Nor can they eat air to satisfy their hunger. Hence, a faith without works is empty and dead.

## SHOWING FAITH BY WORKS

Verse 18 says, "But someone will say, You have faith, and I have works; show me your faith without the works, and I will show you my faith by my works." If a vain and boastful person keeps on boasting, someone will eventually rise up and say, "You say that you have faith. But where is it? You should be quiet. You have faith, but I have works." Notice that this one does not say that he has works only; he does not say that he is without faith. This is not what a Christian would say. He says, "You have faith, and I have works. I have provided some-one a meal today. I have given someone clothing today. Please show me your faith without works. What good is it if you only talk about these things?" Can you see the meaning in these words? When you read them, you must pay attention to the tone. When you read James, the most important thing is to take note of the tone. If you pay attention to the tone here, you have to admit that this word is spoken to the vain and boastful person. James is speaking here about practice; he is not dealing with justification by faith.

We must take note of the word "show" here. This person says, "Show me," and, "I will show you." Hence, James 2 is not talking about whether or not a man has faith before God. It is not dealing with our faith before God at all; rather, it is dealing with our faith before man. If someone boasts before man that he has faith, you should say to such a one, "Show me your faith without works." James 2 deals with the problem of faith before man. No one can see whether or not you have faith. Others see only if you have works, that is, if you feed others and give others clothes to wear. Do you realize that this requires faith also? Suppose that there is a brother or sister here tonight who lacks clothes or food. If I say to him or her that as long as we believe, we will be clothed and fed, that is not sufficient. James says that we have to feed him and clothe him, and at the same time we should have faith. Do you realize that it takes faith to give to others? This faith comes from two sides. If I do not have much money, perhaps only a few coins in my pocket, and I see someone without food and clothing, I have to exercise faith. I do not need to have faith for others; for them I need works only. But for myself, I need faith. If I do not have faith within me, I will probably not be able to give away these few coins until I have reconsidered and counted them a few more times. I will wonder if I will be able to get back what I would give away. But if I can spontaneously give away the few coins, it must mean that I have faith. Hence, when you see a poor man and give him food and clothing, you must have faith before you can have works. Without works, your faith cannot be manifested. Furthermore, even if you are rich and it does not take much faith for you to give away a little, how do you know that after you have given the money, it would not spoil the receiver and cause him to look to you again the next time to bear his burden? If you do good to others indiscriminately, would it not cause others to look to man continually for help? Many times we do not give something to beggars because we are afraid that doing so would cause them to be beggars forever. Thus, even if you are a rich person, you have to have faith that God can keep a person from developing a bad habit of depending and relying on others. You have to believe that God would not make you bear this person's burden continually. This is a work, but it is a work of faith. It is a work that comes out of faith.

He who makes big promises and speaks empty words appears to have great faith. But actually, he has no faith at all. If you have faith, you should take off your coat and let another put it on. You should invite others to eat your food. If you only talk about faith, you do not have it. Hence, James concluded that this kind of talk is sin. The point here is not that faith is wrong, but that speaking empty words is wrong. Last night we talked about faith. The night before last we also talked about faith. But we have not paid attention to this kind of faith yet. Inasmuch as James was opposed to it, we are opposed to it, too. It is useless to speak empty words.

Verse 19 says, "You believe that God is one. You do well; the demons also believe and shudder." This is a very strong word. You believe that God is one. You do well to believe this. The demons believe this too, but they shudder. Please take note of the word "and." The question today is not whether or not you believe. If you say that you believe, no one can say that you do not. The problem is that even the demons believe. But they do not have peace. The apostles did not write to the demons, saying, "Peace be unto you. May God bless you and the fallen angels with you." Although the demons believe, they shudder. That kind of faith does them no good. Their faith makes them shudder and lose their peace. If you say that you believe, is your believing the kind of believing that the demons have? James's words are very strong and sharp. Undoubtedly, you do believe in God. But the demons believe, too. You say you believe, but at the same time you shudder, fear, and are nervous. Therefore, you are standing on the same ground as the demons. When we read on, we

understand what James is against. James is not against faith
at all. He is against a certain kind of faith. James is not
saying that faith will not justify. He is merely saying that this
certain kind of faith will not justify.

In verse 20 James calls these people by their names. He
calls them what they are. He does not call them brothers and
sisters. He does not call them his beloved, as Paul did; nor
does he call them fathers or little children, as John did.
Rather, he calls them vain men. "But are you willing to know,
O vain man, that faith without its works is useless?" Notice
the words "are you willing" here. That James says this proves
how hard their attitude is. When others speak God's Word to
them and warn them, they still will not believe. Hence, James
asks if they are willing to know that this kind of faith is dead.
It is not that they are unable to know or that they are unable
to be clear. It is not that no one will teach them how to know.
It is simply a matter of their not being willing to know. Suppose I try to speak to a brother, and he looks away. When I try
again, he looks the other way. When I try a third time, he
begins to talk to another brother. I would then say, "Brother,
are you willing to listen or not?" This is what James is saying
here. Are you willing to know that this kind of faith without
works is dead?

When we read the Bible, we have to ask God to show us
the circumstances under which the portion was written.
James calls this kind of people vain men. They put everything
out in the open for others to see and talk about and thus
exhibit themselves. They want to have a share in everything.
They want to speak up wherever they are. James says that
this kind of person must be subdued. O vain man, are you
willing to know that this kind of faith is useless? Because
they will not listen after he has spoken so much to them, he
has to taunt them and shout at them a little.

### THE EXAMPLE OF ABRAHAM'S JUSTIFICATION

In verses 21 through 25, two examples are given. Both are
very meaningful. They show us what justification by faith
really is. Verse 21 says, "Was not Abraham our father justified
by works in that he offered up Isaac his son upon the altar?"

James 2 mentions the case of Abraham. Galatians 3 and Romans 4 also mention the case of Abraham. Paul says that man is justified by faith, not by works, and he uses the case of Abraham as proof. Both Romans 4 and Galatians 3 prove that man is justified by faith rather than by works. James also mentions the case of Abraham, but he uses it to prove that man is justified not only by faith, but by works as well. If he had used other persons, we might not understand this matter. But in mentioning the case of Abraham, we can surely understand what justification by faith really is.

In using the case of Abraham, Paul refers to Genesis 15, whereas James refers to Genesis 22. In Genesis 15 God promised Abraham that his seed would be like the stars in heaven. In Galatians 3, Paul puts strong emphasis on God's promise to Abraham. In the book of Galatians, Paul repeatedly talks about the promise. The word *promise* is used very frequently in the book of Galatians. Paul uplifts the promise in Galatians.

Do you know what a promise is? In the whole world, there is only one way for man to receive a promise, and that is by faith. There is no other way for a man to receive a promise. There is only this one condition. If God says that we must do something and we do it, it is work. But God did not tell Abraham that He would give him something if Abraham did this or that. Rather, God said that He would give him descendants. How did Abraham receive the promise? There was no other way but by faith. Suppose a brother tells his son that if he memorizes a list of vocabulary words tonight, he will receive five pieces of candy tomorrow. If the son is to receive the five pieces of candy, he has to memorize the words. This is work. But if the brother simply promises his son five pieces of candy, what does his son have to do? Will he say, "I have to do this or that before I can get the candy"? The child does not have to do anything. All he has to do is believe that his father will do it for him. In Genesis 15 God did not give Abraham one single thing to do. It is as if God said, "I will do it for you. I will give you descendants." Abraham believed in God, and that was reckoned to him as righteousness (Gen. 15:6). Going back to the example of the brother's son, the child may say, "Will my father really give me five pieces of candy? It does not

seem like such a good thing could ever happen." If he thinks
this way, he does not have faith. Everyone who wants to
understand the book of Galatians must realize that a promise
is without condition and without work. One does not have to
do anything. The Father has done everything. Thank the Lord
that everything that God promises He will accomplish. As
long as God is trustworthy, everything is fine. Even if one
tries to do a work, it will not avail.

In Genesis 15 God promised Abraham that He would give
him many descendants. Abraham had everything. But he did
not have a son. He had cattle, he had sheep, and he had tents.
But he did not have a son. However, Abraham believed God.
He believed that God would give him a son. He merely
believed God. He did not do any work. In chapter twenty-two,
after God had given him a son, He said to Abraham, "Take
now thy son, thine only son Isaac, whom thou lovest, and get
thee into the land of Moriah; and offer him there for a burnt
offering upon one of the mountains which I will tell thee of"
(v. 2). Then Abraham got up early in the morning and took his
son to Mount Moriah. He laid the wood for the burnt offering
on his son Isaac's back, and Isaac bore the wood for the burnt
offering, in the same way that the Lord Jesus bore the cross.
When they reached the mountain, Abraham built an altar,
laid his son on the altar, and was about to kill him. This is the
incident that James recounts when he refers to Abraham's
justification. In Genesis 15 God's justification of Abraham
was related to his son. And in Genesis 22 God's justification
of him was also related to his son.

In Genesis 15 Abraham had no son. But he believed in his
heart that if God said He would give him a son, he would
surely have a son. In chapter twenty-two he did have a son,
but God wanted him to offer up this son. If Abraham had not
had faith, he would have said, "God, You told me that You
would give me many descendants. Now if I kill my son, will I
not lose them all? It is not that I am unwilling to do this; I
just want to see Your promise fulfilled. It is not that I dare
not do it; I just want to preserve Your faithfulness." Do you
think that Abraham's offering of Isaac was a work or an act of
faith? What good work is it to kill one's son? What is there to

praise about in killing one's own son? That Abraham raised the knife to offer up his son shows that he still believed the promise of chapter fifteen. God had promised to give him many descendants, and to this end He had given him one son. Now if God wanted him to kill this son, it must be that God would raise him up from the dead. This is what Abraham had in mind when he was about to kill his son. His willingness to kill his son shows that he believed that Isaac would be raised from the dead. The faith in Genesis 15 is a faith in Him who calls things not being into being, while the faith in Genesis 22 is a faith in Him who raises people from the dead (Rom. 4:17). In both instances, what Abraham did was not something of work, but of faith. Abraham's act proved that he had faith. This does not mean that Abraham could be justified by killing his son. It means that in pulling out his knife, he proved that he had faith. The proof of Abraham's faith lies in his willingness to offer up his son.

Hence, James did not say that one cannot be justified by faith. Paul says strongly that justification is not by works, but James could not strongly say that justification is not by faith. If the two contradict each other, we would expect one to say, "Justification is of faith, not of works," and the other to say, "Justification is of works, not of faith." But James does not say this. We must not say what James has not said. James does not say that we should not have faith; he says that one should *prove* his faith with his work. Paul is the one who talks about the principle, so he can boldly declare that justification is of faith and not of works. James is a man of practice. Thus, he says that one must not have faith *only,* but should have works as well. Only when there are works can a man prove that his faith is genuine. Let us read James 2:21 again: "Was not Abraham our father justified by works in that he offered up Isaac his son upon the altar?" His offering up of his son was a work, and it was this work that proved that he had faith.

Verse 22 says, "You see that faith worked together with his works." Paul is bold to say that one can have faith alone, without works. But James does not dare to say that one should have works alone, without faith. He indicates that the faith in

Genesis 15 and the work in Genesis 22 go hand in hand. Then he adds another clause. He does not say that justification comes through faith plus work. Rather, he says, "And by these works faith was perfected." In Genesis 15 we see that because Abraham had faith, he was justified before God. In Genesis 22 we see that because Abraham had works, he was justified before men. Abraham's justification was perfected by his work in Genesis 22. The offering up of Isaac in Genesis 22 manifested the faith in Genesis 15, and the faith in Genesis 15 was perfected by the work in Genesis 22.

In verse 23 our brother James also quotes from Genesis 15. In Romans 4 Paul quotes from Genesis 15 to prove that one needs faith only, not works. Now our brother James quotes the same word that Paul does: "And the Scripture was fulfilled which says, 'And Abraham believed God, and it was accounted to him as righteousness.'" In James the word *it* refers to the act on the mount in Genesis 22. Abraham's offering of Isaac in Genesis 22 was an offering of faith. It was a work that manifested his faith. It was a fulfillment of the words in Genesis 15 that say that Abraham believed God and it was counted to him for righteousness. In Genesis 15 God justified Abraham due to his faith. Abraham's work in Genesis 22 fulfilled God's promise in Genesis 15. Hence, we cannot say that faith alone does not save and that there is the need of works as well. The condition for salvation is faith, not works. But if there is faith, then spontaneously there will be a change in works.

Suppose there is a man whose occupation is to make paper money to be burned to idols. One day he hears the gospel and believes. But after he believes, he continues to make paper money. Is this wrong? He realizes within that the paper money is for idol worship and that a Christian cannot do such work. If you ask whether or not he believes in the Lord Jesus, he would say yes. But if he gives up his paper money business, how will he support himself? He confesses that he is a Christian, but we cannot say with certainty that he is saved. We do not know if he has been saved before God, if he has faith or not. If we see a person who believes that the Lord Jesus is the Son of God and that He was crucified for him, and believes in the gospel of God fully, yet will not give up such a business for fear that he would lose his livelihood, we have no way to tell if he is actually saved. Perhaps he has faith before God. Though the seed has been sown, the sprout has not yet come out. We can only know with certainty after the leaves come out. I do not say that he is not saved. I say only that we are not certain whether he is saved or not. Here lies the difference. There is no question about being saved by faith. But if no work issues from faith, others will not know about that faith. This is absolutely not a matter of good or bad behavior. Please note this carefully. James 2 is absolutely not on good or bad behavior. The emphasis in James 2 is on the works that prove one's faith. James 2 does not tell us to focus our attention on good works or bad works. What it emphasizes are the works that issue from faith. Many people are very good in their works. But these works do not manifest their faith. These are works without faith; these are not what James was concerned with.

Verse 24 is very good: "A man is justified by works and not by faith only." See how careful James is? He says man is justified by works and not by faith alone. Paul is able to say that man is justified by faith and not by works at all. But James never says that man is justified by works alone and not by faith at all. If he were to say that, we would have to conclude that the two apostles have divergent views on doctrine. James says that man is justified by works. But following that he adds another word, that it is not by faith alone. When one has works, it proves that he has faith. This does not mean that one should have good works only, but that one should have works of faith.

## THE EXAMPLE OF RAHAB'S JUSTIFICATION

James was afraid that we would not be clear about the case of Abraham, so in verse 25 we see another illustration. He mentions the case of a prostitute. Rahab was not an honorable woman. There was nothing of merit in her works. Therefore, we see that justification is not a matter of good works, but of works of faith. I have repeated this a few times already. At issue is works of faith, not works of morality. "And

in like manner was not also Rahab the harlot justified by
works in that she received the messengers and sent them out
by a different way?" What kind of good works is this? The
Israelites were crossing the Jordan River to attack Jericho. If
Rahab had been even slightly patriotic, she would have
handed over the two spies. But when the king of Jericho sent
men to look for them, Rahab hid them upstairs. Later she let
them get away. James tells us that this woman's work justified her. What work did she have? Her work was to lie. The
men were obviously there, but she said that they were not. Is
lying a good work? Every Christian knows that lying is not
good. Yet Rahab was justified by her work of lying. If some
say that this is justification by works, it is something that
they themselves are saying; it is not what James is saying.
They are merely saying in the name of James what they want
to say. But what does James himself say? He says that when
Rahab let the two men who spied out Jericho get away, it was
reckoned to her as righteousness.

What does James mean? When the Israelites left Egypt
and went into the wilderness, they could not settle down anywhere, but had to wander for forty years. What good is such a
nation? At least there was a wall around Rahab's Jericho. All
that the Israelites had was sand under their feet. At least
there were houses in Jericho. All that the Israelites had were
tents. Even their God had to dwell in a tent. What was so special about such a nation? However, when the two spies came
and told her how God had cared for them, performed miracles
for them, and had promised that Jericho, and even the whole
land of Canaan, would be delivered to them, their words
caused Rahab to believe. She put her own future, her life, and
even her whole family in their trust. She was even willing to
do something against her own country. God does not say that
this was a good work; He says that this work was the expression of her faith. If the walls of Jericho had been made of
straw or chicken feathers, we might think that the walls
could have indeed fallen. But the walls of Jericho were as
high as heaven. Its gates were fortified with brass bars. How
could it have been taken easily? How could Rahab have committed herself to the two spies? This was a work out of faith,

and God says that what justifies a person is this kind of work. It is not a question of good or bad. To have good works is not the issue at all. To have bad works is neither the issue. The flesh is absolutely useless before God. It has no place at all. Every work in Adam, whether good or bad, is rejected by God. If a man tells others that only good works save, such a person does not know what the flesh is. Hence, it is not an issue of works. Good works cannot justify. Neither can bad works.

Hence, James 2 is on works of faith. It is not on anything else. Rahab was there risking her life. If the men sent by the king of Jericho had found the spies in her house, immediately she would have lost her life. But her hope was to be saved through the spies of Israel. She committed her own life and future into their hands. Hence, at issue is not good works or bad works, but having faith or not having faith. It is faith that justifies. Although James says that Rahab was justified by works, her works were but a manifestation of her faith.

Finally, verse 26 says, "For just as the body without the spirit is dead, so also faith without works is dead." Our spirit resides inside our body. Hence, we can say that our spirit is the spirit of our body. We say that evil spirits are spirits that have left their body, for they are without a body. There is a kind of work that requires faith and must be linked to faith. There is a kind of work that comes out from faith and that issues from faith. If faith is without works, it is dead in the same way that a body without a spirit is dead. Hence, we are saved through faith, we are justified through faith, and we also receive life through faith. Although there are many different ways to express faith, the source is still faith. Some express it by forsaking their profession. Others express it by not following in the footsteps of their parents. Still others express it by not going along with their husband in certain things or by forsaking their position. There are all kinds of expressions of faith. The question is not good or bad works, but faith. What James is saying is that when the opportunity arises, our faith should be expressed.

Hence, we cannot say that salvation is of works. Hebrews

6:1 mentions the word of the beginning of the Christ. The foundation of the word of Christ is repentance from dead works. What is repentance from dead works? It is repentance from what we have done when we were dead. In the Bible, there are two things that we have to repent for. One is sin. The other is dead works. Everything that is wrong morally is a sin and a transgression. If a man believes in the Lord, he must surely repent and deal with these sins. Furthermore, we must also hate and repent for what we did as dead persons. What are these dead works? They are all the good works that we were able to do by ourselves before we were saved, before we became the children of God, before we received the new life, and before we became a new race. One sees his sins and transgressions for what they are. But one does not see the things that he considers moral and noble as things to be repented of. God says that these are dead works. They were performed when we were dead. We must repent for all these works, not depending on them for salvation.

When we are saved, there are two great repentances. One is repentance for all the things that should not have been done. But when someone understands the gospel and sees the complete work of the cross of the Son of God, he repents for the other things also, which are all the good works that he has formerly done. Formerly, we tried our best to do good, as if God would save us if He were only impressed enough by our good works. Today, however, we have become Christians. We must not only repent for our sins; we have to repent for our dead works as well. Hence, dead works cannot help us to be saved. You may say that one should believe in the Lord Jesus, but one should also have good works. But God sees you as a torn rag. The righteousness that God gives us far exceeds the righteousness of the law. Hence, if we want to come to God, not only must we not bring our sins along, we also must not bring our works along. If we wish to talk about works, then our works must be as perfect as Christ's are before God, before they can be acceptable.

My friends, you must see that salvation is not of yourselves. You must realize from your heart that everything is of the Lord Jesus. Faith is not a virtue. Faith is just receiving.

One of our gospel hymns says, "Working will not save me" and "Weeping will not save me" (#1000 in *Hymns,* published by Living Stream Ministry). The last stanza says, "Faith in Christ will save me." When I first saw this line, immediately I crossed it out and replaced it with "Jesus alone will save me." Faith is not a virtue. Faith is just to allow the Lord to save us. It is like a person who falls into the sea. When someone comes to save him by throwing him a net, he does not have to do anything. As long as he does not jump out of the net, he will be fine. Everything is done by the Lord Jesus. Hallelujah! I say again, never misunderstand James 2. Work in James 2 is not a question of being good or bad, but of having or not having faith.

# CHAPTER ELEVEN

# THE WAY OF SALVATION—
# FAITH VERSUS REPENTANCE

In the past two messages, we have seen that the way of salvation on man's side is through faith, rather than the law or works. We have seen that salvation is by faith alone. It is not by faith with the law, nor is it by faith with works (Eph. 2:8-9). However, besides the law and works, man still tries to use other ways to obtain God's salvation. Although we cannot cover these ways in detail, we hope that we can enumerate all of them in the coming two messages. Besides the law and works, repentance also is often considered by man as a very important condition. Man thinks that if he does not repent, he will not be saved. Those who are acquainted with the Bible dare not say that repentance is the only condition for salvation, but they would say that a man is saved by faith with repentance, or through repenting and believing. I admit that the subject of repentance is not easy to understand in the New Testament. But if one would consider the Word of God itself, he would understand the real meaning of repentance and would find out quickly if repentance is a condition for salvation.

## THE THREE BOOKS ON SALVATION IN THE BIBLE
## NOT LISTING REPENTANCE
## AS THE CONDITION FOR SALVATION

Before we talk about the meaning of repentance in the Bible and its relationship with faith and salvation, we should first clarify a few things concerning repentance. After that, we will consider what the Bible says about repentance. In the entire Bible, there is only one book that tells us how we receive eternal life. This book is the Gospel of John. From the very beginning to the very end of the Gospel of John, we cannot find a single occurrence of the word *repentance*. The word *repentance* never occurs in this book at all. This book tells us how we can have eternal life (3:15, 16b, 36), but nothing is mentioned about repentance. It mentions repeatedly that man receives eternal life through faith. When a man believes, he has eternal life. It never mentions repentance. Not only does it not mention repentance directly, it does not mention repentance even indirectly or metaphorically. This is a fact that we have to remember.

Second, there are two books which tell us how man is justified before God. They are Romans and Galatians. The book of Romans does mention repentance, but it never makes repentance a condition for salvation. Neither of these books has ever made repentance a condition for salvation and promise. Hence, we have to remember that of the three books in the Bible that deal specifically with salvation, eternal life, and justification, not once is repentance mentioned as a condition for salvation. In all three books, faith is mentioned every time as the only condition. This shows us clearly that man is saved by faith and not by works.

### MAN EMPHASIZING REPENTANCE
### THROUGH A MIND FILLED WITH
### THE LAW AND WORKS

Why does man pay so much attention to repentance? This is because man's mind has the poison of the law and works remaining in it. Salvation is free, but because man's mind is full of the law and works, he never considers that God would give salvation to him freely. He never thinks that God would freely bear man's burden. He always thinks that he has to do something good before he can be saved. Whether it is the keeping of the law, the performing of good works, or the need for repentance, man always thinks that he has to do something. It seems as if man is never willing to be an unconditional beneficiary. He never wants to stand in a position of receiving. Although he realizes that it is impossible to do everything, he thinks that he must at least do something. It is precisely this doing that has twisted the biblical meaning of repentance. It turns repentance into *our* repentance.

Please remember that the repentance mentioned in the Bible and the repentance that we talk about are two different things. What is repentance according to man's mind? According to the human concept, repentance is improvement. According to his mind, repentance is not something for the past, but is something to deal with the present and the future. Formerly, I was sinful, fallen, degraded, and weak. Now I want to be saved. Hence, I have to improve myself from today on and make myself look better.

The Chinese word for repentance is *hwe-gai. Hwe* means to feel sorry, and *gai* means to change. Some have invented a new doctrine, unknown to the New Testament, based on this Chinese word, saying that some people only *hwe* but do not *gai.* Hence, they say that it is not enough just to feel sorry; there must also be a change. Why does man pay so much attention to change? It is because man's thought is full of works. This is why he emphasizes works so much. He says that since everything he did before was wrong, he must no longer be wrong. He realizes that he was bad and that he was a sinner, but now, he should not be bad and should no longer be a sinner. Formerly he sinned, and before God he was clothed in rags; he had squandered all of his Father's possessions. How then can he be accepted when he returns home? Surely he has to do business, and make some money. Surely he should have on the best robe and a pair of shoes before he can return home. Man's thought is that he needs a certain degree of improvement before he can return home. If his clothes are not proper and he looks the same as before, perhaps the Father would not accept him. If he would improve somewhat, although there is still no assurance whether the Father would accept him, at least there is a better and greater chance. Man never considers that it is possible to go to God and receive salvation in his present condition. He always wants to improve himself. He admits that he cannot be perfect in his conduct. But he thinks that he still has to have something and trust in the Lord for the rest. To him, it is like gambling; he has to place a bet before he can gamble. This bet which he places is the repentance that man talks about.

## REPENTANCE IN MAN'S MIND
## DIFFERENT FROM REPENTANCE IN THE BIBLE

The repentance that man talks about simply speaks of one thing: he is not willing to lower himself to the bottom rung. He thinks that he should be at least one rung higher before God would grant him salvation. This is repentance according to man's mind. It is not the repentance in the Bible. I am not saying that there is no doctrine of repentance in the Bible. There is the doctrine of repentance in the Bible. The Bible even demands that man should repent. But the repentance that the Bible talks about is different from the repentance that we talk about today. What then is the repentance that the Bible talks about? Let us now look at it.

First, the meaning of the word *repentance* in Greek is a turning of the mind. The mind is the thinking organ within man. Hence, repentance as taught in the Bible is not a change in conduct, but a change in mind. The word *repentance* just means a change in one's thoughts and has nothing to do with works. It does not have any connotation of a change in conduct. This is as far as the meaning of the word goes.

Second, in the New Testament, repentance is always used in reference to our past. It concerns what we have done in the past, what we have thought and said, and what we were as persons in the past. Formerly, we had certain kinds of concepts and certain views which we considered good and glorious. Now, through the enlightening of God, our mind has a great turn. It is not a turn with a view to future conduct, but a change from things of the past. We change our view and evaluation concerning many things. Originally, we thought that it was a glory and a joy to deceive others and that the one who was deceived was such a fool because he was ignorant of being cheated. One might delight and glory in this. But what he once considered glorious, now he considers shameful. Repentance is not for the good of tomorrow, but for the wrong of yesterday. Repentance is not saying what one should do in the future; it is a reevaluation in the mind, a changed view, and a different judgment concerning the things of the past.

In Luke 13:3 the Lord Jesus told the Jews that if they did not repent of what they did, they would die like the Galileans did. Hence, repentance is to take a different view than before. It is to see things in God's light, a light that is from above.

Let us go on. In Acts we see the word *repentance* used many times. Acts 8:22 says, "Repent therefore from this wickedness of yours and beseech the Lord if perhaps the intent of your heart may be forgiven you." Simon was trying to buy the gift of the Holy Spirit with money, and Peter replied with a very strong word. He told Simon that he had to repent of his wickedness. This does not mean that Simon should do better in the future. It means that Simon should repent of what he has just done, what he has just said, and what his thoughts have been. Repentance is to deal with one's problems of the past. It means that there were great mistakes in what we did and that we should now have a different view. Formerly, the thought was to spend a little money to buy the Holy Spirit. Now, this is seen as a sin. What should be done? There is now the need for a new view and a renewed evaluation. This is repentance. By this we receive forgiveness.

The word *repentance* appears frequently in Revelation 2 and 3 in a particular way. There, the Lord was dealing with the works of the past. He was calling for men to have a different view concerning their past works. Revelation 2:5 says, "Remember therefore where you have fallen from and repent and do the first works; but if not, I am coming to you and will remove your lampstand out of its place, unless you repent." The Lord said this because they had left their first love. They did not do the first works. They had to remember from whence they had fallen. This is repentance. After this, they have to do the first works which are something of the future. One has to repent of what he did in the past. The works in the future are a different matter altogether.

Verse 16 says, "Repent therefore; but if not, I am coming to you quickly, and I will make war with them with the sword of My mouth." The Lord was speaking here to the church in Pergamos. Some had followed the teaching of the Nicolaitans. They considered this teaching to be good. That is why the Lord said that they needed to repent. They needed to consider that the work of the Nicolaitans was evil. They needed to change their view and their concepts.

Verse 21 says, "And I gave her time that she might repent, and she is not willing to repent of her fornication." She had committed fornication, but she would not consider that as wrong. She would not judge that as improper. Verse 22 says, "Behold, I cast her into a bed, and those who commit adultery with her, into great tribulation, unless they repent of her works." This again shows us that they needed to repent of their past deeds. If they did not repent, the Lord would cast them into great tribulation.

Revelation 3:3 says, "Remember therefore how you have received and heard, and keep it and repent." Here, the Lord is again calling them to repent, that is, to change their view concerning their behavior.

Verse 19 says, "As many as I love I rebuke and discipline; be zealous therefore and repent."

After seeing how the word is used in Luke, Acts, and Revelation, we can now understand what repentance really means in the Bible. Repentance is a change of mind. But it is always used in reference to the deeds of the past and is never used in reference to conduct in the future. Repentance is a change in one's own mind, but what it deals with is in respect to the failures, the sins, the mistakes, the lack of zeal, and the ungodliness of the past. This means that we now see all these as wrong and improper. This is the meaning of repentance. We may say that faith is our looking up to Christ, and repentance is our looking at ourselves in the light of Christ. While we are still sinners, the Holy Spirit shines into us and shows us ourselves. This is repentance. This is most necessary and is indispensable. Without the enlightening of the Holy Spirit and the realization of ourselves, we cannot lift our eyes to the Lord Jesus.

The work of repentance is similar to the work of the law that we have discussed in the last few messages. God's purpose is that man would receive His grace. But man has sinned. He has no light concerning himself. He does not know what kind of person he is. He does not know that he is condemned before God, that he is absolutely useless, and that he is, therefore, unable to receive God's grace. Let us suppose that you are very sick, and your two lungs are completely diseased. You may say that you still have a fair complexion and that there is color in your face. You may not think that some good medicine or a good doctor is necessary. Now suppose you go to have an x-ray. After you see the result of your own x-ray, you will admit that you are a sick man and that you need rest and treatment. Hence, repentance is God's goal in giving the law. Through repentance, we see by the enlightening of God, the shining of the Holy Spirit, and God's Word, that our past deeds were all wrong and that our lifestyle was improper. God has diagnosed our illness, and we have to admit that we are wrong. This is repentance.

There was a brother who always carried others' heavy luggage when he traveled together with them. He volunteered because he thought that others were not healthy, but that he was in good health. Once, after he had completed a heavy task, I suggested that he should go to the hospital and have an x-ray taken. At the beginning he refused. We argued that it would do him no harm, even if he was not sick. So, he went. He found out that he had tuberculosis. From that point on, his behavior completely changed. He dared not do anything anymore. When we asked him to do anything, he would do his best to decline. His change was so drastic that it was as if he were two different persons on the same day. At one moment he thought that he was so healthy and had such good lungs. At another moment his evaluation of himself changed completely. He had a different view and a different evaluation of himself. This is called repentance. Repentance is necessary. It is the goal which God wants to attain through the law.

If we misunderstand repentance to think that it is a change of our future behavior, we are absolutely ignorant of God's salvation. God's salvation never attempts to improve the Adamic nature. If repentance referred to the future, it would mean that old Adam and the fleshly man still have the possibility of improvement and advancement. But the Lord Jesus said, "That which is born of the flesh is flesh" (John 3:6). The flesh will never advance to become the spirit. Only that which is begotten of the Spirit is spirit. If repentance refers to the future, then the foundation of God's salvation is completely torn down. Not only are we not able to improve ourselves, on the contrary, we need to be removed. God's salvation leaves no room for the fleshly man. It removes the man completely. When the Lord Jesus was crucified, all men were crucified with Him. Our old man has been crucified on the cross.

Thank God that the Lord Jesus is a tailor who *makes* clothes. He is not a mender who mends clothes. It is not that our clothing is torn and the Lord Jesus comes to mend it for us. The Lord Jesus only makes new clothes; He does not mend old clothes. Perhaps we are poor, and we are willing to wear old clothes. But in the house of God, no one wears a mended garment. There is no such thing in God's salvation. God said that the first Adam is finished and that all behavior in the first Adam is also finished. Now, we are in the last Adam. Today everything has been accomplished by the Lord Jesus; He wants to be the new life within us. Therefore, repentance in the Bible does not refer to future behavior. Rather, it refers to a change in concept concerning our past. Biblical repentance is a view concerning past deeds rather than future behavior.

## REPENTANCE BEING NECESSARY IN RECEIVING GOD'S SALVATION

When a farmer plants seed, can he sow it on a field without doing anything first to the ground? Wheat grows very easily. Even for us to grow wheat, we have to plow the field and till the soil first. In the same way, there must first be the tilling work in God's salvation before the plants will grow in a deep way. Hence, those who never feel that they have sinned will not be saved, and neither will those who never feel that they are wrong. Perhaps after such a one hears the full gospel as we are preaching now, he would become clear concerning God's work in Christ and would gladly receive the gospel. I dare not say that he has no repentance. Perhaps he has repentance. But the repentance is not deep. There is not much operation of the Holy Spirit in him. He does not see that he is a weak, filthy, and useless sinner before God. Such a one has to go through the experience of Romans 7 in his later years. What is the experience of Romans 7? It is the make-up lesson for a Christian who has not repented. If a man has passed through repentance when he comes to God, there is no need for the experience of Romans 7. If a man has not repented, and does not know that he is desolate before God, but receives the full gospel readily when he hears it, in his future experience, God still has to show him his desolation. It is necessary for one to know himself, either from the beginning or somewhere along the way. God never allows a Christian not to know himself.

Hence, we can see the true meaning of repentance according to the Bible. It is a new concept of one's past. Repentance sees oneself, in the same way that faith sees the Lord Jesus. When one believes, he sees the work that the Lord Jesus has done for him. When he repents, he sees the deeds that he himself has done in the past. To see what one has done in the past is repentance; to see what the Lord Jesus has done on the cross is faith. If we want to see what the Lord Jesus has done for us, we must first see what we have done ourselves. Unless the thief who was crucified next to Jesus had said clearly with his own mouth that what he was suffering was what he deserved, he could not have said to the One crucified next to him, "Remember me when You come into Your kingdom" (Luke 23:42). If he were to curse the magistrates as agents of the imperialists, and if he had not seen that what he suffered was what he deserved, he would not have seen who the Lord was. When we do not see ourselves, we do not see the Lord. When we see ourselves, we see the Lord. This is repentance.

Hence, we can see that repentance does not carry any element of our self, our work, or our behavior. Many people say that I do not believe in repentance. That is not true. I believe in repentance with my whole heart. But I believe in the biblical repentance. I do not believe in the mental repentance that some have had. If it is a repentance according to the Bible, I will gladly believe, for it is real. It gives us a new view and a new perception. Only in this way can we receive the Lord by faith in the presence of God.

## THE PLACE OF REPENTANCE
## BEING IN FAITH AND SALVATION

How then is man saved? The Gospel of John tells us clearly that it is by faith. The books of Romans and Galatians also tell us clearly that it is by faith. Galatians tells us that it is only by faith. In the whole New Testament, there are only these three books that deal with the question of salvation. All three books tell us that salvation is by faith only and is not of the law. Repentance does not come into consideration. What place then does repentance hold? If we read the Bible, we will find out that repentance is never detached from faith. Repentance is never separated from faith. This does not mean that one is saved by faith *and* repentance. Repentance is included in faith and is included in salvation already. When a man believes in the Lord Jesus, the element of repentance is included there already. If one says that he is saved, then his salvation includes repentance. Repentance is never detached from faith. It is always included in salvation.

Now, let us consider if repentance is a condition. In the New Testament, by the time of the book of Acts, the Holy Spirit had come and the full gospel was preached. The book of Acts seems to show us that repentance is a condition for salvation. Many have misunderstood the matter because they have not seen the place of repentance. No doubt, the Old Testament speaks of the teaching of repentance also. Jonah preached to the men of Nineveh that unless they repented, God would destroy them (Jonah 1:1-2). They repented, put on sackcloth, sat in ashes, and fasted. This was for their past deeds. The putting on of the sackcloth and the sitting in ashes were not for future behavior. If they were for future acts, what did sackcloth and ashes have to do with it? Repentance is to feel sorry for and to condemn one's past behavior. One puts on sackcloth and sits in ashes because he realizes that he is wrong before God. Formerly, he thought he was living. Now, he knows that he was dead. Hence, he mourns for his past wrongdoings. This is repentance. This was what Jonah preached. Before the gospel of the Lord Jesus came, we did not see salvation by faith. What we had then was only repentance for past deeds.

Later, John the Baptist came. He did not preach faith. He only preached repentance, that is, a repentance for past actions and past wrongdoings. In Matthew 3:8, he said one very good thing: "Produce then fruit worthy of your repentance." He also said that "he who has two tunics, let him share with the one who has none; and he who has food, let him do likewise" (Luke 3:11). We have to realize that this is not repentance. Rather, this is the fruit of repentance. Repentance is for the past, and the fruit of repentance is for the future. At John's time, the complete gospel was not yet preached, and the light of the truth was not fully revealed. In order to lead men to God, he had to bring them to a different view of the past.

Following this, the Lord Jesus Himself came. The Gospel of John is different from the other three Gospels. The first three Gospels talk about what the Lord Jesus did in time. The Gospel of John talks about what He does in eternity. Every reader of the Bible knows that the Gospel of John does not talk about things in time. Rather, it talks about things of eternity. It begins with "the beginning" and ends with the receiving of eternal life (1:1; 20:22). The first of the three books speaks of the Son of David, the Son of Abraham (Matt. 1:1). It shows us the Christ in time. John tells us about the Christ in eternity (3:13). The first three books are transitional. Hence, they talk about repentance. But why did the Lord talk about repentance also (Matt. 4:17)? It was because the kingdom of the heavens had drawn near. Because the kingdom has drawn near, we have to repent. But in the Gospel of John, after the full gospel has been preached, there is no more mention of repentance. In Acts, some verses also say that salvation must be by faith. Acts 16:31 says, "Believe on the Lord Jesus, and you shall be saved, you and your household." However, in a few places in Acts, repentance is mentioned by itself; there is no mention of faith. This is why some believers misunderstand repentance as a condition for salvation.

## THE TRUE MEANING OF REPENTANCE

Let us study a few passages to see what repentance is. Acts 2:37-38 says, "And when they heard this, they were pricked in their heart, and they said to Peter and the rest of the apostles, What should we do, brothers? And Peter said to them, Repent and each one of you be baptized upon the name of Jesus Christ for the forgiveness of your sins, and you will receive the gift of the Holy Spirit." When some read these verses, they may say that faith is not even mentioned. All that is mentioned is to repent, to be baptized upon the name of Jesus Christ for the forgiveness of sins, and to receive the promised Spirit. Faith is not mentioned at all; instead, only repentance is mentioned. But this was not what was spoken prior to this. The apostle did not begin with repentance, baptism, forgiveness of sins, and the receiving of the Holy Spirit. This was not the day of Pentecost. It was not the first word that Peter preached. It was the last word Peter spoke after he gave his message. Prior to this, Peter had said, "Men of Israel, hear these words: Jesus the Nazarene, a man shown by God to you to be approved by works of power and wonders and signs, which God did through Him in your midst, even as you yourselves know—this man...you, through the hand of lawless men, nailed to a cross and killed; whom God has raised up" (vv. 22-24). Peter was saying, "This is our testimony. God has even exalted Him to the heavens and has made Him Lord and Christ. This is the testimony of the Holy Spirit. God has sent us, the apostles, to testify to the resurrection of Jesus of Nazareth. The Holy Spirit has been poured out, giving the one hundred and twenty the gift of tongues. This is the testimony of the Holy Spirit, testifying that the Lord Jesus has been glorified." There are two testimonies here. The apostles testify of resurrection, while the Holy Spirit testifies of glorification. The apostle Peter preached to them the word of God and showed them what they had done to the Lord Jesus and what God had done to Him. Verse 36 says, "Therefore let all the house of Israel know assuredly that God has made Him both Lord and Christ, this Jesus whom you have crucified." The word of God had been preached, and the apostles had shown them what God had done and what they had done.

Please remember that slightly more than a month before Pentecost, the same group of people were shouting, "Take

Him away! Take Him away! Crucify Him!" (John 19:15). They were instrumental in His murder and crucifixion. Formerly, they considered the Lord Jesus as worthy of death; they shouted to crucify Him and to release Barabbas instead (Luke 23:18). What had happened? Acts 2:37 says, "When they heard this, they were pricked in their heart, and they said to Peter and the rest of the apostles, What should we do, brothers?" This is to believe in the word of God. The word of God was preached, and they received it. They realized that what God had done to the Lord Jesus was very different from what men had done to Him. Moreover, the Holy Spirit was also there testifying. They could not refuse that testimony. Hence, they spoke this pleading word, asking what they should do now that they had crucified the Lord Jesus. If they had not crucified the Lord, there would still be the chance of restitution. But once the Lord Jesus was crucified, what should they do? They accepted the apostle's testimony. As a result, the apostle told them that they had to repent. They had to repent because of their concepts and view concerning the Lord Jesus. In addition, they had to be baptized upon the name of Jesus Christ. To be baptized is to receive Him, to believe in Him, and to confess Him. The meaning of being in the Lord's name is to believe in the Lord. When they do this, their sins will be forgiven, and they will receive the gift of the Holy Spirit.

We can now realize that this is a group of people who had received the word of God. Since they had believed that much already, the apostle was able to tell them to repent. This did not touch their behavior, but their view. The apostle was not saying that if they did not change their former conduct, they could not be saved. This is absolutely not a matter of dealing with a person's conduct. What they had to do was judge themselves and be baptized upon the name of the Lord Jesus as an expression of their faith in Him. In this way, their sins would be forgiven, and the Holy Spirit would be received by them. Hence, the condition for our salvation is faith alone. Salvation is given to us freely. We need not do anything to come to God. It is God Himself who has come to save us because of His Son Jesus Christ.

Acts 3:19-20 says, "Repent therefore and turn, that your sins may be wiped away, so that seasons of refreshing may come from the presence of the Lord." When we read this verse, we may think that repentance is a condition for salvation. It is true that verse 19 seems to indicate that repentance is a condition of salvation. But we must pay attention to the whole passage from verse 1 on. We cannot read verse 19 alone. It would be wrong for us to start from verse 19 and explain it according to our thought. From verse 1 on, we find the story of a lame man being healed. When this lame man looked at Peter, Peter said to him, "Silver and gold I do not possess, but what I have, this I give to you: In the name of Jesus Christ the Nazarene rise up and walk" (v. 6). When all the people saw a man who was born lame begin to walk, they marveled. Peter then stood up to give a message. First, he explained that this was not his work, and it was not through his godliness that such a person was made to walk. In verses 15-20 he said, "And the Author of life you killed, whom God has raised from the dead, of which we are witnesses. And upon faith in His name, His name has made this man strong....Repent therefore and turn, that your sins may be wiped away, so that seasons of refreshing may come from the presence of the Lord." What was he saying? He was talking about faith. He was saying that we believe in His being raised from the dead, that we believe in His name, and that His name had made the man strong. Here was a lame man that everyone knew. It was faith from the Lord that had made this man whole. If we want to believe, just as they had believed, we have to repent. If we want faith, we have to pay attention to repentance. If we want to receive Him, we must have a new view and a new evaluation concerning Him. We must have this qualification.

I mentioned earlier that repentance can never be separated from faith; it is included in faith. Before man repents, he cannot believe. After a man has some faith, he must repent. If a man has a certain amount of faith in God's word, he must repent. One cannot cut the matter neatly with a pair of scissors, with one side being faith and the other side being repentance. This resembles the salvation experience of many people. If you ask one hundred people when they were saved, perhaps only fifty can give you the exact date and year of their salvation. The other half would not know when they were saved. They do not know how they received God's salvation. To them it matters little how they were saved. The important thing is that they are saved. It is all right if they do not know the date of their birth. As long as they are born, they feel that it is good enough. Hence, we can see that at the beginning, the word of God was first preached (2:16). If they had not believed, why would they be pricked in their hearts?

We may ask that if they had indeed believed, why would Peter have said that they must repent and be baptized before their sins could be forgiven and the Holy Spirit be poured out? If they had believed, why were their sins not forgiven yet, and why was the Holy Spirit not poured out yet? If we say that they had not believed, then why were they so concerned after they heard God's word? Why did they ask what they must do? We have to realize that when the word of God is preached, different people have different reactions according to their own condition. The condition in Acts was different. Some sinners feel that they have sinned, and they are sorrowful for their sins. When we preach the gospel to such people, we may never mention repentance. But some people come to believe in Him without having realized their sins. Such people must be brought back to the point of repentance. Hence, when we preach the gospel, we have to pay attention to this difference. Some have come to the Lord through repentance. We only have to ask them to believe. For others, we have to lead them to repentance and conviction concerning themselves. Even after God has given them faith and they have believed, we still must persuade them to be baptized and have a heart of repentance before their sins can be forgiven and the Holy Spirit can be poured upon them. Hence, we see that repentance can be included in faith. If a man does not repent, how can he believe? If a man does not realize that he is sick, he will not be willing to see a doctor. Moreover, repentance can also be included in salvation. Man is to believe in God's word, be forgiven, and receive the Holy Spirit after he repents. Hence, we see that Acts 3 speaks of faith also. This man is saved and healed by faith. It is so clear that what is spoken of here is faith.

When we come to chapter seventeen we see something else. Acts 17:30 says, "Therefore, having overlooked the times of ignorance, God now charges all men everywhere to repent." Here, God does not tell man to believe. If it were up to us, we would surely have changed the word "repent" to "believe." But what Paul was talking about in the following verses was not a question of faith. If he were to tell us that man has sinned and that the Son of God has accomplished the work of redemption and has solved the problem of sin, then he would have to mention faith. But here Paul was talking about judgment. Verse 31 says, "Because He has set a day in which He is to judge the world in righteousness by the man whom He has designated, having furnished proof to all by raising Him from the dead." God has designated the Lord Jesus as the Judge to judge all men. At the same time, in order to let everyone know that He has designated the Lord Jesus as the Judge, God has raised Jesus from among the dead as a proof of their faith. This is why it says that we have to repent. So, this is not a question of faith here. Through His resurrection from the dead, the Lord Jesus has become a proof of our faith. He is worthy of our belief already. Now there is no need to talk about faith anymore. The resurrection of the Lord Jesus is here as a proof; it is clear and beyond doubt. Now what we must do is repent for the things that we have done. Then we will be able to believe. The Lord Jesus is worthy of our belief. As long as we repent, we can believe.

Acts 26:19-20 says, "Therefore, King Agrippa, I was not disobedient to the heavenly vision, but declared both to those in Damascus first and in Jerusalem and throughout all the country of Judea and to the Gentiles that they should repent and turn to God, doing works worthy of repentance." If we read these two verses only, we would think that the only thing that Paul was preaching was repentance. Paul confessed before King Agrippa's judgment that his work was to cause men to repent and turn to God and do works worthy of repentance. If that was all, then the gospel according to Acts would not be a gospel of faith. In order to understand this verse, we must look at the previous passage. We cannot take a portion of Scripture out of context. It is unfair to do this. Verses 14-20 say, "And when we all fell to the ground, I heard a voice saying to me in the Hebrew dialect, Saul, Saul, why are you persecuting Me? It is hard for you to kick against the goads. And I said, Who are You, Lord? And the Lord said, I am Jesus, whom you persecute. But rise up and stand on your feet; for I have appeared to you for this purpose, to appoint you as a minister and a witness both of the things in which you have seen Me and of the things in which I will appear to you; delivering you from the people and from the Gentiles, to whom I send you, to open their eyes, to turn them from darkness to light and from the authority of Satan to God, that they may receive forgiveness of sins and an inheritance among those who have been sanctified by *faith in Me*. Therefore, King Agrippa, I was not disobedient to the heavenly vision, but declared both to those in Damascus first and in Jerusalem and throughout all the country of Judea and to the Gentiles that they should repent." Why do they have to repent? It is because the Lord Jesus has accomplished the work of redemption. All those who believe in Him will surely obtain this redemption. Repentance is something for the believing ones. Everything is done. Now, all that is needed is to repent. What is to repent? Formerly, one says that there is no need to believe. Now, he says that he will believe. This is repentance.

Suppose I see a person today, and I preach the gospel to him, telling him that the Lord Jesus has accomplished everything. I may say, "My friend, you have to repent and believe in the Lord. As soon as you believe, you will be saved. You have to have a different view towards sin. You also have to have a different view towards faith in the Lord Jesus. You have to repent of your inward condition; in this way you will be able to believe." We can see that the repentance spoken of here is not a matter of works. How do we know that it is not a matter of works? It is because repentance is included in God's salvation. Repentance is a part of salvation. Not only does this repentance have nothing to do with man's work, but it becomes one item within the scope of faith. In the few verses that we just read, we can see one mysterious thing—that repenting is a part of believing. Without repentance, there cannot be faith. Hence, faith includes repentance, and repentance is in faith.

## REPENTANCE BEING GIVEN BY GOD

Another verse tells us that repentance is not only related to faith but is related to salvation as well. Acts 5:31 says, "This One God has exalted to His right hand as Leader and Savior, to give repentance to Israel and forgiveness of sins." We see here that repentance is given by God in the same way that forgiveness is given by God. In the Bible a few times repentance and forgiveness are joined together. Acts 2 says that repentance is for the forgiveness of sins (v. 38). Acts 3 says that repentance results in our sins being wiped away (v. 19). Two other places mention repentance without forgiveness. In two of these four instances, repentance and forgiveness are joined together. Repentance is linked to salvation. Forgiveness is something God initiates. Repentance is also something God initiates. The gift of forgiveness is given by God. A heart of repentance is also given by God. Therefore, repentance is a part within faith and a part of salvation. Both of these are something that God initiates. God gives man repentance in the same way that He gives him forgiveness. It is God's word that comes to us. It is God that enlightens us and tells us that our past was wrong. It is God who gives us a heart of repentance, who commands us to repent. I marvel at this. This is salvation. Because we do not see our past, God shines His light on us. This is God's way of working.

If a child's face is dirty, his mother would not ask him to earn some money to buy a towel to wipe it clean. Instead, the mother would find a towel and tell the child to use it. When God wants us to repent, He Himself gives us repentance in the same way that He gives us forgiveness. God Himself gives us repentance so that we would see our past and realize how low, weak, and corrupt we were. After this, He tells us to repent.

Luke 24:45-47 is a most amazing passage. It says, "Then He opened their mind to understand the Scriptures; and He

said to them, Thus it is written, that the Christ would suffer
and rise up from the dead on the third day, and that repentance for forgiveness of sins would be proclaimed in His
name." The ones mentioned here preached repentance for forgiveness. We should preach forgiveness in His name. We also
should preach repentance in His name. Today we can repent
in the Lord's name because the Lord has given us repentance.
It is similar to God's creating two eyes for us and then asking
us to see. If we did not have two eyes, it would be difficult
for us to see. Thank the Lord that He first gives us eyes and
then asks us to see. First, He gives us feet and then asks us to
walk. It is the same with repentance. First, He gives us repentance, and then He asks us to repent. All of this is done by
God. Hence, when we preach the gospel, we can say that as we
have forgiveness through the Lord Jesus, in the same way
we have repentance through Him. If a man says that he
cannot repent, that he still considers sin attractive, and that
he does not feel that he is a sinner, we can tell him, "This is
all right. I am now preaching the gospel to you in the name of
Jesus. God will give you repentance. It is a part of salvation.
Just as you receive life and are justified before God, in the
same way you receive repentance."

How did we repent? When we heard the preachers telling us of the evilness and loathsomeness of sin and the
redemption of the Lord Jesus, we wanted to repent and
believe in Jesus. We were not sitting in a corner, telling ourselves how corrupted we were or what sinners we were. Even
if we were to repeat this over and over again, this speaking
would not make us feel that we were sinners. Would you
feel that you were wrong by merely speaking about it? No
one among us repented this way. When we first heard the
gospel, we opposed it and criticized it; we did not want to
accept it. If we chose to argue, we could have put forth many
arguments. On the day that we were saved, the gospel that
was preached to us may not have been that prevailing. But
while we were there or after we had returned to work, or while
we were walking on the street or reading a book, we were convicted. Spontaneously we repented, and then we were saved.
We ourselves repented; no one forced us, reminded us, or

pressured us to repent. It was God who gave us the repentance, and it was we who said, "I repent." Hence, this is God's work. This is why the Bible says that repentance is given by God.

In Acts 11, after Peter preached the gospel in the house of Cornelius, the Jewish brothers rebuked him for going to the house of a Gentile. Peter then related to them how he had preached the gospel. Verse 18 says, "And when they heard these things, they became silent and glorified God, saying, Then to the Gentiles also God has given repentance unto life." Please notice that God has *given* the Gentiles repentance unto life. Hence, we see that repentance is a part of God's grace. It is a part within God's salvation. This is something done by God.

Second Timothy 2:25 says, "In meekness correcting those who oppose, if perhaps God may give them repentance unto the full knowledge of the truth." Many oppose the truth and will not accept God's truth. We can ask God to give them repentance so that they would come to the knowledge of the truth. This is also something that God has done.

What then is repentance? After reading all of these Scriptures, we must draw a conclusion. The question of repentance is not as clear-cut as other truths in the Bible. It seems to be quite ill-defined. On the one hand, a man is not saved through repentance but through faith. This is the truth shown to us by the Gospel of John, the book of Romans, and the book of Galatians. We cannot make any mistake about this. But on the other hand, without repentance a man cannot believe. So, in our preaching, many times we tell people to repent. It does not mean that repentance alone will save us. Rather, it means that repentance will bring forth faith. If a man has not repented, he will not be able to believe. But repentance is not works. The Bible says that repentance is given by God. God tells us to repent. We do not sit in a corner thinking that we have to repent, that we have to hate our sins and judge ourselves. We have to realize that no one can do this. I am afraid no one in the entire world can do this. Even if some are able to do this, it is not worth anything. Repentance is a gift from God. Even in the Gospels, when the Lord Jesus came to preach the gospel, not only did He preach forgiveness but repentance as well. He is the One who enables us to repent. Those who repent are the believing ones and the saved ones. If there are those here who have not yet been saved and who do not know how to receive God's grace, we must say that God desires to give you grace. He desires to give you repentance. He is leading you into salvation through repentance.

Lastly there is another verse telling us that it is God's goodness and kindness that is leading us to repentance. The last clause of Romans 2:4 says that "God's kindness is leading you to repentance." May God grant us a spirit of repentance. May God be gracious to us and show us the meaning of repentance and make known to us whether we are saved through repentance or through the Lord Jesus.

# CHAPTER TWELVE

# THE WAY OF SALVATION—
# NOT BEING CONFESSION OR PRAYER

We have seen in the past few evenings that the way for a person to be saved is not through law-keeping, good works, or repentance. I must make one point clear; that is, we are only discussing the way of salvation and not the condition for salvation. This is due to the fact that there simply are no conditions required of man for him to be saved. God has fulfilled all the requirements. The question before us tonight is this: What is the way for us to be saved? We are not dealing with the matter of condition, for that implies that one has to work for his salvation.

## THE WAY OF SALVATION NOT BEING CONFESSION

Tonight we are going to consider the fourth "not being." We thank God that in recent years He has moved in many places to make many people realize in their conscience what sin is, and thus their need of the Lord Jesus to be their Savior. However, without an understanding of the Bible, they often add their own words to those of the Scriptures. In so doing, they invent different ways to salvation, such as the keeping of the law, good works, repentance, and so forth. A popular method happens to be the confession of one's sins. There are those who advocate that salvation is by confession, that it is necessary for man not only to repent, but to confess his sins. I once heard one who was quite used by the Lord say that when Jesus died, He plastered onto the cross pieces of paper on which our sins are inscribed. He said that when we receive the Lord Jesus as Savior, we must confess our sins either before God or before men. Once a confession is made regarding a certain sin, the record of that sin would be removed from the cross. Each additional confession would remove another piece of paper. You would finally be saved when you had finished confessing all of your sins and all the sheets of paper had been torn away. What this man preached was not the gospel of God nor that of the New Testament; he had brought in a human gospel which asserts that unless a person makes confession to man and to God, his sins have yet to be removed from the cross. He utterly failed to realize what the Lord Jesus has accomplished.

I can still remember the case of a rather uneducated brother from Kuling who happened to be in Shanghai a few weeks ago. He is an electrician who installs light fixtures. He was hardly literate until recent days. Some time ago he could identify only the character "I" and not "We." He was unable to recognize most of the words in a Bible verse and needed to ask for help seven or eight times in reading a single verse. Once he said to me, "I went to listen to a sermon by a very famous person. This man maintained that we must confess our sins in public so that each sin we confess will be nailed to the cross. If we do not confess our sins openly to crucify them, we cannot be saved. He said that we must believe in the word of the cross, and that if we did not nail our sins to the cross by way of confession, there would be no way for us to be saved, for that would mean that we do not trust the cross. After his sermon, the speaker sought questions from the audience to see if there were things we were unclear about."

"Mr. Nee," the brother continued, "I am uneducated. If I were to stand up in that meeting to read a verse from the Scriptures, the people would probably have to adjust me seven or eight times. But the more I listened to the man speak, the more I felt something pounding in me. I felt that the Holy Spirit would not let me go unless I stood up. But I really did not know what to say. Eventually, I rose up. The speaker was on the platform, and I was standing on my chair! I asked, 'Sir, according to your speech, are we saved by our own cross or by the cross of Christ?' Then I sat down. Mr. Nee, can you tell me if I asked the right question?"

I told the brother that neither a doctor of divinity nor an overseer of a parish had that kind of clarity. This is the key question: Are we saved by our own cross or the cross of Christ? Does Christ's cross or my own cross save me? That sermon was undoubtedly a word of the cross, but whose cross was it? When Paul said, "For I did not determine to know anything among you except Jesus Christ, and this One crucified" (1 Cor. 2:2), he did not allude to Christ and a cross but to Christ and His cross. Dear friends, we are not saved by our own works but by the cross of Christ. Yet man equates confession of sins with works and attempts to be saved through such confession. This is the reason we must see what the Bible says regarding confession. We shall look into the Scriptures thoroughly to find out the proper position we should take in this matter.

## Confession in the Bible

Let me first say a few words lest you think that I do not believe in confession or restitution. Christians ought to confess their sins and make restitution. I admit that these are truths in the Bible, and as such, they should be applied. But I must add that the Bible never considers confession to be a way of salvation. If we think that we can be saved through confession, then the solution to the problem of our sins is still not clear to us. We are presuming that there is another method of redemption apart from the cross of Christ. We may even surmise that we can deal with our own sins before God and man without the cross of Christ.

## 1 John 1:9

Let us come to a verse many love to quote, that is, 1 John 1:9, which says, "If we confess our sins, He is faithful and righteous to forgive us our sins and cleanse us from all unrighteousness." There are a number who, based on this verse, state that confession is indeed a requirement for salvation. However, I must draw your attention to several points in this verse. First, what is mentioned here is definitely not public confession. First John 1:9 deals with our problem before God when it says, "If we confess our sins." This differs from the current practice of open confession before men. First John 1:9 does not say anything about open confession.

Second, the pronoun "we" in this verse is not like the same pronoun used in the books of Romans and Galatians in that it has nothing to do with the Jews. The Epistle of 1 John is also different from the Gospel of John. John's Gospel shows us how an unbeliever can obtain life, whereas his Epistle tells us how one who has life proves before man that he possesses that life in fact. His Gospel reveals the way to receive life, whereas his Epistle discloses how one who possesses such a life goes about demonstrating what he possesses. Thus, properly expounded, the "we" in this verse does not refer to sinners, but to believers. The Gospel of John describes the way a sinner is justified by God, but 1 John indicates how a Christian may restore his fellowship with God. The Word here does not discuss how the world can believe in Jesus to have eternal life. It indicates how a person who has eternal life and is a child of God can have his sins forgiven by God and have his unrighteousness cleansed when he fails. Hence, this verse makes reference to the believers alone, those who have been saved and justified, those who possess eternal life.

Remember that, whereas an unsaved person is forgiven of his sins by faith, a saved one is forgiven by confessing his sins. Sinners are pardoned by believing in the Lord, and Christians are forgiven by confessing their sins before their Father. First John 1:9 does not deal with the sins of a sinner but with those of a believer, not with the sins committed before one's salvation, but with those committed after one has been saved. Consequently, this verse has nothing to do with our present subject.

I would not be so strict as to say that this verse can be applied only to Christians. Rather, I would admit that one may borrow from a host of Scriptures and utilize them to get people saved. Recently a sister told me that a lady was saved by reading the phrase, "The seed is the word of God" (Luke 8:11). I do not know how this could have happened. When I first preached the gospel, I was convinced that it takes clear gospel Scriptures to get people saved. However, much experience in recent years has taught me, and I say this reverently, that many are actually saved by strange verses. One cannot imagine that verses as strange as some are can save people. I am not insisting that no sinner could be saved by 1 John 1:9. I am saying that when John was moved by the Holy Spirit to write his Epistle, in his mind the ones referred to in this verse were Christians and not sinners. He originally intended them to be for Christians. Although one may temporarily borrow this word and apply it to a sinner, he should not keep on borrowing it. Strictly speaking, such a verse refers to Christians and does not imply that one must confess his sins publicly and make restitution to others in order to be forgiven.

## Matthew 3:5 and 6

There are another two verses which seem even more obvious than 1 John 1:9. They are Matthew 3:5 and 6, which say, "At that time Jerusalem and all Judea and all the surrounding region of the Jordan went out to him, and they were baptized by him in the Jordan River as they confessed their sins." We are told when the people heard John's testimony and realized their own sinfulness, they went out to be baptized by him and confessed their sins while they were being baptized. Again, a few matters should be noted in these verses. First, neither of the two verses indicate that the people took confession as their way to salvation. They did not try to obtain salvation through confession. We are merely told that when they heard John's preaching of repentance, they were compelled by the Spirit to be baptized and to confess their sins. They were in fact looking to the very Lord who was to pass through death and resurrection, and in whom they hoped for their salvation. Though John did baptize, his hands were actually pointing them to the Lord Jesus who was among them. It was he who said, "Behold, the Lamb of God, who takes away the sin of the world!" (John 1:29). In baptisms of the church, and in the baptism of John the Baptist, the Christ who died and rose is referred to. John readily admitted how little he was worth by declaring that "He must increase, but I must decrease" (John 3:30), and that the people should not believe in him but in the coming One. Although he did prepare the way, he was not the way; the way was the coming One to whom he pointed.

How then were the confessions made? Since John did not tell them to come and confess their sins, his listeners must have done it on their own. Let us assume that one of us who is a worker has just finished witnessing for the Lord, and without any kind of urging, charging, demanding, or suggesting, the audience has been deeply enlightened by God in the conscience concerning their sins. They are compelled to rise up to admit that they have committed certain particular sins. To this I would surely say, "Amen" and "Hallelujah!" I would speak praises and never oppose this sort of open confession before men. If John were to say that a man could not be saved or forgiven unless he confessed his sins, and if John actually encouraged, prompted, commanded, and induced the people to confess their sins, then his actions would hardly match the record in Matthew 3:6. According to this verse, his listeners confessed their sins on their own; they were not encouraged by John.

Do not presume that I do not believe in the confession of sins. We have often encouraged the brothers and sisters to make confessions to others. Yet we refuse to accept confession as the means to be saved. There is only one means of salvation prescribed in the Scriptures, and that is faith. The ancient John the Baptist never urged anyone to confess his sins. Neither should any modern John the Baptist urge man to do the same. Of course, if a person, upon realizing his own sins, should stand up to make a confession on his own, we have to let him do so.

You may have heard of the great Welsh revival. I had occasion to study in detail reports on that revival. Many have made studies on it. This greatest of all revivals began between the years of 1904 and 1905. A correspondent of a well-known British newspaper actually went to Wales in 1909 to conduct an investigation of the event. Wales was not a small place. The pastors of one of the cities told the reporter that the number of souls saved had declined to almost nothing during the previous two years. When the correspondent inquired whether the revival was in recession, they replied, "Yes. There is no one around here any longer who is asking to be saved, because everyone has been saved already!" Knowing that the revival began with Evan Roberts, he then asked concerning his whereabouts. They answered, "We have no idea."

When he asked them about their meeting time, they said, "We do not know." Likewise, when he questioned them about the meeting place, they repeated, "We do not know." They did not seem to know who the leader of a revival meeting was, nor the time and place of the meeting. The reporter then asked what he should do, to which they responded, "We meet anywhere at anytime, even at midnight or the early hours of the morning. We do not know where Evan Roberts is, but he may appear at anytime. There is a revival gathering in almost every home. You find people praying in different homes at different hours through the night. But it is difficult to find Evan Roberts. Nobody knows where he will be." The reporter remarked that he had never witnessed revival like this in his entire life. He was determined to find Evan Roberts. His efforts in the next few weeks, however, failed to yield any results.

One day, when someone told him that Evan Roberts was in a small chapel, the reporter dashed off immediately to the place. He remarked that the meeting he came upon was most chaotic. A mother was breast-feeding her baby; a few were running in and out of the meeting as if they were salespersons of some sort; another mother was comforting a crying child, while yet another was using a chair as a cradle, rocking her child to sleep. The place was in a mess. And yet there seemed to be an inexplicable and unique element in the atmosphere. "Where is Evan Roberts?" the reporter asked. "The fourth man on the third row," someone answered. "Mrs. Penn-Lewis is also here. There she is on that row." They were all silent in their seats. Once in a while someone would stand to call a hymn, or another might rise to read a few verses from the Scriptures. When one or two hours went by without a single word from the people, no one dismissed himself. At times some would stand to confess their sins on their own without being admonished to do so.

Friends, such a work is the work of God. It is different from platform sermons concerning deathbed stories with an intention to convince the audience that they must either confess their sins or else not be saved at all. I am not forbidding confession. There are times when one should confess his sins. At times one might even declare to a crowd what kind of person he once was and how God had worked in him. However, none of these should be the result of a preacher's prodding from the platform. Sometimes there is more than prodding; it is as if some are commanding. What is in Matthew 3:6 is indeed public confession, but it is the spontaneous result of the work of the Holy Spirit and not an outcome of John's charge. I am not opposing open confession; I am merely opposing this kind of confession. Much more, I am not opposing the work of the Holy Spirit; I wish there were more of such works! If a person is led by the Spirit to confess his sins, we all have to say, "O God, we thank and praise You, for You have worked among us." But we have to oppose any teaching that says confession must be done in a certain way and to a certain degree before certain results will be achieved. We cannot exchange confession for salvation. We must not take confession of sins as our way of salvation.

We have to note that in the sentence, "And they were baptized by him in the Jordan River as they confessed their sins," the main predicate according to the original language is not "confessed" but "were baptized." Thus, the people were being baptized by John in the Jordan River, and while they were being baptized, they also confessed their sins. We may say that "he spoke, walking," which would mean that the person was speaking and walking at the same time. While both "spoke" and "walking" are verbs, "spoke" is the main predicate and "walking" the subordinate verb. Hence the man was speaking, but he was doing so while he was walking. Similarly, in Matthew 3 they were baptized in the Jordan River as they confessed, meaning that while they were being baptized, they were simultaneously confessing their sins. Such is the original sense in Greek. So you see, the confession there was absolutely not a method, but an action which took place. While the people were being baptized, they were admitting that they were wrong in this and in that. The picture here is one of the Holy Spirit working among them, rather than a work of regulation. They were being baptized and confessing, just like our example of someone speaking and walking at the same time. In any case, public confession was never treated as a way to be saved in this verse.

## Acts 19:18 and 19

There are only three places in the New Testament which record this matter of confession of sins. We come now to the third place, which is in Acts 19:18 and 19, which says, "And many of those who had believed came, confessing and making known their practices. And a considerable number of those who practiced magic brought their books together and burned them before all; and they counted up the price of them and found it to be fifty thousand pieces of silver." Although there is only the word "confessing," without the mentioning of "sins," the same thing is referred to. In 1 John 1 it says "confess our sins," in Matthew 3 it says "confessed their sins," and here it says "confessing" and "making known their practices." First, the confession and the divulgence of their practices were not reckoned as a way to be saved. Second, those who confessed and recounted their practices were not sinners but believers, people who were Christ's. This can be compared to some brothers and sisters standing up in the meetings to give a testimony acknowledging what they have done in times past. It can also be compared to some who testify at their baptism of things done in the past. We are altogether not saved through this kind of confession. Some have believed and have become the Lord's. They now confess their past history. They admit that they were evil. They are no longer afraid to tell the saints that they have been transferred from the miry clay onto a solid rock. When the Ephesians burned their magic books, they were making an open demonstration that though they had practiced these things, they now belonged to the Lord. Third, "And many of those who had believed came." Not all came. Not every saved person needs to confess in the meetings. It is because the Holy Spirit moves strongly to prompt people that they rise to disclose their practices that they may glorify God by showing the extent of God's salvation in them. Friends, you can discover from these three portions of the Word that the way of salvation is through faith and not through public confession.

These are the three portions of the New Testament where confession of sins is specifically covered. There is one other place, in James 5:16, where confession of wrongdoing to one another, rather than confession of sins, is mentioned. James tells us when a brother or sister is sick, the elders of the church should be called to pray over the sick person and anoint him. And if any wrongdoings are involved, there should be mutual confession and forgiveness. This is a different matter from our subject today. We have looked into all the verses in the New Testament concerning the confession of sins. Do you now see the way for one to be saved? It is through faith and not through the confession of sins.

## CONCERNING THE PRACTICE OF CONFESSION

Let me say a few words concerning the practice of confessing sins. We all know whom we have offended and defrauded before we were saved. After we were saved, we felt sorrowful in our heart and wished to confess to those same people. This is something that we should do. God commands, even compels us to do so. It is something taught in the Scriptures. Having seen God's righteousness and the glory in His presence, we now realize that it is unrighteous to be indebted to others. What then shall we do? We refuse to be unrighteous persons. We even tell ourselves, "I am saved. I will be a righteous man. I will thoroughly deal with all the areas in which I have been unrighteous or not right with others so that they may forgive me." There is no problem with your sins being forgiven before God, but you must make confession to men of your offenses to men. However, confession and restitution are absolutely not the way of salvation. You do not need to make confessions and recompense before you can be saved. As a saved person, and one who is just, you are merely asking pardon from people you have wronged.

The thief on the cross must have robbed many and sinned against many. However, he had no opportunity to confess and make recompense to anyone, because he could hardly move on the cross. He was not able to return any item which he had plundered from others. Yet, without any confession or restitution, he still could be saved. The Lord Jesus said to him, "Today you shall be with Me in Paradise" (Luke 23:43). We may consider this robber as the first person to be saved in the

New Testament. He was the first to be saved after the Lord's death. Hence, the problem is not one of confession. The thief on the cross, though deprived of the opportunity of making recompense, was nevertheless saved. If he had lived on, he should have made recompense for righteousness' sake. But the question of his salvation was resolved on the cross in an instant. Confession is something that follows salvation. He was already saved on the cross; his salvation was altogether not due to any kind of confession or restitution. If he confessed his sins again at some later date, it would not have saved him more. Here we are clearly shown that salvation is by faith, whereas confession is a spontaneous expression of Christian living. Since we now know our righteous God, we desire to clear up the problem of our sins before man. Our salvation is totally a matter between us and the Lord Jesus; it is resolved through Him alone.

There are three things here which we must be clear about. First, we confess our sins before God, judging ourselves, repenting, and acknowledging that we are sinners. All these are done before God. This causes us to have faith to receive the Lord Jesus as our Savior. Second, after we are saved, we become aware of our offenses towards others and wish to clear them up. We wish to make recompense and to confess to those whom we have defrauded so that we may live a righteous life on earth. Third, after we are saved, as the Holy Spirit works in us, we want to tell others what kind of sinners we were and how many sins we have committed. We may do this during our baptism, and we may do this after baptism.

I do not know if you are clear or not. Never deem the confessing of sins so highly. We must put it in the place accorded by the Scriptures. Since the Bible never considers it as a way to salvation, neither should we. Thank God it is the Lord Jesus who saved me. I did not save myself. Thank God it is the cross of Christ that saved me. I am not saved by my own cross; the cross of Christ did the saving work.

### THE WAY OF SALVATION NOT BEING PRAYER

We come now to the fifth "not being." There are many people who will add another condition to salvation. It is not law-keeping or good behavior, nor is it repentance or confession. They say that a person must pray in order to be saved. They base their claim on Romans 10: "Whoever calls upon the name of the Lord shall be saved" (v. 13). As a result, some believe that they must beseech God before they can be saved. On a number of occasions I have encountered some people who wanted to be saved. They said, "Daily I plead with God to save me, and I still do not know when He will do so. I have been praying for three months without any inward sensation. I just do not know if God will see fit to save me." I have also met some others who said, "I am waiting for the Holy Spirit to come and move me to my knees to ask Jesus to save me. I am not saved as yet. I must wait for the Spirit to inspire me to pray before I can be saved." For this reason, we need to see whether a man needs to pray before he can be saved.

First, one seeks to be saved through praying and begging because he is entirely ignorant of God's love and God's grace. He thinks that God hates man, and therefore he must pray for God to change His mind before He will save him. He gives himself to pray, without knowing how much he has to pray before God will hear him or listen to him. Remember how Elijah challenged the prophets of Baal on Mount Carmel? He challenged them to ask their god to send down fire. The prophets "cried aloud, and cut themselves after their manner with knives and lancets, till the blood gushed out upon them" (1 Kings 18:29). They supposed that Baal would listen if they would only inflict more pain upon their own bodies. Today there are those who also think that if they bring distress upon themselves and plead enough with God, He will have compassion on them. These kinds of people have never seen the gospel. Because they have never seen God in the light of the gospel, they believe that their begging before God will turn His heart towards them. Actually there is no need for God to turn His heart. His heart has long been turned. We are the ones who need a turn of heart, because we rejected and opposed Him, and we did not believe in Him.

Second Corinthians 5:19 says, "God in Christ was reconciling the world to Himself." God did not wrong man; it is man who has wronged God. There has never been a need for God to be reconciled to man. Rather, man has to be reconciled to God because it is man who is totally at fault. The problem is not with God, but with man. Everyone who desires to understand the gospel ought to know that God is love and that He loves the world. He has no problem with us, and neither do we need to plead with Him.

Second, man thinks that he must pray and plead before he can be saved because he simply does not realize that the Lord Jesus has come; He has died and resurrected, all of sin's problems are solved, and all obstacles to salvation are removed. Not only has the Lord Jesus come, but the Holy Spirit has also come. He came to make manifest in man what God and the Lord Jesus have accomplished. Many sinners pray for their salvation as if they were asking the Lord Jesus to die for them again. They do not realize that He has completely finished the work of redemption. Since He has finished His work, there is absolutely no reason for us to plead with Him. Today is the time for thanksgivings and praises; it is not the time for filing requests and petitions. Suppose your parents have brought you something that you asked for. You may perhaps, out of sincerity, bow to thank them. Certainly you would not kneel down and beg to have that item, saying, "Please give this to me because I need it." It is simply pointless and senseless for you to continue to beg after your parents have already given the item to you. Today God is not speaking about the severity of your sins. If He were, then there may be a reason for you to plead. Rather, God is now saying that He has freely given you His Son. It would be a strange thing indeed if someone gave you something and you were still begging instead of thanking! If you know God's heart, and if you are clear about the Lord Jesus' work, you would never attempt to be saved through prayer. Prayer has no place in this matter. It is better for you to kneel to thank God.

Once after I had shared the gospel with a man, I asked if he would believe. He replied that he would. When I said, "Let us kneel down," he asked if we were going to pray. I told him, "No." He asked, "For what purpose then?" I answered, "Simply to inform the Lord Jesus." There is no need to ask Jesus to die again or to ask God to love, to be gracious, or to forgive us. The Lord has already borne our sins on the cross. Now our only need is to notify Him by saying, "I have believed the Son of God, and I have received the cross of Christ. O God, I thank You." Is this not easy? Yes, to receive salvation is an easy matter. It was, of course, not an easy thing for God to accomplish salvation; it took God four thousand years to accomplish it. After man fell, it took God four thousand years to cause man to realize his sins. He then caused His Son to be born of a woman and to hang on the cross to be judged for sin. In the end He also sent the Holy Spirit. It is only after God has done so much work and expended so much effort that we can receive salvation in such an easy way. He has paid the greatest price to accomplish everything. Now if you have believed and received, all you need to do is to say, "Thank You." This is the way of salvation. There is no place for prayer here.

Why then does Romans 10 bring up the matter of prayer? Romans 10:5 through 7 reads, "For Moses writes concerning the righteousness which is out of the law: 'The man who does them shall live by them.' But the righteousness which is out of faith speaks in this way, 'Do not say in your heart, Who will ascend into heaven?' that is, to bring Christ down; or, 'Who will descend into the abyss?' that is, to bring Christ up from the dead." Two kinds of righteousness are mentioned here. One is the righteousness which is out of the law, and the other, righteousness which is out of faith. The righteousness out of the law results from one's works before God, and the righteousness out of faith is accomplished in us through our believing in the Lord Jesus Christ. The former has everything to do with us, and the latter, everything to do with Christ.

It is absolutely impossible for a man to obtain the righteousness out of the law, because it requires him to be sinless in his thoughts, intentions, words, and behavior for every year, hour, minute, and second of his life from the time he was born. If he breaks any one item of the law, he transgresses the whole. For us, this is simply a hopeless proposition. Since we cannot have the righteousness out of the law, we need to have the righteousness out of faith. This righteousness, as we have mentioned, is the righteousness through which Christ was judged. Since Christ has suffered the punishment, we have this righteousness through faith. This righteousness has absolutely nothing to do with us. The Scriptures say, "'Do not say in your heart, Who will ascend into heaven?' that is, to bring Christ down; or, 'Who will descend into the abyss?' that is, to bring Christ up from the dead." There is no need for us to do this. There is no need to ascend into heaven. This means that there is no need to ask Christ to come to the earth to die for us. There is also no need to descend into the abyss. This implies that the resurrection of Christ is now the basis of our justification. God has already caused the Lord Jesus to die and resurrect, and His resurrection has become the basis of our justification. All that remains for us to do is to believe.

Verse 8 says, "But what does it say?" "It" refers to Moses' word. Paul quoted Moses to show that even Moses preached justification by faith. This is quite amazing, inasmuch as Moses was the promoter of the law and its requirements. But Paul introduced Moses, saying that Moses also spoke concerning justification by faith when he said, "'The word is near you, in your mouth and in your heart,' that is, the word of the faith which we proclaim." Paul maintained that Moses' words refer to justification by faith. To understand this quotation we need to go back to Deuteronomy 29 and 30 in the Old Testament. There Moses passed on all of God's law and commandments to the Israelites, telling them that if they failed to obey those commandments and keep the law, God would punish them by scattering them among the nations; and if their hearts would draw near to God in the dispersion, the word would be near them, even in their mouths and in their hearts. Moses was saying that God's judgment would be present whenever man breaks the law and transgresses. What shall man do then? He needs to receive a righteousness apart from the law, one which is in his mouth and in his heart. Such a grace outside of the law is a gift to us. When Deuteronomy was quoted in Romans 10, a word of explanation was added. "'The word is near you, in your mouth and in your heart,' that is, the word of the faith which we proclaim." There is no thought of work here. The righteousness which is out of the law has been thoroughly transgressed against. When the people were scattered among the nations of the earth as predicted in Deuteronomy 30, they could no longer claim to have any work. The question of work was over. The only word which they had then was the word that was in their mouth and in their heart. Formerly it was a matter of works, and the result was dispersion. Now there are no more works. Hence it is of faith.

Paul continued to define the meaning of "in your mouth" and "in your heart" in verse 9 by saying, "If you confess with your mouth Jesus as Lord and believe in your heart that God has raised Him from the dead, you will be saved." Dear friends, where is your mouth? Each one of us has brought our mouth to this place. None has left his at home. Where our body is, there our mouth is also. At the moment we believed in the Lord Jesus, we spontaneously confessed Him with our mouth. The first words out of Paul's mouth when the Lord confronted him on the road were, "Who are You, Lord?" He had not believed in the Lord before. But at that juncture he did believe. Our confession of Jesus as Lord is made spontaneously from our heart rather than before people. It amazes me to think that some illiterate country folk who have never been exposed to the gospel before can say, "O Lord," upon hearing the good news. This cannot be a work. It is a spontaneous utterance. For one to believe in his heart is not a matter of work. There is no need to take any steps or to spend any money. One only needs to say "O Lord" right where he is, and he will be saved. He can say it audibly or inaudibly. As long as he believes that God has brought Him down from the heavens and has brought Him up from Hades, everything will be worked out. This will prove that he is justified and saved. Our confession can never carry the element of merit. Confession is not a way to salvation; it is merely an expression of salvation. It is a very spontaneous thing. If we call Him Lord with our mouth and believe in Him in our heart, we shall be saved. There is no problem at all.

Verse 10 follows and explains verse 9. Why is one saved when he confesses with his mouth Jesus as Lord and believes in his heart that God has raised Him from the dead? "For with the heart there is believing unto righteousness, and with the mouth there is confession unto salvation." I was always perplexed as to how this matter could be put into people's hearts. I met two people today who consider this word of salvation too far from them. To them, this word is farther than the provinces of Yunnang and Tibet; it is farther than a foreign country. It is simply a word from the heavens. It seems that the word of salvation is so far away that it eludes them. Nevertheless, God says that the way of salvation is not in heaven nor beneath the earth. It is very near, in our mouth and even in our heart. If we had to ascend into the heavens or descend under the earth, we would wonder how anyone could be saved. Today the word is in your mouth and in your heart. As long as a person opens his mouth and believes in his heart, he shall be saved. God has made this salvation so utterly available and convenient that if a person would believe in his heart and confess with his mouth, he shall be saved. Justification here is more a matter before God than before man. When men see you confessing, they will realize that you are saved. When God sees you believing, He justifies you. Verse 11 says, "Everyone who believes on Him shall not be put to shame." Faith alone is enough.

Although the Word of God is abundantly clear, there are still those who like to argue against it. They insist that confession is the way to be saved. I wish to ask them, "If so, what will you do with Romans 10:8: 'The word is near you, in your mouth and in your heart'?" Here it says the word of faith, not the word of confession. The Scriptures say "believe." They do not say "confess." Verse 6 says, "But the righteousness which is out of faith speaks in this way." Verse 6 speaks of the righteousness out of faith, and verse 8, the word of the faith. There is one confession in verse 9 and another in verse 10. Both confessions are with the mouth. However, verse 11 does not say, "Everyone who confesses Him shall not be put to shame." Rather, it says, "Everyone who believes on Him shall not be put to shame." We must recognize the emphasis here. Verses 6, 8, and 11 mention "believe," and verses 9 and 10 mention "confess." Verse 9 first says "confess" and then "believe"; whereas in verse 10 it is first "believe" and then "confess." In this one portion "believe" is used five times and "confess" twice. At the end, the order of "confess" and "believe" is reversed. All this signifies that salvation should be due to faith and not to confession. Confession issues from faith. What one believes in his heart, he utters spontaneously with his mouth. A person will spontaneously say "daddy" when he sees his father. Where there is faith, confession follows immediately.

The end of verse 12 shows us that confession here is the confession of Jesus as Lord. This confession comes from faith. How can we prove this? We may not see this from verses 1 through 11. But verse 12 says, "For there is no distinction between Jew and Greek, for the same Lord is Lord of all and rich to all who call upon Him." Verse 13 says, "Whoever calls upon the name of the Lord shall be saved." Calling upon the Lord's name is equivalent to the confessing of the Lord Jesus in the previous verses. To call on the name of the Lord is to confess Jesus as Lord, to call Him Lord, and to address Him as Lord. By taking care of the context of this passage, we will realize that calling is simply confessing.

Verse 14 says, "How then shall they call upon Him into whom they have not believed?" This is a wonderful word. It shows that calling comes out of believing. Naturally, no one can call without believing. We can see that confessing with the mouth results from faith in the heart. Because a man believes in his heart, he calls with his mouth. He calls because he believes. Do you see this fact? Everything issues from faith; faith is the way of salvation. Although it mentions confession with the mouth, this confession is based upon faith in the heart. It is natural for those who believe to call.

I believe tonight we are all saved ones who have received the Lord Jesus. May I ask how you have received Him? We received Him by faith. Did you also pray? Salvation is due to faith. Prayer is the expression of this faith. Everyone in the world is saved by faith. However, this faith is expressed in prayer. Faith is within and prayer is without. When you believe in your heart that Jesus is the Savior, spontaneously you will pray with your mouth that Jesus is Lord. Whoever believes in his heart will confess with his mouth. But we must always remember that confession is not the way to salvation.

Although the word says "Whoever calls upon the name of the Lord shall be saved," yet calling is not the way to salvation. The reason is that calling comes from faith; it is a spontaneous action, something uttered before God spontaneously.

Let us come back to verse 12: "For there is no distinction between Jew and Greek, for the same Lord is Lord of all." I love the phrase, "There is no distinction." Romans 3:22 and 23 say, "Even the righteousness of God through the faith of Jesus Christ to all those who believe, for there is no distinction. For all have sinned." Here it says, "For there is no distinction between Jew and Greek, for the same Lord is Lord of all." Each one must call upon the Lord, confess with his mouth, and believe in his heart before he can be saved.

May the Lord be gracious to us and show us that the only way of salvation in the Bible is faith and nothing else. Salvation is not by faith plus law-keeping, good works, repentance, confession, or prayer. This is the scriptural truth. We have to stand upon the Bible. The Bible reveals clearly to us that the way of salvation is faith alone.

# CHAPTER THIRTEEN

## THE WAY OF SALVATION—
## FAITH VERSUS LOVING GOD
## OR BEING BAPTIZED

During the past two weeks, we have seen man's need for salvation and God's preparation of this salvation. We have seen the problems God encountered when He prepared this salvation for us and how He completely solved all the problems of sin. We have also seen the way to receive salvation. Because men understood the Bible in an incorrect way, they came up with many conditions for salvation. Some want to have one condition, whereas others want to have another condition. We saw that man is not saved by the law or by works. He is not saved by repentance, prayer, or confession. Man is not saved by anything he has in himself. Other than these human ways, there are still two very common mistakes within the church. The first is the concept that in order to be saved, man has to love God; that is, if a man does not love God, he will not be saved.

### LOVING GOD NOT BEING THE WAY OF SALVATION

I admit that 1 Corinthians 16 tells us that a man has to love God. If he does not love God, he is accursed. This is a fact. But the Bible shows us clearly that man is saved by faith and not by love. Some think that there are evidences in the Bible that prove that man is saved by loving God, and that without loving God a man cannot be saved. There are some sinners, when the gospel of salvation by faith is preached to them, who would say that they cannot be saved because they do not love God at all. They think that if they really love God and are drawn to God, God will save them. To them man is saved by loving God. They do not realize that man is saved not because of loving God, but because God loves him. It is God who loved the world and gave His only begotten Son, that whoever

believes into Him should not perish, but have eternal life
(John 3:16). On God's side, it is love. On our side, it is faith.
Man's side does not have to be the same as God's side. He does
not have to love God as God loves him. It does not say that
man needs to love God so that he would give his son to God, so
that God would trust in him and cause him not to perish, but
to have eternal life. We do not have such a Gospel of John.
Thank God that He loved the world so much that He gave His
only begotten Son. The Bible does not say that we first love
God, but that God first loves us. The basis of salvation is not
that we love God. The basis of salvation is God's loving us. If
we put the basis of salvation on our love for God and our sacrifice to Him, we will immediately see that the salvation we
would have would not be secure. Our hearts are like the sand
of the sea that comes and goes with the tide. If our house is
built on the sand, our fate will follow the flow of the tide.
Thank the Lord. It is not a matter of us loving God, but of God
loving us.

## THE STORY OF THE GOOD SAMARITAN

Although John 3 and other places may say what we have
said, some may ask: "What about Luke 10?" Let us now read
what Luke 10 says. Luke 10:25 begins, "And behold, a certain
lawyer stood up." This man had a wrong profession. "A certain lawyer stood up and put Him to the test." His motive was
wrong. His intention was not right. "Saying, Teacher." He had
a wrong understanding. His understanding concerning the
Lord was wrong. He did not know who the Lord was. "What
should I do to inherit eternal life?" His question was wrong.
This man was wrong in his profession, wrong in his motive,
wrong in his intention, wrong in his understanding of the
Lord, and wrong in the question he asked.

He asked, "What should I do to inherit eternal life?" What
did the Lord Jesus say? "And He said to him, What is written
in the law?" You are a lawyer. You should know what the law
says. "How do you read it?" Something may be written in the
law. But man can be wrong in reading it. The Lord asked a
double question. What is written in the law, and what have
you read from it? Sometimes the law is written one way, but

man reads it another way. "And he answered and said." He answered what the law says, and how he read it. "You shall love the Lord your God from your whole heart and with your whole soul and with your whole strength and with your whole mind, and your neighbor as yourself." This lawyer was well acquainted with the law. He knew that the sum of the law is to love God with our whole heart, our whole soul, our whole strength, and our whole mind, and to love our neighbor as ourselves. He could sum up the whole law in one sentence. This was an intelligent man. Probably everyone who comes to tempt is intelligent. Only the intelligent ones try to tempt. What is it to tempt others? Those who want to be taught ask questions, and those who come to tempt also ask questions. The ones who want to be taught ask questions because they do not understand. The ones who want to tempt ask questions because they do understand. Some ask because they do not understand; they come humbly to be taught. Some ask because they understand; they want to show you how much they understand. This is the meaning of tempting. This man came to the Lord asking how he could be saved. He said that he wanted eternal life and that he wanted the life of God. What then must he do? The Lord said, "What is written in the law? How do you read it?" The man could recite it by heart. He knew it long ago. One has to love God with his whole heart, his whole soul, his whole strength, and his whole mind, and has to love his neighbor as himself. He knew all these. That was why he recited them immediately. When he answered this way, the Lord told him to do it and he would be able to have eternal life.

Here is a problem. Whatever the Lord Jesus may have meant when He spoke to the lawyer, and whatever the circumstances may have been, all those who are not familiar with the truth and the meaning in God's word would say, "Is it not clear enough that to have eternal life, a man must love God and love his neighbor? If a man does not love God and his neighbors, is it not true that he cannot possibly have eternal life?" Although the Gospel of John mentions eighty-six times that eternal life is obtained through faith, some may say that the Gospel of Luke says at least once that eternal life is obtained through loving God. If a man does not love God or his neighbor, he cannot possibly be saved.

If that is the case, I would ask if any one of us has ever loved God this way, that is, with our whole heart, our whole soul, our whole strength, and our whole mind. No, there is no one like this. There is no one who loves God with his whole heart, his whole soul, his whole strength, and his whole mind. No one can say that he loves his neighbor as himself. There is no such person. Since there is no such person, no one would obtain eternal life. We need to understand why the Lord Jesus said that we should love God with our whole heart, our whole soul, our whole strength, and our whole mind. Thank the Lord that the Bible is indeed the revelation of God. There is absolutely no mistake in it. This is the reason I love to read the Bible. If this passage beginning from Luke 10:25 ended with verse 28, the truths of the Bible would contradict one another. If that were the case, man would have to love God with his whole heart, his whole soul, his whole strength, and his whole mind. None of these four "whole's" could be missing. But if that were the case, no one could ever be saved. Thank the Lord that after verse 28 there are many more verses. Let us read on.

It is fortunate that this man was quite bothersome. "But he, wanting to justify himself." He asked this question for no other reason than to justify himself. He said to Jesus, "And who is my neighbor?" Since the Lord said that he had to love the Lord his God with his whole heart, his whole soul, his whole strength, and his whole mind and to love his neighbor as himself, it would have been awkward for him to ask who God was. Did he, a lawyer, not know who his own God was? It would also have been hard for him to ask who he was, for of all the men in the world, only philosophers do not know who they are. With nothing else to ask, he asked who his neighbor was. He seemed to say, "You are saying that I have to love my neighbor as myself, but who is my neighbor?" From verse 30 on, the Lord told him who his neighbor was. He began to tell him a story.

This story is one of the most common and familiar stories in the church. It would be good for us to read it together:

"Jesus, taking up the question, said, A certain man was going down from Jerusalem to Jericho, and he fell among robbers, who having both stripped him and beat him, went away, leaving him half dead. And by coincidence a certain priest was going down on that road; and when he saw him, he passed by on the opposite side. And likewise also a Levite, when he came to the place and saw him, passed by on the opposite side. But a certain Samaritan, who was journeying, came upon him; and when he saw him, he was moved with compassion; and he came to him and bound up his wounds and poured oil and wine on them. And placing him on his own beast, he brought him to an inn and took care of him. And on the next day he took out two denarii and gave them to the innkeeper and said, Take care of him; and whatever you spend in addition to this, when I return, I will repay you. Which of these three, does it seem to you, has become a neighbor to him who fell into the hands of the robbers?"

We are very familiar with this story. Let us spend some time to consider it. This man went from the place of peace to the place of a curse. Jerusalem means peace, and Jericho means a curse. He did not go from Jericho to Jerusalem, a journey that goes up. It was from Jerusalem to Jericho, a journey that goes down. He went from the place of peace to the place of a curse. This man was in a downhill condition. He met robbers on the way. It was not one robber, but a whole gang of robbers, who took away all he had, stripped him of his garments, and left him with no outward covering at all. They beat him until he was half dead; he was wounded in his very life. The Bible shows us that a man's garments are his deeds, and a man's being is his life. Here the shining deeds are stripped away and gone. The life that remains only has a body that is living; the spirit is dead. This is a man half dead. All readers of the Bible know that this is a description of our person. From the time man was tempted by the serpent in the garden of Eden, and since he began to sin, man has never experienced peace in his life journey. Man is continually tempted by Satan. The result is that all his outward deeds are stripped away. Even more his inward spirit is dead. He is living as far as the body goes, but dead as far as the spirit goes. Man can do nothing about his condition. He can only wait for others to come and save him.

A priest came by. When he saw this man, he passed by on the other side. A Levite also came by. After he saw the man, he also passed by on the other side. The priests and the Levites are the two main groups of people in the Old Testament. In the Old Testament, the whole law is in the hands of the priests and the Levites. If you take away the priests and the Levites, there would be no law left. To a half-dead sinner, one who is bound by Satan, waiting to go to destruction, and having no outward virtue, there was nothing to do except to wait to die. What would the priests tell him? The priests would have said, "Love the Lord your God with your whole heart, your whole soul, your whole strength, and your whole mind, and you will rise up and walk." The Levite would also come and say, "That is right. But you must also love your neighbor as yourself." These are their messages. This is what a priest and a Levite would say to a dying man. "It is true that you are half dead and that your shining garments have been stripped away. But if you would do good, you can be saved." This is the meaning of loving God with the whole heart, the whole soul, the whole strength, and the whole mind. This is what it means to love God. If you see one who has not been beaten, that one may still have the heart, the soul, the strength, and the mind to do something. It would still be possible for him to love God with his whole heart, his whole soul, his whole strength, and his whole mind. It would have been possible to tell him this if he were still in Jerusalem. But the problem today is that he is no longer in Jerusalem. He is on a journey, and he is dying. These commandments cannot help him. Therefore, please remember that it is not a question of giving our "whole," but of getting some help. Here is a man who is dying of sickness. He is living in sin. He cannot do anything about his condition. If you tell the sinner to love God with all his heart, soul, strength, and mind, he would say that he has never loved God in his life. If you say that he has to love his neighbor, he would tell you that he has been robbing others all his life. What should you say to a man who is about to step into eternity? At this juncture, the priests and the Levites are of no help. They can only pass by on the other side. When they see this kind of man, they cannot help him.

The word about loving God with our whole heart, soul, strength, and mind, and loving our neighbor as ourself is not to help us to inherit eternal life. It is only to show us the kind of persons we are. If you have never heard a word about loving God, you would not know how important it is to love God. If you have never heard anything about loving your neighbor, you would not know how important it is to love your neighbor. Once you have heard the word about loving your neighbor, you will realize that you have never loved your neighbor. Actually, the words in the law such as loving God, loving the neighbors, not coveting or killing, are there only to expose our sinfulness. They show us our condition. The end of the law, as James has said, is simply to serve as a mirror. It shows you who you are. You do not know what your face looks like. But if you look in a mirror, you see what you look like. Formerly, you did not know that you do not love God. Now you know. Not only is there no love with the whole heart, whole soul, whole strength, and whole mind, there is not any love for God at all. Not only is there no love for God, there is not even love for one's neighbor. You have been robbed by the robbers already. Yet you still do not know what has happened. With the law, you know. You were beaten by the robbers, left half dead, and stripped of your garments, and you did not even know it. Now you know. What then did the priests and the Levites do? They came to say: "My friend, do you not know that you have been beaten by the robbers? Do you not know that your garments have been stripped off? Do you not know that you are half dead?"

After a while, another one came. This was the good Samaritan. "But a certain Samaritan, who was journeying, came upon him." Unlike the other two, this one came journeying. The priest came by coincidence. The Levite also came by coincidence. But the Samaritan came journeying. He came purposely to save him. "And when he saw him, he was moved with compassion." He had love, and he had compassion. At the same time, he had oil and wine with him. Hence, he could heal the one beaten by the robbers. Who is this Samaritan? John 4:9 tells us that the Jews had no dealings with the Samaritans. Everyone mentioned in this story was a Jew. The one beaten up by the robbers was a Jew. The priest was a Jew. The Levite was a Jew. What do the Jews represent? And what does the Samaritan represent? The Jews represent us human beings. What about the Samaritan? The Samaritans have no dealings with the Jews. They do not mix in with the Jews. They are apart from the Jews and above the Jews. We know that this One is the Lord Jesus. One day when the Lord Jesus was on earth, a group of Jews criticized the Lord Jesus and reviled Him with two very strong statements, saying that He was a Samaritan and one who had a demon (John 8:48). Please notice that in Jesus' answer He said that He did not have a demon. The Jews said that He was a Samaritan and had a demon. The Lord denied that He had a demon but did not deny that He was a Samaritan. Hence, the Samaritan here refers to the Lord Jesus. John shows us that in type He is a Samaritan.

This Samaritan came purposely to this half-dead man. When he saw the man, he was moved with compassion, and he saved him with two things. One was wine, and the other was oil. He poured out the oil and the wine, put them on the wounds, and bound up the wounds. We have to see that this is after Golgotha and after Pentecost. This is not at Bethlehem. If it were at Bethlehem, it would have been the wine on the oil. But since Jerusalem and since the house of Cornelius, it is the oil on the wine. Wine represents the work of Golgotha. Oil represents the work on the day of resurrection and the day of Pentecost. Wine is symbolized by the cup at the Lord's table. When you become sick, what the elders bring to your house is the oil. What is represented there is what is spoken of here. In other words, wine is the work of redemption, and oil is the work of fellowship. Wine symbolizes the blood of the Lord in redeeming us, and oil symbolizes the Holy Spirit applying the work of the Lord to us. This is very meaningful. If it were only the oil poured without the wine, there would be no foundation for our salvation. If there were no oil, salvation would not have any effect. Without the cross, it would have been unrighteous for God to forgive our sins. It would mean that He was dealing with our sins in a loose way. It would mean that He was glossing over our sins. But without the oil, though God may have accomplished redemption in His Son and may have solved the problem of our sins, that work could not be applied to us; we would still be wounded.

Here we see that there is oil, and there is wine. Furthermore, the oil is mentioned first. It is the Holy Spirit who has applied the work of the Lord upon us. This is the procedure of salvation. It is the oil that is mingled into the wine. The Holy Spirit does nothing other than convey the Lord's work to us. How wonderful this is! Many of our sisters are nurses. We also have two brothers here who are doctors. Do you know that the function of the wine is altogether negative? It is used as a disinfectant. This means that the redemption of the Lord is to deal with past filth and past sins. The oil is there to help the wine. Here, on the one hand, there is the removal of what was in the first Adam. On the other hand, there is the new life from the Holy Spirit. Only by this can the dying man be healed. I will speak more concerning this matter if I have an opportunity later.

After the good Samaritan bound up the wounds of the man beaten by the robbers, what happened next? He placed him on his own beast. The beast denotes traveling. With a beast, you can travel without exerting much effort. When there is a beast, I do not have to travel by my own effort; the beast will carry me. Where did the beast go? It went to the inn. This inn is the house of God. When this man is brought to God, God cares for him.

What is the meaning of two denarii? All the metals in the Bible have their meanings. Gold in the Bible signifies God's nature, life, glory, and righteousness. Brass in the Bible signifies God's judgment. All the places in the Bible that require judgment have brass. The altar was brass, the laver was brass, and the brass serpent was brass. The Lord's feet were as shining brass; they are for trampling. In the Bible iron signifies political authority. But silver throughout the Bible signifies redemption. Every time redemption is mentioned, silver is there. In the Old Testament, the money paid for redemption was silver. The two denarii here signify the price of redemption. The two denarii were handed to the innkeeper. This is our salvation. Because of this, God has accepted all those that trust in Him. Spiritually speaking, the inn signifies God's heavenly house. Physically speaking, it signifies the church. "Whatever you spend in addition to this, when I return, I will repay you." After we are saved, we are in the church, waiting for the Lord's return. These points are not my main subject, but I mention them in passing.

The lawyer asked the Lord, "Who is my neighbor?" After the Lord told him this story, He replied to the lawyer with a question, "Which of these three, does it seem to you, has become a neighbor to him who fell into the hands of the robbers?" If you listen carefully to this word, you will realize that the Lord is telling the lawyer that he was the one who fell into the hands of the robbers.

Many today apply this passage incorrectly. They think that the Lord Jesus wants us to love our neighbor as ourself. Whether it is the Bible schools, the Sunday schools, or the Sunday pulpits, they all tell people that one has to be a good Samaritan. You have to love your neighbors, to show mercy to them, and to help them. To them, who is the neighbor? It is the one who was wounded by the robbers. And who are we? We are the good Samaritan. But this is exactly the opposite of what the Lord Jesus was saying. What the Lord meant was that we are the ones wounded by the robbers. Who then is our neighbor? Our neighbor is the good Samaritan. We think that we are the good Samaritan. We can move. We can walk. When we see those bound by sin, we are able to help them. But the Lord Jesus said that we are not the good Samaritan. Rather, we need the good Samaritan. We are the man wounded by robbers on the journey. We are those who are waiting to die. We do not have any good works. Who is our neighbor? He is the good Samaritan. What is it to love our neighbor as ourselves? It does not say that we have to love others as ourselves. It means that we have to love the Savior as ourselves. It does not mean that we must first love others before we can inherit eternal life. Rather, it means that if we love the Savior, the Samaritan, we will surely have eternal life.

The problem today is that man continually thinks of works. When he reads Luke 10, he says to himself: "Someone is wounded. Someone is dying. If I care for him and love him, I will be a good Samaritan, and I will have eternal life." We think that when we help others, we will inherit eternal life. But the Lord Jesus said if you allow someone to help you, you will have eternal life. None among us is qualified to be the good Samaritan. Thank the Lord, we do not have to be the good Samaritan. We have a good Samaritan already. This Samaritan, who formerly had no dealings with us, has now come. He has died and has solved the problem of our sins. He is now resurrected, and He has given us a new life. This One has bound up our wounds. He has given us redemption. He is helping us and is bringing us to heaven, that God would accept us and care for us.

Finally, we have verse 37: "And he said, The one who showed mercy to him." This time the lawyer answered correctly. He answered that it is the One who showed mercy to him. The One who shows mercy to me is my neighbor. My neighbor is the Samaritan who stopped to bind up my wounds with the oil and the wine, who put me on the beast and brought me to the inn. My friends, the whole question is not to be the neighbor of someone else. Rather, it is the One who showed mercy to you becoming your neighbor.

The Lord Jesus said, "Go, and you do likewise." This word confuses many people. They think that the Lord is telling us to help others. But what this word means is that your neighbor is the good Samaritan. Therefore you should accept Him as your Savior. Since your neighbor is the good Samaritan, you must be the one wounded by the robbers. This shows us that while we were lying there, He came and saved us. Never say that we can do anything ourselves. Never say that we have the way. He is showing us that we have to let Him do everything. We have to let Him pour the oil and the wine on our wounds. We have to let Him bind up our wounds. We have to let Him put us up on the beast and bring us to the inn. We have to let Him do the work of taking care of us. We have to be like the one wounded. We do not have to be like the Samaritan. Man's greatest failure is to think that he should do something. Man always wants to be his own savior. He always wants to save others. But God has not appointed us to be the savior. God says that we are the ones to be saved.

Hence, the Lord's word fully answered the lawyer's question. It does not mean that one should not love God with his whole heart, his whole soul, his whole strength, and his whole mind. The question is whether or not he can do it. We cannot do it either. We have a wounded life. Actually, our real condition is that we are dead. Our body is living, but our spirit is dead. We need salvation. We cannot help God. Neither can we help man. If we think that we can do something, we will not experience the forgiveness of sins. The work of the cross and the work of the Holy Spirit will not come upon us.

Hence, remember that Luke 10:25-37 never tells us that man is saved through loving God. On the contrary, it says that the Samaritan was first moved with compassion before we could love. He loves first, and then we can love. Before He has loved, we cannot love. It is true that if any man does not love the Lord, he is accursed. In Luke 7, the Lord Jesus told Simon that he who has been forgiven the most loves the most, and he who has been forgiven little loves little. Love comes after forgiveness. It is not a matter that he who loves much receives much forgiveness, and he who loves little receives little forgiveness. However much a person is forgiven, that is how much he loves. A Christian loves the Lord because He has saved him. If you cannot even love the Samaritan, then I do not know what I can say of you. There is no such person on earth. There is no one on earth who does not love the Lord at all; everyone has to love Him at least a little. The Lord said that he who has been forgiven little loves little. It does not say that there is no love. Everyone loves Him to a greater or lesser extent. However, the condition of salvation is not our love. If I am saved because I love the Lord, then one can see that this is very unreliable. Within two or three days, I can change so many times. I am one who has been wounded by the robbers. I am lying there. I can do nothing at all. I am at the end of myself. I do not love God with all my heart, and I do not love my neighbor. But now I allow Him to save me. After He has saved me, I can love Him. We love Him because He has first loved us. It is God's love in us that has produced our love for Him. It is utterly impossible for us by ourselves to produce a love for God.

## SALVATION NOT BEING THROUGH BAPTISM

Now we have to consider another question. Some people say that a man cannot be saved without being baptized. Perhaps those among us would not say this. But some who have been affected by the poison of Roman Catholic tradition may be full of this kind of thought. Recently, a few co-workers and I met a few western missionaries in Canton. They all paid much attention to this matter of baptism. There is a certain missionary in Hong Kong who is very strong about this matter. They certainly have their scriptural basis, which is Mark 16:16: "He who believes and is baptized shall be saved, but he who does not believe shall be condemned." Some would argue that this means if a man has believed but has not been baptized, he is still not saved, because this verse clearly says that he who believes and is baptized shall be saved.

Here I would like to ask a question. What does salvation mean here? It says: "He who believes and is baptized shall be saved." But following this it says: "He who does not believe shall be condemned." From this we see that the salvation here must not refer merely to deliverance from condemnation. We must be careful here. The Lord says he who believes and is baptized shall be saved. The corresponding sentence should be that he who does not believe shall not be saved. But it is so strange that it says he who does not believe is condemned. Hence, the salvation in the first clause must not refer to the not being condemned in the second clause. We have to see that not only does salvation refer to a man's salvation before God, but it also refers to his salvation before men. Before God, it is a question of condemnation or no condemnation. Before men, it is a question of being saved or not being saved. Before God, all those who believe in the Lord Jesus are not condemned. He who does not believe is condemned already. This is the word of John 3:18. But one cannot say that he who believes and is baptized shall not be condemned. We can say that he who believes and is baptized shall be saved, but not that he who believes and is baptized shall not be condemned. This is because condemnation has to do with God. Salvation here does not have to do with God. Salvation has to do with man. That is why the question of baptism comes in. To be condemned or not is a matter before God. That is why there is only the difference between believing and not believing. To be saved or not is not before God; it is something for man to see. That is why there is the difference between baptism and no baptism.

When we read the Bible, we have to take care of these distinctions. We will take John 3 again as an example. The Lord Jesus said in verse 5: "Unless one is born of water and the Spirit, he cannot enter into the kingdom of God." Then in verses 6 and 8, when it mentions this matter again, it mentions only being born of the Spirit, without mentioning being born of water. The reason for this is that there are two sides to the kingdom of God. One side is spiritual, and the other side is earthly. Spiritually speaking, if a man is not born again, he cannot enter into the kingdom of God. This is a fact. But there is still the human side. On the human side, there is not only the need to be born of the Spirit, but the need to be born of water also. What is the Spirit like? It says the wind blows where it wills. We can also say that the Spirit blows where it wills. In the original language, wind and spirit are the same word. Both are *pneuma*. The Spirit blows where He wills. One does not know where He comes from or where He is going. Man cannot control the wind in the sky. When it comes, it simply comes. When it goes, it simply goes. Many times, we only hear the sound of the wind, and know that it is here, or that it is gone. We cannot control the wind in the sky, but we can control the water on the ground. I have no way to control the wind blowing on my face. But I can determine whether I want to go into the water or not. The wind blows where it wills, but the water goes where I will. I cannot order the Spirit in heaven to put me into the kingdom. But I can manage to get myself into the water. I can have a part in the kingdom of God on earth. When I am baptized, no one can say that I do not belong to the Lord. This is why the Lord said in Mark 16 that he who believes and is baptized shall be saved.

What is the difference between being saved and not coming into condemnation? Please remember that condemnation is something strictly before God, but salvation is relative; it is something before God and something before man as well. Whether I am condemned or not is a matter before God. But whether I am saved or not has to do with God and has to do also with man. Salvation is toward God and man; condemnation is strictly toward God. Once a man believes, he will not be condemned before God. He who does not believe has been condemned already. Those who are in Christ shall not be condemned. But those who do not believe have been condemned already. This is the question before God all the time. But thank the Lord, salvation is with God and with man as well. On the one hand, we have to believe, so that we can be saved before God. On the other hand, we have to be baptized, so that we can be saved before man.

If there is a man today who continues to be a Christian secretly, should we acknowledge him as a Christian? He has believed and is no longer condemned before God. But one cannot say that he is saved before man. Before God we have to be delivered from condemnation. But before man we have to be saved. If there is a person who has genuinely believed in the Son of God and has genuinely believed in the work of the Lord's cross, yet he never confesses with his mouth, nor has he ever been baptized, others will not know if he is saved. There is only one condition to be saved before God and to come out of condemnation before God, which is to believe. But to be saved before man there is another condition, which is to be baptized. I am not saying that baptism is not necessary. We definitely need to be baptized. Baptism has to do with our salvation. But this salvation is not what some people think. This is absolutely not a question of coming under condemnation. It does not say that if you are not baptized, you will be condemned. Rather, it says that if you do not believe, you will be condemned. Before God there is no question of baptism; there is only the question of faith. Once there is faith, everything is settled. Baptism is not for God. Baptism is for man. It is a testimony among men, testifying of the position that one stands upon. Are you a person in Adam? Or are you a person in Christ? This fact is testified by baptism.

Thank God that the thief next to the Lord's cross went to Paradise. At that time, Peter was not there yet. Neither was John or Paul. Right after the Lord went to Paradise, the thief followed Him. But he was not baptized. Before God, whoever calls on His name shall be saved. Why does a person call on His name? It is because he has believed. But whether those on earth will say that such a person is saved or not is another question. In the next few evenings I will make a clear distinction for you. It seems that in the Bible, justification, forgiveness, and coming out of condemnation are all before God. But salvation is before God and before man as well. If you are not clear about these things, you will create many problems. In the Bible, many places refer to what happens before man. Many other places refer to what happens before God. If we confuse the two, we will fall into error.

I have said that baptism refers to a man's coming out of Adam and into Christ. On one side is Adam. On the other side is Christ. We have to get out of Adam and into Christ. How do we get out? We were a part of Adam. How can we now come out of Adam and into Christ? Let me first ask one question: How did we get into Adam? If I ask how we can get out of Adam, some would say that they do not know. That is why I ask how we got into Adam. The way we enter in will be the way we get out. How did we get into Adam? The Lord Jesus said in John 3:6 that that which is born of the flesh is flesh. How did I become a part of Adam? I was born into him. Now that you know how you got in, you will know how you can get out. If you got into him by birth, you have to get out of him by death. This is quite obvious. But how do we die? God crucified us when the Lord Jesus was crucified on the cross. Therefore, in Christ we have died to Adam. How then do we get into Christ? The Lord goes on to say that that which is born of the Spirit is spirit. I get into Christ by birth. Peter said that we are regenerated through the resurrection of Jesus Christ from among the dead (1 Pet. 1:3). Hence, it is His resurrection that has regenerated us. Here we see two things: through the death of the Lord, we are delivered from the family of Adam.

Through resurrection, we have entered into Christ. Through death, we are delivered from the first Adam. Through resurrection, we have entered into the second Man. All of these are accomplished by the Lord Jesus. He has died on the cross. As a result we also have died. He has resurrected. As a result we have entered into the new creation.

The death is spiritual, and the resurrection is also spiritual. But our baptism is physical. What then is baptism? Baptism is our acting out. Through His servants, His apostles, the Lord Jesus told us of His work: When He died on the cross, we were also included in His death. What should we do after we have heard this? According to history, this happened two thousand years ago. We were already crucified two thousand years ago on the cross of our Lord Jesus. His word is now preached to us. It tells us that we have died. What then should we do now? I once asked a village woman this question. She answered, "If the Lord Jesus has crucified me, then I need to buy a coffin." This is altogether right! The Lord Jesus has crucified me. Why should I not buy a coffin? Since He has crucified me, I must hurry to bury myself. Baptism is my request to be buried in the water because I have been crucified by the Lord. Baptism is a response to God's crucifixion of us. God has preached the gospel to you and told you that you are dead. Your response is that since you have been crucified, you will find someone to bury you. Hence, baptism means that we are dead in Adam already. Others are taking me out to be buried. Now we are on the ground of resurrection. Hence, death is our exit from Adam, and resurrection is our entrance into Christ. Baptism is our burial. Death is the termination of Adam, and resurrection is the new beginning in Christ. Baptism is the bridge between these two sides. Through baptism we pass from death to resurrection.

My friends, the Lord Jesus has accomplished everything. There is no condition required for us to be saved. All we have to do is to simply believe. To believe is to receive. I need only to receive because the Lord has done everything. I no longer have to do anything. Baptism is through faith. It is an acting out. Let me ask: If there is no plot, how can we perform? Do we have a plot first and then an act, or do we have an act first and then a plot? All plays exist because there was a plot already. Because there is a spiritual fact before God already, we can act it out through baptism.

May the Lord be gracious to us and show us that nothing other than faith can be a condition for salvation. Baptism has absolutely nothing to do with salvation or condemnation before God. We come out of condemnation before God through faith. Our acting out at baptism is only for our salvation before man. May the Lord be gracious to us and make us clear about our salvation.

# CHAPTER FOURTEEN

# THE WAY OF SALVATION—FAITH

## GOD'S SALVATION BEING FOR EVERYONE
## THROUGH FAITH

Over the past few evenings, we have looked at the things that man considers to be ways of salvation. If we do not twist the Word of God but trust in it, we will see from it that none of those things are a condition for salvation. As we have mentioned already, according to the Bible there is only one condition for salvation—faith. Together the words *faith* and *believe* occur in the Bible over five hundred times. Among these many verses, over a hundred verses tell us that salvation is by believing, that justification is by believing, and that we receive life by believing. In over thirty places we are told that through faith we receive this or that from God. These places show us that man is favored by God through faith and nothing else.

Why does the Bible put so much emphasis on faith? Tonight we will consider why faith has to be the way of salvation. But we must first ask a question. Is salvation a work of man or a work of God? Is it man's plan or is it God's plan? Does it originate with man or with God? Those who do not know God do not know salvation. Only those who know God know God's salvation. Those who know God have to admit that it is God who has initiated salvation. It is God who has planned it, and it is God who has accomplished this plan. As we have mentioned before, everything is done by God. On our side, we do not have to do anything except believe.

Why do we have to believe? It is because redemption is accomplished by Christ. God wants to make the method of salvation so simple that everyone can obtain it. That is why He requires only faith. If salvation is from God, it must be universal. If God's salvation were just for a certain group of people, God would be partial. If God's way of salvation required something from us, that something would become an obstacle to our salvation. If there were the simple requirement that man had to wait five minutes before he could be saved, even that would greatly diminish the number of saved ones in the world. Many people do not have even five minutes to wait. God would not have to require even perfect righteousness. If He were to require righteousness in only one thing, perhaps you could render Him this righteousness, but hundreds of thousands of people on earth might not be able to do so. If such were the case, salvation would not be so simple.

In America there was a famous preacher named Dr. Jowett. He had a co-worker named Mr. Barry. Mr. Barry was a pastor in a church, but he had not yet been saved. One night someone rang the doorbell of his church. After letting the bell ring for a long time, Mr. Barry reluctantly put on his night robe and went to see who it was. At the door was a young, improperly dressed girl. When he asked her bluntly what she wanted, the girl asked, "Are you the pastor?" When he admitted that he was, the girl said, "I need help to get my mother in." He thought that a girl dressed in such a way must have a terrible home. He thought that perhaps her mother was drunk, and she needed help to get her mother back into the house. He told the girl to call the police, but the girl insisted that he go. He tried his best to turn her down and told her to go to the pastor of the church nearest her. But the girl said, "Your church is the nearest church." Then he said, "It is too late now. Come back tomorrow." But she insisted that he go at once. Mr. Barry thought for a while. He was a pastor of a church with over twelve hundred members. If one of them saw him walking with this young girl dressed in that kind of way in the middle of the night, what would they think? But the girl insisted and said that if he would not go, she would not leave. Finally, he gave in and went upstairs to change. Mr. Barry later told Dr. Jowett that while he was walking to the girl's house, he pulled his hat down very low to cover his face and tucked in his coat for fear that others might see him. The place where they went was not in a nice area. When he stopped before the house that they were to enter, he saw that it was not a decent place at all. Then he asked the girl, "Why do you want me to come to such a place?" The girl answered, "My mother is very sick. She is in terrible danger. She said that she wants to get into the kingdom of God. Please get her in." Mr. Barry could not do anything except step into the house. The girl and her mother lived in a very small and dingy room. Their home was very poor. When the sick woman saw him coming, she cried out, "Please help me to get in. I cannot get in." He thought for a while and wondered what he should do. He was a pastor and a preacher, and here was a woman who was dying. She wanted to enter the kingdom of God; she wanted to be taught how to get in. What could he do? He did not know what to do. So he spoke to her in the way he spoke to his congregation. He began to tell her that Jesus was a perfect man, that He was our model, that He sacrificed Himself, that He displayed such benevolence, and that Jesus went about helping people. If men follow in His footsteps to sacrifice themselves, to love and help others, and to serve society, they would uplift their humanity and others' humanity. Mr. Barry was talking to her with his eyes closed. When he finished, she became mad. She cried out, "No, no! This is not what I want you to speak about." Her tears began to fall. She said, "Sir, tonight is my last night on earth. Now is the time for me to settle the question of eternal perdition or entry into God's kingdom. This is my last chance. Don't try to take me for a ride or play games with me. I have sinned my whole life long. And not only have I sinned, but I have also taught my daughter to sin. Now I am dying. What can I do? Don't play games with me. All my life I have done nothing but sin. Everything I did was unclean. I never knew what being moral meant. I never knew what it was to be clean. I never knew what it was to have a conscience. Now you are telling such a sinner as me, in the state that I am in tonight, to take Jesus as my model! How much work would I have to do before I could take Jesus as my model! You told me that I have to follow in the footsteps of Jesus. But how much would I have to do before I could follow in His footsteps! Don't play games with me at this hour so crucial to my eternity. Just tell me how I can get into God's kingdom. What you told me will not work for me. I cannot do any of those things." Mr. Barry was taken by surprise. He thought to himself, "These are the things that I learned in theological school. I studied them for my doctorate in theology. I have been preaching them for the past seventeen or eighteen years. And these are the things I have read out of the Bible. But here is a woman who wants to get in, and I cannot help her." So he said, "To tell you the truth, I don't know how to get in. I only know that Jesus was a good man, that we have to imitate Him, that He was benevolent, and that He sacrificed Himself to help others. All I know is that if a man takes Jesus as his example and walks as He walked, he will be a Christian." In tears the woman said, "Can you do nothing for a woman who has been sinful all her life to help her enter God's kingdom at the last hour? Is that all you can do to help a dying woman to get into God's kingdom, who will have no tomorrow and who will have no second chance?" Mr. Barry was stuck. He had nothing more to say. He thought, "I am a servant of Christ. I am a doctor of theology. I am a pastor of a twelve hundred member church. But here is a woman on her deathbed, and I cannot help her at all. She even thinks that I am playing games with her." But then Mr. Barry remembered something he had heard from his mother while sitting on her lap when he was seven years old. She had told him that Jesus of Nazareth is the Son of God, that He was crucified, and that He shed His blood to cleanse us from sins. Jesus of Nazareth died for our sins on the cross and has become the propitiatory sacrifice. He remembered these words then. He had neglected these words all his life, but that day these words came back to him. Then he rose up and said, "Yes, I have something for you. You do not have to do anything, but God has done everything in His Son. He has dealt with our sins in His Son. God's Son has taken away all our sins. The One who demands the payment became the One who pays. The One who was offended became the One who suffered for the offense. The Judge has become the judged." At that word, the woman's face showed signs of joy. He went on to tell her all that his mother had told him. Then, suddenly the woman's face turned from joy to tears, and she cried,

"Why didn't you tell me this earlier? What should I do now?" He then told her that she needed only to believe and to receive. At that word, the woman died. Later Mr. Barry told Dr. Jowett that on that night the woman entered in and he also entered in.

I have been touched in my heart many times by this story. If there is salvation, it should be available to anyone. If you say that one must be baptized before he can be saved, then the thief on the cross could not be saved, because he was not baptized. If you say that one cannot be saved unless he makes restitution, then the thief on the cross could not have been saved, because both his hands and feet were nailed firmly to the cross. I am not saying that we should not be baptized or make restitution. But the condition for salvation is not restitution, baptism, confession, or repentance. Repentance is nothing but a changed view about one's past. If it were a matter of law and work, who could fulfill it? This woman is the best example of God's salvation being for everyone.

## BELIEVING IN THE LORD'S DEATH
## AND RESURRECTION

The only condition for God's salvation is faith. Faith is saying that you are willing and that you want it. What is the faith that the Bible talks about? First, God has accomplished redemption by the death of His Son Jesus Christ on the cross. His work on the cross has been completed. Why has it been completed? I do not know why. Neither do you. Only God knows why. How can the blood of the Lord Jesus redeem us from our sins? Why is the Lord's redemption effective? We do not need to ask these questions. These are matters for God. The Lord's work on the cross has been accomplished, and God's heart is satisfied.

The cross of the Lord Jesus is not for satisfying our heart. It is for satisfying God's heart. Does the settlement of a debt satisfy the heart of the creditor or the heart of the debtor? If God feels that something is sufficient for Him, we also should feel that it is sufficient. God is righteous. If He says that the Lord's work is able to redeem us from sin, it is surely able to redeem us. Whether or not you think that the work is sufficient is irrelevant. What matters is that God thinks that the work is sufficient. It is not just a matter of whether or not the money has been paid. What matters is whether or not the creditor considers the money paid. If the money you pay satisfies his heart, you will have no problems. I wish I could repeat this a hundred times. The work of the Lord Jesus is not to satisfy our heart. The work of the Lord is first for the satisfaction of God's heart. It is God who demands the judgment on sins. It is God who requires that sins be dealt with. It is God who said that without the blood there is no remission of sins. If God were unconcerned, the blood would be unnecessary. The blood is there because God is concerned. If God were unconcerned, the cross would be unnecessary. There is the need of the cross because God is righteous.

The Lord has accomplished all the work on the cross. Hence, God raised Him from the dead. The resurrection of the Lord Jesus is the proof that God is satisfied with the Lord's work on the cross. Although we do not understand how the cross has satisfied God's heart, we know that Jesus of Nazareth has risen from the grave. Was it the death of Jesus of Nazareth that the apostles went all over the world to preach? Have you heard such a gospel? I have never heard such a gospel. They went all over the world only to tell others that Jesus of Nazareth has been resurrected. If you read the book of Acts, you will see that the apostles did not preach the death of Jesus for our sins. What they told people everywhere is that this man had resurrected. They preached this because the fact of the Lord's resurrection proves that His death has glorified God. The Lord Jesus was resurrected because His work had been accepted before God. His redemption is complete, and we can now be saved. If the Lord's work had not been completed, He would have been left in the grave. Hence, resurrection is nothing other than the Lord Jesus satisfying God's heart. The Lord Jesus has resurrected from the dead. The apostles preach this to us as a proof for our faith, calling us to believe in the Lord Jesus. On the one hand, salvation has to do with the Lord's death. On the other hand, it has to do with the Lord's resurrection. His death is for the settlement of our debt and the forgiveness of our sins. By this death the problem of our sins is solved. His resurrection is the proof that His work of death has satisfied God's heart. God considers His work right and proper.

I have used an illustration before, which I will use again for the sake of the many new ones with us. If I have sinned, I should go to jail. But suppose a friend of mine volunteers to go in my place. Because he goes to jail, I am released. But it is not until he is released that I know my case is settled. Only then will my heart be relieved. My body is released because his is imprisoned. But my heart is released only when he comes out. Until the case is over, he will still be inside. If he is still in jail, I will not know if he has borne my punishment or if I will still be wanted. When he is out of prison, I will know that the case is settled. In the same way, as soon as the Lord Jesus died, the problem of my sin was solved. But the Lord Jesus had to resurrect before I could know that the problem of sin was solved. He was delivered for our transgressions and was resurrected for our justification. He resurrected because the problem of our justification was solved. We can go to the world to tell everyone of the work God has accomplished through the death of His Son Jesus Christ. At the same time, we can tell others that through the resurrection of the Lord, God has given us a receipt and a proof. It informs us that the task is finished. Today we do not merely believe in the cross. Rather, we believe also in the resurrection.

Can you find one verse in the Bible that tells man to believe in the cross? It is very strange that we are always told to believe in the resurrection. If you meet a nominal Christian today who may have been a member of a church for ten, twenty, or thirty years and talk with him a little, you will realize that there is a big difference between believing in the cross and believing in the resurrection. I met a member of a denomination once who had been an elder for thirty-eight years and a "Christian" for fifty or sixty years. When I asked if he believed in the Lord Jesus, he said, "Yes." But when I asked if he knew that his sins were forgiven, he dared not say yes. Then I asked him if Jesus was his Savior, and he said, "Yes." But when I asked him if he was saved, he said that he did not know. When I asked him if he believed that the Lord

Jesus had been judged on the cross for our sins, he readily said that he did. Not only does the Bible say this, even our hymn book says it. It says that thousands of bulls and goats on the Jewish altar will not forgive us of our sins, but the one sacrifice of the Lord cleanses us from all sin. When I asked this man if he were cleansed from his sins, he said he believed that the crucifixion of the Lord was for his sins, but he dared not say that his sins were washed away. I cannot blame him for being unclear. It is true that the Lord Jesus died on the cross. But how can one know that this cross counts? He believes in the cross, but how does he know that the cross has solved all his problems and settled his case? Although the settlement for sin happened on the cross, what makes us clear is the resurrection. If you repay someone some money, how do you know that the amount paid is sufficient and that the bank notes are genuine? What if the notes are counterfeit? Only one thing will assure you that the amount has been fully paid—a receipt from your creditor saying that the amount has been paid in full. When you pay the money, the creditor clears your account, and you know that the matter is settled. In the same way, the death of the Lord Jesus speaks of what He has done for God, while His resurrection speaks of what God has done for us. Death is the settlement between Him and God, but resurrection is the announcement to us of the settlement between God and His Son. God said that the debt has been cleared. If you believe that the Lord's death is for your sins, the Lord's resurrection will then declare that your sin record has been cleared. Many people say that we have to settle our sin account, and that if it is not settled, we cannot be saved. Thank the Lord that my sin account was settled before I was even born. Even the receipt was issued. The death of the Lord Jesus was the settlement of the debt, and the resurrection of the Lord Jesus was the proof of this settlement. Resurrection is the proof of justification. We are justified because God has been gracious to us and has redeemed us from sin. The death of the Lord Jesus was for the solution of sin. The resurrection of the Lord Jesus was for the proof of justification. Hence, our faith rests on the resurrection of the Lord Jesus.

This is not all that resurrection accomplished. If we think that it is, we are wrong. This is only the objective aspect of resurrection. There is still the subjective aspect. Objectively speaking, the resurrection of the Lord becomes the proof of our salvation. If anyone were to ask me how I know that I am saved, I would tell him that I have the proof. This proof proves that I am saved. You may tell me that you were saved on a certain date in a certain year because that was when you received the Lord. I would then ask how you could know that was sufficient. You may say that you confessed your sins that day, but how do you know that confession is sufficient? You may say that you cried for your sins that day, but how do you know that your tears will wash your sins away? You may say that you have repented, confessed your sins, and accepted the Lord Jesus, but how do you know that this repentance, confession, and receiving of the Lord is sufficient? If you asked me, I would answer that I am actually saved because of the Lord's death, but I know that I am saved because of the Lord's resurrection. My friends, you have to differentiate between the two. I am saved because of the Lord's death, but I have the assurance and clear knowledge that I am saved because of the Lord's resurrection. When I pay the money, I settle my debt. I know that I have settled the debt because I have a receipt. Thank God that He has given us a proof and a receipt. His Son has paid the debt for all our sins on the cross, and through the resurrection of His Son, He has informed us that the matter is fully settled. Hence, all of the Lord's work is now finished.

If there is anyone here tonight who still doubts that he is saved, I only need to ask him what he has believed in and what he has received. It is not sufficient for a person just to believe in the cross and to receive the redemption of the Lord on the cross. One must also believe in His resurrection. The resurrection of the Lord Jesus is God's message to us. It shows us that God has accepted the Lord's work. Thank God that the cross has satisfied God's heart. That is why there is the resurrection. Thus, the foundation of our faith is the death of Christ, but our faith is also based on the proof of resurrection. Death is His work of redeeming us. Resurrection is the proof of His having redeemed us. Notice that here I have said "having redeemed." Death is His work of redeeming us, and resurrection is the proof of His having redeemed us.

## RECEIVING THE LORD'S WORK
## THROUGH FAITH IN GOD'S WORD

The work of the Lord is now complete. His death has taken place, and His resurrection has also taken place. What happens next? The Bible shows clearly that God has put all His Son's work in His Word. What is the Bible, and what is God's Word? Many times I like to think of God's Word as God's pocket for His work. God put all His work into His Word. If God were standing among us today, and He wanted to show us His Son's work and the proof of this work, how could He do it? He put the work of His Son's cross in His Word. He also put the proof of His Son's resurrection in His Word. Today God communicates all these things to us through His Word. When we receive His Word, we receive the proof of His work. Behind the Word are the facts. If there were no facts behind the words, the words would be empty. Behind the words there surely are the facts.

In winter, everyone, both male and female, wears gloves. God's Word is God's glove. All His works are contained in it. One day I met a western female missionary. She did not know what it was to believe in God's Word. She thought that all she needed to do was to believe in God, in His Son Jesus Christ, and in God's work. I told her that without God's Word there is no way to believe in God, in His Son Jesus Christ, and in God's work. Once we believe in God's Word, all these items become effective to us. After two hours of talking, I still could not get through with her. Later, she was about to leave. She had on a pair of deerskin gloves. She was about to take off the gloves to shake hands with me. I said, "You don't have to take them off. I can shake with your gloves on." To her this was quite impolite. Perhaps she considered that I was a Chinese and that I did not know proper manners. When I shook her hand I asked, "What am I holding now, the hand or the glove?" Immediately she understood what I meant. I told her that the hand was in the glove. When I shook the glove, I was shaking the hand. I shook the glove, because in it was the hand. This is like the Word of God. God has put Himself and all the work of His Son's cross in His Word. When you hand me God's Word, you are handing me God in His Word, plus all the work of His Son. When she left, she told me that everything else that had been said was useless. This one word cleared her up.

Today we preach to others the work of God's Son and the testimony of His resurrection. However, it is by His Word that we preach these things. If a man receives God's Word, he receives God's work and God's grace. God's Word is precious because in it there is the substance. What use is it if the gloves are empty? Even if you squeeze them all day long, it is useless. They are useful only when the hands are there. Without the Lord Jesus, the Word of God is dead letters. Without the Lord Jesus, I would surely burn this book.

Hence, what is faith? It is nothing other than the receiving of God's testimony for the work of His Son. God has placed the work of His Son in the Word and has communicated this Word to us. When we believe in His Word, we are believing in Him. First John 5:9 says, "If we receive the testimony of men, the testimony of God is greater." What is the characteristic of God's testimony? "This is the testimony of God that He has testified concerning His Son." The Word of God is concerning His Son. Please read verse 10: "He who believes into the Son of God has the testimony in himself; he who does not believe God has made Him a liar." Please notice the next clause: "Because he has not believed in the testimony which God has testified concerning His Son." What is it to not believe in God? It is to not believe in God's testimony of His Son. What is to believe in God? It is to believe in the words God has spoken, the testimony that He has made concerning His Son. Hence, to believe in God is nothing other than to believe in God's testimony. In the past two weeks, we have seen God's testimony. We have seen what God has done for us, what problems He has solved through His Son, and what proofs He has given us. God has spoken to us His Word. What should we do now? We should believe in Him, that is, we should receive the testimony He has concerning His Son. If there are some here who have not been saved, some may have told you already that you should believe. But what should you believe in? You do not have to believe in a Christ that is sitting in heaven. That is too far away. All you have to do is to believe in this book. This is so near. God's hand is already in the glove. The glove is God's Word. When you believe in God's Word, you are believing in God's Son. When you receive the words of the Bible, you are receiving everything in the Word. Over the past eighteen hundred years, George Müller may be considered as one of the men with the greatest faith. When others asked him what faith was, he answered that faith is when God says something, I say the same. Faith is to believe in God's Word. It is to believe in God through His Word.

## THE HOLY SPIRIT COMMUNICATING GOD'S WORK TO US

There is another matter related to faith in God's Word. How can God's work become ours? The key is the Holy Spirit. The Holy Spirit has come. The Holy Spirit is the keeper of God's Word. The Word of God is living because the Holy Spirit is keeping watch over it. God has placed all His works in His Word. The Holy Spirit is keeping watch over it on the side. Whenever man receives God's Word by faith, the Holy Spirit comes and applies all of God's works to him. Here we see how complete the work of the Triune God is. It is God who has loved us and who has purposed the work of redemption. It is the Son who has accomplished the work of redemption. It is God who has placed the work of the Son in the Word, and it is God who communicates to us through the Holy Spirit all the works of the Son contained in the Word. The greatest problem of man, and his most foolish thought as well, is to be confused about the condition for the Holy Spirit's work. Man thinks that if he repents God will work, or if he is baptized God will work, or if he confesses his sins or does good works, God will work. But there is not such a thing. The Bible tells us clearly that only the Holy Spirit can communicate the Lord's work to us. The characteristic of the Holy Spirit's work is fellowship. After the Lord Jesus accomplished all the work, the Holy Spirit came and communicated this work to us. If there were only the accomplished work of the Lord Jesus without the fellowshipping work of the Holy Spirit, it would still be useless to us. Without the Father, man cannot be saved. Without the Son, man cannot be saved. Likewise, without the Holy Spirit, man cannot be saved. Although there is the work of the Father and the Son, there is still the need of the Holy Spirit to communicate these works to us and to cause the objective matters to become subjective.

The question is now what we should do in order for the Holy Spirit to work on us. The Bible shows us clearly that there is only one condition for the Holy Spirit to work—faith. Do we receive the Holy Spirit by the works of the law or by faith? It is by faith. This is what Paul told us in the book of Galatians. When we believe in God's Word, the Holy Spirit will apply this word to us. That is why I said that the Holy Spirit is the keeper of God's Word.

If there is anyone here tonight who is not yet saved, I hope that you will open your heart to receive God's testimony. You do not have to worry about who the Lord Jesus is. You do not have to worry about who God is. What relates to you directly is the Word of God. If you have a proper relationship with the Word of God, the Holy Spirit will communicate to you all the works of God and the Lord Jesus. If you open your heart and call on Him and invoke Him, like the publican who prayed for God to be merciful to him, or more accurately translated, to be propitiated to him, you will be justified. Once you open your heart to call on Him, the Holy Spirit will communicate God's work to you. This is the work of the Holy Spirit.

Tonight I am only speaking about the initial things of salvation. Actually, all the works of the Holy Spirit follow this principle. Whenever you come to God to receive His Word, the Holy Spirit will make this Word come alive. It may seem that what you receive are dead things, but when the Holy Spirit comes, He will make them alive in you. Do not try to accomplish anything yourself. Do not think that the Holy Spirit is ignorant of your faith in God's Word. No, as soon as you believe, He comes in immediately to work. There is nothing that He does not know. This is the work of the Holy Spirit in redemption. The Triune God has accomplished all the work of salvation for us in order that we may be saved.

## THE FUNCTION OF FAITH—
### SUBSTANTIATION

Perhaps you may ask, "Why would the Holy Spirit communicate to us all of God's work in His Word when we believe in this Word?" The words in 1 John that we just read tell us what faith is. That is the work of faith. But what is the function of faith? The function of faith is the substantiation of the Lord's work in us. This is what Hebrews 11 shows us. Hebrews 11:1 says, "Now faith is the substantiation of things hoped for." The King James Version translates this word as the noun "substance," but in the original language it is not a noun but a gerund, a verbal noun. Darby's translation renders it "substantiating." This is not a noun but a gerund from a verb. This kind of gerund is used often. For example, in the church there is the "overseeing" by the elders. This overseeing is not a noun but a gerund. "Substantiating" is also used in the same way. Faith is a substantiating. Do not underestimate this translation. I have been looking for ten years without finding a suitable word. Then, when I discovered Darby's use of "substantiating," I think I came across the best translation. Everything in the world, whether animals, plants, or minerals, has to be substantiated by us. While we live on the earth, we are constantly substantiating things around us. My eyes substantiate every sight and color. While I am speaking here, some brothers and sisters who are hard of hearing do not know what I am talking about. They only see my mouth moving. I have the words, but they lack the substantiating. I have the substance, but they do not have the power of substantiating it. They cannot substantiate my word in themselves. If there were a singer or some wonderful music here, I could substantiate it with my ears. When our hands touch something, we know that it is smooth or coarse. Our nose can identify a good or a bad smell. Our tongue can identify a sweet or a salty taste. All these are substantiations. All the organs in the human body are doing the work of substantiating.

What is faith? Faith is not making something out of nothing. Faith is substantiating what is there. Faith is not daydreaming or the speaking of a dream. Faith is to manifest what is there already. This is why Hebrews says that faith is the substantiating of things hoped for. The word "things" should be translated "substance." Although they cannot be seen, it does not mean that they are not there. The greatest problem of man today is that he does not have the substantiating ability. As a result, he doubts the reality of the things. If you tell a person who has lost his taste buds to take a sweet drink, he will say that it tastes like some soy sauce he just drank. This is to have the substance without the substantiation. All the spiritual things are there. God has placed all His works in His Word. If you have faith, you will substantiate them.

We who are preaching the gospel are not preaching nonexistent things. The problem today is that many will not substantiate them. In Christ I am full of substance. But many would not substantiate these things. Tonight we have two brothers here who cannot see. I can say that this book is black and that book is brown. When they touch these books, the two are the same to them. You can tell that one is black and another is brown because you can see, but to them there is no distinction between black and brown. If they ask me what black is, I can only say that black is black. I cannot explain it. There is no way to explain it. What is the difficulty? The difficulty lies in their lack of the substantiating ability. It is the same way with us before God. Many are like deaf or blind people. When you talk to them about spiritual things, they say that they do not feel this or that. They have no way to substantiate those things.

Hence, what is faith? The apostle told us clearly that the function of faith is to substantiate the spiritual things. Something was not there with you. Now it is there. Today we are living in a physical world, but God has put all the spiritual things in His Word. The Word of God is full of the things of God. Do not take the Word of God that lightly. Even eternity is in the Word of God. What is the function of faith? The function of faith is to manifest spiritual things in the same way that eyes manifest shapes and colors, ears manifest sounds, and the nose manifests smells. Faith manifests spiritual things. This is why God wants us to have faith.

## RECEIVING BY BELIEVING THAT WE HAVE RECEIVED

Now we have to see how we have to believe. In the Bible, faith has its own laws. In the whole New Testament, there is only one place that tells us the function of faith—Hebrews 11:1. At the same time, in the whole New Testament, there is only one place that tells us how to believe—Mark 11:24: "For this reason I say to you, All things that you pray and ask, believe that you have received them, and you will have them." Here it tells us what it is to believe. What is faith? Faith is to believe in the Word of God. "Believe that you have received them." We have to pay attention to the word "received." It is in the past tense. If you meet a man today who says that he will receive, immediately you know that he does not have faith. If you ask someone if he has believed in the Lord Jesus and if he has been saved, and if he tells you that he hopes to be saved, then he surely is not saved. All those who say that they want to receive or that they hope to receive do not have faith. Mark 11:24 shows us clearly that faith is to believe that we have received. Faith is not to believe that we will receive. It is not to believe that we shall receive, are about to receive, or can receive. All these "wills," "cans," and "shalls" are not faith. Only the faith that believes that one has received is the faith that the Bible talks about.

Many times when I preached the gospel to someone, he would hear about the work of God and realize that all has been done. I would show him his corruption, his weakness, his sins, and his degradation. As a result, he would confess his sins and come to see the work of the Lord Jesus. After this we would kneel down to pray. First I would pray for him. Then he would pray himself. He would confess that he is a sinner and that he has committed many sins. He would ask for forgiveness and ask for the Lord to give him life. After he prayed in this way, I would ask, "Are your sins now forgiven?" If he said, "I believe that God will forgive my sins," I would say to myself, "Forget it. Here is another dead case." If he said, "I believe fully that God will forgive my sins," I would know immediately that he did not have faith.

When will a preacher rejoice over a listener? It is when such a one prays and says, perhaps in tears, that he is clear about everything now. You know that such a one has passed the gate and has obtained eternal life. He may say, "Thank the Lord, the problem of my sins has been solved," or he may say, "Thank the Lord, He has accepted me," or "Thank the Lord, God has forgiven all my sins on account of His Son." When you hear this, you know that such a one has believed and is saved. There is only one kind of faith in the Bible—the faith that believes that one has received. Everyone who says that he will receive, can receive, shall receive, and must receive, has not received.

My friends, this is the way to believe in all the facts in the Bible. With some people, after you pray with them, you know if they have passed from death to life and if they are saved. Many hope to be saved. This is not the real faith. Once I talked with a man who said that he fully believed that he would be saved. I said, "You had better change your wording a little. You should say, "I fully hope" instead of "I fully believe." If you fully believe, then you have received it already. Hence, anyone who has not put the word "have" or "already" into the word of God has not believed. If you say that your sins have been forgiven, this shows that you have believed. If you say that you have overcome your sins, this also shows that you have believed. Or if you say that you have received, this again shows that you have believed. Whenever you can say that you have received, at that time you have truly received. My friends, the matter today is very simple. I will not lower the standard of the Bible. All of God's works are accomplished. The Word of God has been preached to us. The Son of God has died. The Lord Jesus has resurrected. What should we say now? We should say, "Thank the Lord, I have received." This is good enough. Sometimes, when I attend revival meetings, I can almost cry. When the people there cry, I also cry. They cry for themselves, but I cry for God's salvation. They plead to

God saying, "Oh God, save me," as if by this begging, God would be touched to love them or to turn and save them.

Thank the Lord. Those who have faith do not need to pray. Those who have faith are full of praises. Never say that prayer is a sign of faith. Please remember that, on the contrary, prayer is a sign of lack of faith. All experienced Christians know that where there is faith, there is praise. One hymn [*Hymns*, #690] says,

> Hear the message from the throne,
> Claim the promise, doubting one;
> God hath spoken, "It is done."
> Faith has answered, "It is done."
> Prayer is over, praise begun.
> Hallelujah, "It is done."

You cannot say, "It will be done." All those who say it will be done do not have faith. God said that everything is done. You also must say that everything is done. God said that He has accomplished everything, and I believe in this. This is all that matters.

The greatest problem today is that when you go to many denominations, you meet hundreds of church members who say that they believe that Jesus will save them. They believe that Jesus will and can save them, but this is not faith. This is hope. To do this is to annul the Word of God. For example, if I give this book to Brother Hu and he says, "I believe that you will give it to me tomorrow," this is not politeness but an insult to me. Today God has sent His Son to accomplish redemption. If we still say, "Please save me," what is this? What we ought to say is, "God, I thank You because You have taken care of all my sins on the cross." My friends, a sinner cannot be saved by prayer. A sinner can only believe that Jesus has saved him.

Faith is not a merit. Never consider faith a work. Some say that they do not know if their faith is strong enough. God has made faith so simple for you, but man has made a simple thing very complicated. Suppose I have a brother who is short of money and has become very poor. Now I want to give him some money. I tell him, "You do not have to do anything. You

cannot afford even to work. Here, take this money and go."
By doing this, I am making the matter most simple. However,
suppose his mind is very complicated. Suppose he would ask,
"If my brother is going to give me money, should I take it with
my left hand, or should I take it with my right hand? Should I
take it at noon, or should I take it in the afternoon? Should
I take it standing up, or should I take it sitting down?" He
wants to study how he can take it. This would be the greatest
mistake in the whole world.

While I was in Chefoo, I met a sister. I told her that if she
would believe, she would receive. She said, "I have been doing
this for a week. I still do not know how I can believe. I do not
know if this is the right way or that is the right way to believe.
I do not know if my faith is strong enough." I told her that
God has accomplished all the work. She only needs to believe
in a simple way. But she was too analytical. She made faith a
work.

Thank the Lord that it is the simplest thing on earth to
receive salvation. We do not have to do anything. It does not
mean that nothing has to be done. It only means that the
Lord Jesus has done everything. God says that He has died.
I say that I believe He has died. God says that the Lord Jesus
has resurrected and become a proof. I say, "Yes" and agree
that His resurrection has become a proof of my justification.
He says that my sins are forgiven, that He has saved me.
I will not wait. I believe, and the matter is settled. When I
believe, I have received. Thank the Lord. This is all. We have
passed from death to life. There is no need to feel anything or
to wait for any peace or joy to come.

A few years ago, I preached the gospel to one person. He
told me that he believed in the Lord Jesus, that he believed
that he was a sinner, and that he believed the Lord Jesus had
forgiven his sins. But he had a problem. He did not feel that
the Holy Spirit was working mightily in him like he thought
He was working in other Christians. I asked if his sins were
forgiven. He answered, "No." I asked him why. He said that
he did not feel the Holy Spirit working in him yet. I said,
"My friend, you are absolutely wrong. The Bible does not say
that whoever feels that he has believed in the Son of God has

eternal life. We do not believe by our feelings. Rather, we believe by the Word of God." When a person gives this book to me, I do not have to feel anything. I only have to believe in his word. Salvation is without any condition. There is, however, the proper procedure. The procedure of salvation is not work; it is simply to believe and to receive. Whatever God says, I say the same. This is to receive. Thank the Lord that His grace is sufficient for us.